THE
ULTIMATE
MONEY GUIDE
FOR CANADIANS

THE ULTIMATE MONEY GUIDE FOR CANADIANS

Investment Strategies That Really Work

JERRY WHITE

John Wiley & Sons

Toronto • New York • Chichester • Brisbane • Singapore

John Wiley & Sons Canada Limited
22 Worcester Road
Rexdale, Ontario
M9W 1L1

Canadian Cataloguing in Publication Data

White, Jerry, 1946–
    The ultimate money guide for Canadians: investment strategies that really work

ISBN 0-471-64092-1

1. Saving and investment – Canada.   2. Finance, Personal – Canada.   3. Financial security.
I. Title.

HG5152.W55 1994   332.6'0971   C94-930220-1

Production Credits
Cover design: Selwyn Simon
Cover Photo: Greg Tjepkema
Text design: Selwyn Simon and JAQ
Printer: Tri-graphic Printing Limited

Printed and bound in Canada
10 9 8 7 6 5 4 3 2 1

To every bank who told me, "No!"

To every teacher who said I wouldn't amount to anything because I had a sense of humour.

To every boss who said it was wrong to be too entrepreneurial and innovative.

To every academic colleague who told me an individual could not make a difference!

SEE!

And to Robert Walker:
student, employee, partner, friend.

CONTENTS

As an economist, financial journalist, and business person, I have observed that the 1990s so far have been like no other period I have ever experienced. The decline since 1988 has left nearly one in six Canadians in the labour force unemployed or underemployed. One person in nine is receiving social assistance, and I could argue that the economy has experienced as many as four dips during this economic restructuring. Interest rates are at a 29-year low, yet despite this, Canadian business and personal borrowing is at a 30-month low.

Because of Canadians' fixation on fixed income securities and real estate, we have been greatly affected by the lower interest rates and resulting decline in income from interest sources—a drop of 57% since 1991—while, at the same time, dealing with a decrease in income from real estate—as much as 50%. The Gross Domestic Product will not return to its 1980s pace. The loss of 450,000 industrial jobs, the aging of the population, high deficits, ever higher taxes, and globalization of the world's economy ensure that neither economic growth nor inflation will be strategic factors to help offset poor investment decisions.

Inflation was the cornerstone of Canadian investment for more than a decade. High inflation aided real estate values, as well as all other capital assets. It encouraged high borrowing levels and provided double-digit fixed income returns, making investment and financial planning seem unnecessary for most people. However, due to the continued expectation of low inflation rates for the rest of the 1990s, Canadians are now being forced to take action.

We do not believe in equities as a nation. Canadians generally have been shy of the stock market. Until 1992, 85% of investment holdings were in fixed income securities and real estate. We choose not to support Canadian business or invest in our friends and neighbours. In 1994, ignoring the stock market will no longer be viable. The strong performance of equities, the 400% increase in mutual fund sales in the last three years, the lack of options, and the globalization of investing have all had an impact on our investment decisions.

Canadians are older, less confident, and less financially secure than ever before. In April 1993, 87% of those responding to a national Angus Reid survey said they felt they could no longer rely on government for their retirement. Those hardest hit by all these changes are people—the baby boomers and older members of the population—who have lost jobs and income late in life, as well as the under-30 population (labelled "Generation X"), whom experts have suggested will never have the assets or income of their parents.

For retired Canadians, this period has been devastating. Many have lost more than half of their cash flow from investments. They have always assumed that they were limited to fixed income investments because of a distaste for risk and a lack of knowledge of the options. Many above the age of 65 feel that they are too old to invest or seek financial advice.

The 45- to 59-year olds feel paralysed by a fear of job insecurity, declining housing prices, and a loss of confidence in the many corner-stones they had counted on. Less than half of this group have Registered Retirement Savings Plans (RRSPs) and few, less than 20%, planned properly for retirement. To save companies money, employer pension plans now are being recast from defined benefit plans to money purchase plans with minimum annual employee contributions required. The defined benefit plans are more costly to employers, but more beneficial to the employees, guaranteeing the amount of the final pay-out on retirement. However, the money purchase plans, which require the employee to make contributions, are more expensive for the employee; this kind of plan also gives no assurances on the final value of the members' retirement funds because the plan is structured in such a way that the ultimate pay-out relies on the investment returns. Unfortunately, many pension plans have been tied to real estate investments and mortgages, which resulted in poor returns during the recent decline in the real estate market.

There is concern among the younger generation, too, whose work lives will be subject to much more uncertainty than their parents' because of relatively high unemployment and taxation. These young adults, who also face an increasingly complex world of investment and money management, must improve their inadequate knowledge in these areas.

The economic restructuring we have been witnessing has not only affected individuals, but has altered the traditional family structure. Since 1972, thousands of adult male workers earning $30 per hour have been replaced by the two-income family with one spouse earning $18 per hour and the other, $12 per hour. After taking inflation and taxation into account, real income for Canadian families did not grow from 1972 to 1991 and has declined by 3% in the last two years. It will probably drop by another 7% before the end of the decade unless there is a proactive effort to generate investment returns.

Income from salaried employment is not a growth option. With this in mind, entrepreneurship, self-employment, and home businesses will be the primary source of income for 20% of Canadian households by 1996, partially because there are few other options.

Personal financial planning and investing will be and must be the primary source of real income, wealth, and personal security enhancement for 80% or more of Canadians. Either you will earn income from investing and entrepreneurship or you will not advance financially. It is the way of the 1990s.

My own preference always has been to teach and help my fellow Canadians to improve their lot. I undertook this role more than 23 years ago as a personal battle against big government's assault on the small business and the individual Canadian's income. If I could show Canadians the proper utilization of the six elements of financial planning, as well as conduct research and provide education in entrepreneurship, I could not only increase Canada's potential as a nation, but also defeat those bureaucratic, restrictive elements in both the public and private sectors that have debilitated us as a people.

I want Canadians to succeed as individuals and as a unified people. To me, in 1968, Canada was the finest nation on Earth with the best quality of life. But 1968 was also the beginning of the Canadian social welfare state and big deficits, big inflation, and high unemployment. It began a 25-year period of social decline where Canadians began to believe that society owed them a job and that government should take care of them for life. We developed a sense of entitlement and lost our sense of peoplehood—who we were as a nation. There was no longer a common vision or identity as Canadians. We built massive governments, racked up deficits that exceeded our GDP, and rejected our entrepreneurs. We are now paying the price for this period of self-indulgence.

I want Canadians to be rich! But through personal vision and responsibility, not government hand-outs. I sincerely believe that you can still make the choice, regardless of your age, to become at least financially secure. You can choose to become rich.

The concept of *The Ultimate Money Guide for Canadians* is that each of you can make conscious choices, at any time in your life, which will make you richer or poorer. There are specific strategies and financial knowledge that, if followed properly, have the potential to double your net worth every three years, producing returns of 30% or better per annum. These strategies do not necessarily involve significantly greater risk. There is always risk. But do you not consider a 57% decline in returns on fixed income securities to be a sign of a risky and poor investment?

If you combine good strategies based on empirical research with personal discipline, sound financial planning, and good financial advisers, you have a greater probability of achieving the wealth-doubling goal.

However, the first words that Canadians learn as children is not "Momma" or "Da Da", but "No." Most people reject new ideas outright and refuse to act. You must choose to act and learn to say "Yes" to new ideas. As a result, you can choose to be rich.

Yes, salaried middle-income earners can retire as multimillionaires if they make the choice. Just making maximum RRSP contributions during your entire working life, with your funds invested at only 12% returns, will yield a $10 million retirement fund for the middle-income earner.

Many of the concepts and strategies presented in this book are new, based on original research. The goal is to present new ideas in clear and simple ways without the jargon, the complexity of the tax and investment professions, and the confusion of the academics. Investing is not complex or painful. It is a process that can be learned. It is dynamic and, most importantly, fun.

Investing is both evolutionary and revolutionary. The evolutionary process involves expanding on previous concepts, gradually developing ideas such as portfolio management, risk management, globalization, and asset allocation. Investors are now looking at the strategy of maintaining a "portfolio of portfolios" to mitigate risk and increase returns. This concept helps lower investment risk and create above-average long-term financial returns through broad-based diversification and asset allocation.

Investing also has a revolutionary aspect, requiring a major break with the past, relinquishing dependence on government or employers, and recognizing the need to educate yourself and take personal responsibility. Self-help, however, should be supplemented by expert advice for maximum effect. Unfortunately, only 5% of Canadians have used the services of a financial planner or expert adviser. Less than 3% of taxpayers use tax shelters. And, as of August 1993, we still had less than 10% of assets in equities.

Anyone who says change is easy is either a liar or consultant or both. To change one individual is hard. To change an entire population is next to impossible.

This is a book about action plans and doing, about choices and decisions, about wealth and poverty. It is not a rehash of old ideas and traditional concepts. I assume you have actually heard about equities, mutual funds, and RRSPs, and you are buying this book because you are looking for new ideas and approaches that do work. You are tired of clichés, repetition, and media that repeat themselves every year on the same issues.

After years of hearing or reading about RRSPs, you have a vague idea of what they are, how they work, and why you need one. What is important is to have the right RRSP strategies in the context of a total financial planning program, not in isolation.

This book is not about one product or service or act or decision. It is about a commitment to total financial planning in view of a highly taxed, deficit-driven, low-growth, low-inflation economy. All strategies need a context. This is ours—an economic mess we let happen and now we are forced to act. Taking action is not something most people like to do. Most people prefer reacting.

The total synergistic approach to planning assumes that all six elements—cash management, income and insurance protection, investment strategies, retirement planning, estate planning, and tax planning—are interrelated and inseparable. If you apply them all concurrently, together they produce a financial return that will be greater than the sum of their individual parts.

By making investment decisions within the context of new economic realities, you make choices based on: the cash consequences of the decision; the tax benefits; the impact on retirement and the estate; and the ability of the investment strategy to help maintain your personal security and provide income protection. The result of the decision is not a series of 4%, 6% or 8% per annum returns, but rather reasonably consistent after-tax returns of 25% to 35% per annum, resulting in a doubling of net worth every three years.

In understanding the optimal investment options available and their interrelationship and synergistic potential, you can produce these high returns. Such results are reasonable and attainable.

Most of the financial planners with whom I work tell me that minimum returns of 15% to 20% are possible, but 30% is attainable with professional assistance. When I demonstrate the returns in the total context, they recognize that I'm correct and that the returns are no exaggeration.

You must, however, act and learn to say yes to new ideas.

The New Canadian Economy to the Year 2000

I have to confess that I am an optimist by birth. I see opportunity everywhere. Even in bad times, I continuously look for the silver lining.

Trying to escape the constant barrage of negative books that have proliferated of late is difficult. We are told of the coming world bankruptcy in 1995, the world financial collapse, and the forecasted depression for the balance of the 1990s. Canadians have to prepare themselves for an environment of low growth, low inflation, low interest rates, and high unemployment.

I have included on the next page a summary table of economic forecasts that were compiled in August 1993 for 1993-94 from 11 independent sources.

Even as a true optimist, I think these economic forecasts are still too positive. The Canadian economy, which has shown a real weakness, has to contend with an uncertain political situation and heavy tax burden that seem to be further impeding economic recovery. Disappointing housing and construction statistics, a personal crisis of confidence, lack of job security, changing demographics, an aging population, and low demand for business loans have caused the economy not to respond to record-low interest rates that normally would stimulate spending.

20 Symptoms of a Long-Term Downturn

1) Commodity prices enter a long cyclical downtrend.

2) Financial institutions have difficulty obtaining repayment of loans.

3) Personal and business bankruptcies rise.

ECONOMIC FORECASTS FOR 1993–94

FORECASTER	GDP % chg. 1993	GDP % chg. 1994	Unemployment rate % 1993	Unemployment rate % 1994	CPI Inflation rate % 1993	CPI Inflation rate % 1994	3 mon. T-bill yield % Q4-93	3 mon. T-bill yield % Q4-94	C$ in US ¢ Q4-93	C$ in US ¢ Q4-94
Conference Board	2.8	3.0	11.3	11.1	2.1	2.2	4.06	4.39	77.6	80.9
WEFA Canada	2.9	4.5	11.4	11.7	1.9	1.8	4.63	4.43	77.9	76.7
DRI Canada	2.7	4.4	11.2	11.1	3.3	1.7	n/a	n/a	78.3	79.5
Inst. Policy Analysis	3.2	4.7	11.1	10.8	1.8	1.7	n/a	n/a	77.8	n/a
ScotiaMcLeod	2.5	3.6	11.0	10.5	2.0	2.2	4.25	5.25	76.0	79.0
Caisse Desjardins	3.1	3.5	11.1	10.5	1.9	2.2	4.75	5.80	77.0	80.0
Royal Bank	3.5	4.2	11.0	10.5	2.5	2.5	4.75	5.75	79.0	80.0
TD Bank	2.7	3.8	11.3	11.1	2.0	2.3	4.80	5.00	77.2	77.7
Richardson Greenshields	3.6	3.9	n/a	n/a	2.7	2.5	5.00	6.00	79.0	80.0
Bank of Nova Scotia	2.5	3.0	11.2	10.8	2.0	2.0	4.50*	5.00*	77.0*	76.0*
Burns Fry	3.0	3.4	11.1	10.5	1.8	2.0	4.55	n/a	77.7	n/a
AVERAGE	**3.0**	**3.8**	**11.2**	**10.9**	**2.2**	**2.1**	**4.59**	**5.20**	**77.7**	**78.9**
1992 ACTUAL	0.7		11.3		1.5		7.29		79.3	

* Second half

TABLE 1–1

4) Earnings of life insurance companies fall.

5) The creation of debt is abhorrent. (For example, in Canada in 1993, we had a 2h-year low in borrowing despite the lowest interest rates in 29 years.)

6) Government has difficulty in collecting taxes.

7) Overall tax revenue declines. (This has contributed dramatically to our deficit.)

8) Jobs disappear and many self-respecting citizens are forced onto public assistance for income. (Nearly 35% of the unemployed are white-collar workers and managers.)

9) Salaries stagnate while prices fall.

10) Salaries for the skilled in high-tech industries rise sharply.

11) Promotions are slow; layoffs are common.

12) Farmers are among the worst hit.

13) The standard of living in industrial areas declines sharply.

14) Construction in urban centres goes through extreme swings, with aggressive over-construction and then sudden halts.

15) Cash is hoarded and savings rise.

16) Interest rates fall. (In Canada, they are now at a 29-year low.)

17) There is a sharp drop in labour-intensive work, while do-it-your-self projects proliferate.

18) Property prices fall steadily.

19) Rents fall and there is an over-abundance (20% to 27% surplus) of commercial property.

20) Price deflation occurs and fortunes are lost in collectibles.

THE NEW REALITIES: GETTING READY FOR MORE BAD TIMES

Let us examine where we are as a country, people, and economy—Canada in the 1990s. Canadians are either ignorant of their economic plight or simply don't want to know the economic realities. Yet no one aspiring to personal financial security can achieve this goal without understanding our economy.

Unlike our parents' generation, which saw real earnings increase an average of 3% annually, most workers now barely keep pace with inflation. Today's employees cannot count on steadily rising incomes to boost their standard of living and enable them at the same time to save for their future. Most Canadians under the age of 40 will never be as well off as their parents. This is one of the new realities and financial challenges we will have to face.

In terms of positive developments, Canada has beaten inflation down to less than 2% a year, meaning that retired individuals on fixed incomes need not fear the threat of inflation as much. However, the massive increase in taxation combined with low returns on fixed income securities have put us in a position where we have to apply new strategies that are both entrepreneurial and innovative.

Here are the particulars.

1) There has been no rise in personal income "in real terms" for most Canadians since 1972. In fact, the average Canadian family has had a $3,000 net loss of disposable income in the last ten years, because of tax increases. Most middle-class families now depend on two wage earners to cover their day-to-day living expenses. Furthermore, the middle-income taxpayer pays the bulk of the taxes collected in Canada, the highest component in the seven most industrialized nations in the world (the G-7).

2) Sixty percent of mothers of young children are currently in the workforce. Divorce, job loss, disability, or death of a spouse can bring on financial ruin. Meanwhile, adding to the family's ex-

penses are child care, medical and dental costs, and college and university tuition, which are rising at twice the rate of inflation.

3) A secure retirement is a receding dream for most of us. Employers are cutting back on defined benefit pension plans (which gurantee a fixed pay-out based on final salary and seniority) and are replacing them with defined contribution plans (which allow individuals to invest their own money in company-sponsored investment options but with no assurances as to how much money the investments will ultimately pay out). The other problem is the Canada Pension Plan. Today's retirees are receiving $4 in income for every dollar they have contributed. Tomorrow's retirees will get back only $1 for every dollar they contribute. The government, spending between 25% and 30% of its income on unnecessary national debt, cannot afford to pay for the same standards of pensions, health care, and welfare to which we have become accustomed.

4) The heyday of high-yielding, low-risk investments (Certificates of Deposit issued by banks, money market funds, and residential real estate) has ended. CD rates will only approximate the inflation rates while over-building and a lower rate of new household formation have flattened house values and wiped out equity in most parts of Canada.

5) Eighty percent of the white-collar unemployed (35% of the overall unemployed) will not find re-employment in a large corporation or government.

6) Income from fixed income securities has declined by 57% since January 1, 1991.

7) Canadians have roughly 80% of their cash or liquid assests placed in bank deposits or short-termed fixed income securities. Less than 10% of the population have ever owned equities.

8) The only real growth in incomes and personal security will come from successful investing.

9) Approximately 600,000 women have selected the home business as their source of income.

10) The governments in Canada are essentially insolvent.

If you read my previous book, *Strategic Personal Investing*, you may also recall the list of the 21 threats to personal financial security that have changed the 1990s.

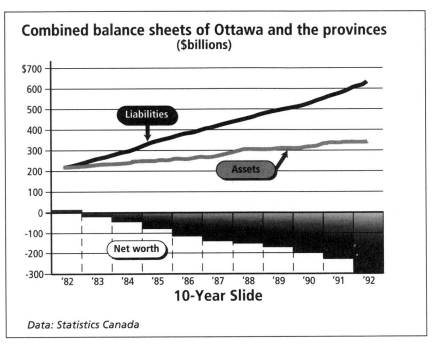

Combined balance sheets of Ottawa and the provinces
($billions)

Liabilities

Assets

Net worth

'82 '83 '84 '85 '86 '87 '88 '89 '90 '91 '92
10-Year Slide

Data: Statistics Canada

Figure 1–1

INTEREST RATES HAVE FALLEN MORE THAN 57%

Interest Rates

December	1990	1991	1992	1993
5 Year GIC	10.25%	8.25%	7.25%	6.00%
CSB	10.75%	7.50%	6.00%	6.00%
T-Bills	11.51%	7.43%	6.04%	4.14%
Savings Accounts	10.56%	6.35%	5.07%	2.00%

Percent Drop

	1 Year	2 Year	3 Year
5 Year GIC	–12%	–29%	–41%
CSB	–20%	–44%	–44%
T-Bills	–19%	–48%	–60%
Savings Accounts	–20%	–52%	–80%
AVERAGE	–18%	–43%	–57%

Table 1–2

21 Threats To Financial Security

1) Decline of fixed yield securities income by 57% in 30 months.

2) Low interest rates—the lowest in 29 years.

3) Loss of consumer purchasing power—worse off than in 1980.

4) Increased personal debt—$100 billion of credit card debt (at 16% rate of interest) that is non-deductible interest expense.

5) Collapse of real estate as a store of value, especially in Central Canada.

6) Household difficulty in saving—after discounting the financial contribution of a second wage earner in a family, net disposable income per family is at the same level in inflation-adjusted dollars as in 1973.

7) Increasing personal and consumption taxes.

8) Rising health and insurance costs because of the aging of the population.

9) A declining standard of living and expectations.

10) Falling wage scales and fewer corporate benefits.

11) Increasing job insecurity—double-digit unemployment will be here for several years.

12) Earlier retirements (forced and chosen) especially among the middle-income white-collar worker.

13) Rising education costs and the need to re-educate ourselves.

14) Increasing government debt and shrinking social security net.

15) Minimal inflation and "real dollar" cost of servicing the personal debt.

16) Collectibles moving out of reach.

17) Investment scams—too many bad deals.

18) Fewer tax planning options—what the Feds give back, the provinces take away.

19) Changing demographics (older parents, younger children).

20) Need for incremental income from investment sources to offset the loss of disposable income from employment.

21) Rising costs for financial services—bank charges rose 67% in five years versus a 29% inflation rate.

THE GOVERNMENT MESS

One of the most important things to happen in the past five years regarding the personal finances of Canadians has been the widespread realization that we cannot rely on anyone but ourselves to look after our financial future.

According to any reasonable standard of financial management, the federal government and most provincial governments are broke. Canadians are finally waking up to the reality. This situation is important for two reasons. First, as government debt grows, most of the social programs many Canadians rely upon for financial assistance will gradually disappear. Secondly, as government debt grows, personal income taxes will continue to rise and prevent Canadians from being able to accumulate enough wealth to look after themselves in their later years.

The government will no longer look after us. With the high deficits and national debt, our governments are having difficulty coping with the ever-increasing strains of growing demands on unemployment insurance, welfare, pensions, and health care. The direct thrust of government is to tax the individual and consumption.

I would summarize the key issues facing our government as follows.

1) The government has increased the national debt to a per capita level that is six times the U.S. level, yet seems incapable of cutting expenditures to reduce the growing debt. Therefore, despite protestations of "no new taxes," neither the GST nor the old taxes are making any inroads into the national debt problem.

2) Compared with national pension plans in other industrialized countries, the Canada Pension Plan has been grossly underfunded. This has placed a greater burden on Canadians to provide for their own retirement. However, the majority of Canadians have done little if any retirement or estate planning. Given current demographics, 65% will end up under government care or under assistance from others when they reach age 70. Furthermore, only about one-third of taxpayers will contribute to RRSPs, and most of them will not make a meaningful contribution (say, 50% or more of the taxpayers' available limit).

3) The need to contain costs associated with our health care system will force provincial and federal governments to eliminate medical benefits for Canadians living or travelling outside Canada. Unless these people purchase coverage from private insurance companies, medical costs will largely be the responsibility of the individual in future years.

HOW OUR TAX DOLLAR IS SPENT

Payments to individuals	27¢
Public debt charges	25¢
Payments to provinces	15¢
Government operations	12¢
Defence	8¢
Other economic social payments	8¢
Crown corporations	3¢
Aid to less developed countries	2¢

Data: February 1992 Budget Projection

TABLE 1–3

4) The federal government and most provincial governments in Canada have dramatically reduced personal tax planning opportunities for Canadians. They have done this by consistently working to reduce income-splitting options for spouses, increasing attribution rules, reducing tax avoidance strategies, and increasing both the dollar amounts and frequency of tax installment payments. All this means is that our governments have continually restricted the ability of Canadians to protect their income and save money for the future. The consequence will be that most of us will have to prepare for a significant decline in our personal assets and living standard in our retirement years.

5) The government introduced a goods and services tax on consumption.

6) The government increased personal tax rates at the provincial level to offset the federal reductions.

7) Fees for services, licences, and permits from governments have been dramatically increased.

8) The government eliminated the $100,000 capital gains exemption on real estate (excluding the principle residence).

9) During the 1970s and 1980s, many wage contracts and government programs (e.g., pensions, unemployment insurance, and welfare) were indexed. That is, they included a provision for automatic annual salary or payment increases, based on the increase in cost of living and other factors. However, indexation, as a governing principle for protecting income from the negative effects of inflation, has now been dramatically

reduced. Therefore, Canadians who are living on fixed incomes from various government programs will see more and more of their income being eroded from inflation. Many of these people will be unable to earn additional income from other sources to make up the difference, especially if they are senior citizens.

10) The government controls the returns on Canada Pension by borrowing the money at below-market rates. Provinces do the same with the pension funds of provincial employees and teachers.

Everybody hates paying taxes, but most Canadians really do not have a detailed understanding of how their purchasing power and personal savings are affected by our tax laws. The best way of understanding the extent to which our governments have their hands in our wallets is the concept of "Tax Freedom Days." This day simply represents the date in the year after which our personal income has paid all taxes and actually goes into our own pockets. As taxes have increased steadily over recent years, this date has tended to move later and later in the year, leaving us with less and less annual personal income. Table 1–4 identifies the tax freedom day for each of the ten provinces, as well as for Canada in general, over a nine-year period.

TAX FREEDOM DAYS

	1993	1992	1991	1984
Newfoundland	May 11	May 12	May 6	May 15
P.E.I.[1]	May 8	May 13	May 18	May 18
Nova Scotia[1]	June 2	June 5	June 8	June 14
New Brunswick	May 30	May 22	May 22	May 17
Quebec	June 21	June 21	June 12	May 17
Ontario	June 16	June 16	June 14	May 29
Manitoba	June 10	June 12	June 14	June 13
Saskatchewan[2]	July 8	June 27	June 7	June 17
Alberta[2]	June 19	June 22	June 7	Sept. 23
B.C.[2]	June 24	June 23	June 8	June 4
CANADA[2]	June 11	June 12	June 10	May 25

[1] Based on 1992 budgets

[2] Excluding natural resource royalties, 1993 TFD is June 8 for Canada, June 27 for Saskatchewan, May 31 for Alberta and June 17 for B.C.

Source: Fraser Institute

TABLE 1–4

TAXES OF THE AVERAGE FAMILY IN 1993

Province	Average cash income	Profits tax	Income tax	Sales tax	Liquor, tobacco etc.	Auto, fuel, licence	Social security, pension, medical	Property tax	Natural[1] res. taxes	Import duties	Other taxes	Total taxes
Newfoundland	46,475	745	5,692	3,809	1,301	747	2,483	630	120	286	838	16,652
P.E.I.[2]	45,481	668	6,028	3,423	1,366	689	2,588	725	14	319	68	15,887
Nova Scotia[2]	42,164	882	6,928	3,305	1,224	696	2,810	1,069	29	359	324	17,627
New Brunswick	44,488	1,008	6,387	3,797	1,052	772	2,733	1,550	161	326	502	18,288
Quebec	48,487	1,796	8,155	3,846	1,039	686	4,271	2,153	43	404	402	22,793
Ontario	59,580	1,723	10,112	4,136	1,304	843	4,929	2,758	75	500	853	27,233
Manitoba	45,410	1,235	7,015	3,150	1,427	680	3,777	1,673	190	394	402	19,943
Saskatchewan	44,714	2,456	6,938	3,299	1,362	1,141	2,383	3,157	1,381	370	670	23,159
Alberta	51,594	1,717	8,168	1,711	1,503	671	3,870	2,725	2,746	435	501	24,047
B.C.	49,004	1,548	8,482	3,691	1,538	644	3,689	2,064	1,008	440	421	23,525
CANADA	51,797	1,449	8,381	3,611	1,254	743	4,123	2,040	363	428	555	22,946

1 - Natural resource taxes are treated as though they were paid by the people of the province.

2 - Based on 1992 budgets

TABLE 1-5

The tax assault on Canadians by all levels of government continues unabated. Given the enormity of this tax grab, you must realize that it is consuming an average of 44% of your total cash flow. As a result, the financial services industry is growing. Yet most people assume that tax planning only involves going to a tax preparation service in April, whereas proper planning should be a year-round concern. No investment/financial planning strategy would be complete without an extensive array of tax advice.

I am not a believer in "tax minutiae"—doing a large number of things to save a little. Rather a comprehensive tax plan needs to fit into a total financial planning strategy. This will produce an increased cash flow, more dollars to invest, reduced liabilities, increased returns on investment, and more secure retirement planning with a well protected estate. This is synergistic planning. The whole is greater than the sum of the parts. Your net return will be dramatically greater if you follow through the six elements of financial planning outlined in Chapter 2.

By understanding the new realities of the Canadian economy, and the need to change your own financial/economic destiny, you can enhance your returns after tax by 25–30% or more. The goal is simply to enhance your net worth in three years by 100% to ensure your high standard of living, personal security, and long-term financial well-being. This means it is your patriotic duty to succeed, create wealth, and overcome the government's failing in the economy.

REAL ESTATE AS AN INVESTMENT

Another new financial challenge that we must face concerns the issue of real estate as an investment. In assembling any material or position on real estate, I always ignore those individuals who have a vested interest in perpetuating a myth about it. This includes real estate agents, bankers, and lawyers. None of these groups has proven to be a reliable predictor of market trends and opportunities.

Real estate has been the downfall of many Canadian trust and insurance companies, as well as major corporate conglomerates who had access to all the sage advice of the groups mentioned above.

Far more reliable has been the performance of demographers, economists, some real estate developers, and a few financial planners and investment counsellors. Without spending excess time and space on their analyses, the essence of their current views includes the following ideas.

1) In North America, the economic and industrial expansion is both westward and southward as well as to secondary and tertiary economic centres that offer low costs, low taxation, and lower costs of living for workers.

2) Demographics indicate the lowest level of new family formation and population growth rates in nearly 50 years. This means that the demand for traditional detached, single-family-owned dwellings will continue to decline in many markets until 1997 at the earliest and 2005 as the most likely, when a new population group of today's teenagers will be in a position to acquire housing.

3) Today's children will never be as well off as their parents. Called Generation X by demographers, they have lower expectations as to earnings, less chance at stable long-term employment, and fewer housing needs.

4) The loss of 2.7 million middle-management jobs creates a direct long-term impact on mid-priced housing.

5) The 50- to 79-year-old set that controls 65% of the disposable income for housing will need small, redesigned, senior-compatible housing with different amenities. Retirement housing will continue its upward trend.

6) States and provinces offering the lowest taxes and costs for serviceable land will experience the only continuous reliable real estate markets. These locations include (in no particular order): Utah, Arizona, Nevada, New Mexico, Idaho, Gulf Coast and Northern Florida, North Carolina, Alberta, Interior British Columbia and Victoria, South Carolina, Georgia, and Alabama. Other suitable markets are St. Martin, Puerto Rico, U.S. Virgin Islands, St. Lucia, Bermuda, and Cayman Islands.

7) On a global basis, the most dynamic markets in the world will be in the following locations.

   a) Mainland China in the new economic zones should show 15% to 20% growth per annum for the next 10 years
   b) Singapore
   c) Vietnam after the U.S. embargo is lifted
   d) England—the six-year fall in real estate is over and prices will begin to rise
   e) Poland, Hungary, and the Czech Republic have been undervalued for years—the return of a free-enterprise economy will boost productivity in future years

The availability of China-based mutual funds that include real estate stocks will allow us access to this market. I have been recommending mutuals in the areas where they have yielded 30% or more growth for the last three years.

8) Most Canadians still hold non-performing real estate, including their principal residence, in their asset portfolio. This means, if your children are grown and out of the house, you have a non-performing asset that will not even outperform inflation. At today's low interest rates, you can borrow against this asset at a net cash cost of 3% after tax, as it is fully deductible interest. In addition, modest leveraging should free up about $50,000 on the average residence, which can be invested to accelerate your portfolio appreciation. Those who choose not to act will find that their primary focus will be asset preservation, not asset growth. If the house is not necessary, then its liquidation—tax free—will produce a large pool of cash that can be distributed across the portfolio.

9) The cottage or summer residence will be an unaffordable luxury for most. High taxes, the 1992 loss of the $100,000 capital gains deduction on secondary real estate holdings, the impoverishment of the middle-income earner, and property tax increases in recreational and resort areas have flattened this market completely.

10) Commercial and industrial real estate and raw land will be the poorest performing real estate categories. Multi-unit residential, retirement, and low-cost housing under $200,000 will be the most exciting areas.

INTEREST RATES: THE FIXATION WITH FIXED YIELD SECURITIES

If you look at the overall performance of fixed income securities over the past 20 to 30 years, you will be sadly disappointed by their actual performance. The 30-year average of these types of investments generally has been an annual rate of a little over 4% (approximately 4.3 %), but if we look at the performance of equity, it has always been consistently and dramatically greater, generally averaging well over 10% even going back to the 1930s. Fixed yield securities in many cases offer reduced risk, and many people believe that the first question always to ask in any investment they make should be: "Is the investment government guaranteed?" ("and therefore has no risk if backed by the government?") Of course, the greater the risk, the greater the return.

The most common attitude among Canadians is that they have worked hard for their money and are seeking "no-risk" investments to preserve their assets. Canada Savings Bonds have been perceived as being the best available no-risk vehicle.

In 1981, the Government of Canada offered a 19.5% Canada Savings Bond. This offering led to the emergence of the expression, "Canadian risk," on Wall Street to describe any government-guaranteed bond paying a ridiculously high rate of interest. Let's look at the economic realities of that brilliant "no-risk" offering.

To begin with, in 1981, the effective tax rate for interest income was approximately 51% for people in the highest income bracket. The individual was left with about 9.5% net yield after tax. The inflation rate in that year was 12%, so the individual actually lost about 2.5% by buying this investment. On the surface, it looked extraordinary, but in terms of the economic return, it was very poor. The subsequent years produced returns in the 10% range in terms of the face rate, but the net yield to most investors, once again, was a negative cash flow after inflation and taxation.

If the rest of the '90s show steady growth and super-low yearly inflation, average interest rates might look like those on the following table.

COMPARING INTEREST RATES FROM 1960 TO 1994				
Year	Prime Rate	5-Year Mortgage	Long Canadian Bonds	Consumer Inflation
1994	5.5–5.0%	8.0%	5.5 - 6.5%	2 - 2.5%
Compare that with past history. There is nothing like it since the good-growth, low-inflation 1960s**.				
1960-72	6.3%	8.0%*	6.1%	2.8%
1973-78	9.3%	10.3%	8.8%	9.0%
1979-82	15.6%	15.8%	13.0%	4.7%
1983-91	11.3%	12.2%	10.6%	4.7%
*Estimate	**Average			

TABLE 1–6

To make bonds even less attractive, the government introduced legislation in 1990 that made Canada Savings Bonds ineligible for the three-year accrual rule. The three-year accrual rule had allowed you to gather interest for three years before you had to pay tax on it. But under the new rules for any fixed income security, interest income would be declared for the year that it is accrued by governmnent and not when actually received. In other words, even though you have not received interest income on the bonds for 11 years, you have had to pay tax on that money (which you have not received yet) each and every year. What a tremendous bargain, what an opportunity of a lifetime, and it was guaranteed! But the only thing that was truly guaranteed was poverty, negative cash flow, and a loss of purchasing power.

Now that interest rates have declined to a 29-year low, many people today are receiving 1% on their daily interest accounts and the money is sitting there, doing absolutely nothing but reducing the account holder's purchasing power. Many individuals still walk in at the end of February to their local bank or trust company, plop down their money, and say, "I want to buy one of these RRSPs." They buy a GIC as if it were the only option. In most cases, people are sadly disappointed to see what they have actually earned on these types of investments. Unfortunately, fixed yield securities are the cornerstone for most Canadians' investments and long-term financial planning.

THE NATIONAL PROPENSITY TO LINE UP

As I indicated earlier, Canadians did line up to buy those 19.5% fixed yield securities. In fact, 1979 was a great year for line-ups. People lined up en masse for gold that year as it traded at $860 (U.S.) an ounce. Everyone was buying—the butcher, the baker, the candlestick maker, and an awful lot of dentists. The only question I asked them was, "Who is going to buy it from you?" The only one making a profit was the bank. Gold fell back quickly to $540, then $400, then $340. Lemmings line up. When the mob is there, there is no longer a profit to be made.

Most investors buy history—where the market has been—and usually enter the market en masse after the profit is gone. I discussed a particular stock on the radio in June 1993. Based on the analysis we did as a firm, I felt that the stock, a highly speculative junior gold, could move up from 72 cents a share to more than $1.50. Our projection held as gold prices soared in June and July on that particular stock. In five weeks, the stock jumped to $2.20, and many listeners made thousands of dollars. That's when the calls started. The average call was, "Now that the stock is up 300%, is it OK to buy it?" The answer, of course, was no.

Canadians lined up by the tens of thousands in October 1981 to buy the Canada Savings Bonds described above because of their 19.5% rate. We sucked $13 billion out of the money supply, eliminated $40 billion in purchasing power, and added greatly to the recession that followed. The analysis illustrated earlier showed that there was no return to be made. Yet everyone was in that line!

Line-ups continued throughout the 1980s, especially in real estate, with most people lining up after the peak of the market in 1988. Lining up seemed to be a great national pastime that year. Every Saturday, people would line up to buy condominiums on speculation of a constant market increase based on further speculation and inflation.

The C.D. Howe study of this period pointed out that the price increases from 1984 were all based on speculation, not underlying value. There were thousands of units being bought without tenants, and there was no one to whom you could sell or rent the units. The market finally collapsed, taking thousands of Canadians with it. But everyone was in the line, therefore the market was gone. The profit was earned between 1984 and 1988. After that, there was no one on whom you could unload the units.

Despite these bad experiences, people continue to line up every February 28th for their RRSPs rather than buying them as a part of a planned strategic investment and tax-planning decision with pre-authorized monthly payments to maximize the long-term returns. Lining up en masse or following the crowd is the opposite of good investment strategy.

Investment and financial planning decisions are personal—subjective and unique to each situation. You set priorities based on your personal income, investment objectives, needs, lifestyle, age, and family circumstances. Proper investing is not a make-shift plan or impulse purchase. Following the crowd is not only inadvisable, it is simply the opposite of the natural investment process and produces disasterous returns.

"The Best of Times"

I believe that there are many of you who, like me, seek the silver lining and believe it is possible to profit during difficult economic times with low inflation. In Canada, the remainder of the 1990s will continue to be the best of times for these winners.

1) People who save

2) Businesses with no debt

3) Quality stocks and bonds

4) Producers of proprietary products that competition cannot erode

5) Low-cost producers

6) Venture capitalists

7) Businesses involved in research and development

8) Entrepreneurs

9) High-volume, low-price retailers

10) Introductions of new products

11) Pensioners (inflation will not erode their income)

12) Marketing people

13) Conservative investment practices

14) Strict family budgeting

15) Specialized and continuing education

16) Education for professional people

17) Consumers with low debt, and high savings

18) Renters

19) Consumers of internationally traded commodities

These are the 1990s. In case you missed it, it's in all the newspapers: these are the 1990s, not the '60s, '70s, '80s. What will be popular during this decade?

- Investment instead of consumption.

- Trading down instead of trading up.

- Warehouse clubs instead of designer boutiques.

- Family vacations instead of private getaways for two.

- Minivans instead of luxury sedans.

- Mutual Funds instead of Canada Savings Bonds.

- Garage sales instead of retail shops.

- Home businesses instead of corporate careers.

In relative terms, the population of Canada is rapidly aging, with older parents and younger children. People seem more concerned about law and order, personal financial responsibility, and entrepreneurship. Individuals are also rapidly becoming disenchanted with big government and the traditional large financial institutions.

Here are the new family values of the 1990s.

1) Preserving value of current assets.

2) Seeking job security for the main breadwinner(s).

3) Retiring in comfort with financial security.

4) Accumulating capital to pay for children's education and perhaps people's own re-education.

These priorities will help shape the economic landscape throughout this decade, as consumer spending shifts to accommodate the new personal values and the new economic realities.

ACTION PLANS FOR FRUGAL TIMES

Don't	Do
• Don't get involved in status symbols	• Savor the simple pleasures
• Don't become involved in debt	• Be flexible, adaptive and responsive
• Don't become too specialized	• Save your money
• Don't become addicted to affluence	• Learn as many skills as you can
• Don't live in areas that depend on support for necessities	• Try to live in areas where there are renewable resources
• Don't buy remote land	• Live near a smaller centre or town
• Don't be greedy and get caught holding a speculation bubble	• Repay your mortgage after you contribute to your RRSP.

TABLE 1 - 7

The strategies presented here are actually relevant regardless of the economy. They are wise and solid ideas from individuals who have predicted where we are today. Add them to your lifestyle and your knowledge of economic issues.

The basic principles of financial planning now are discipline, doggedness, and diversification. The objective is to develop a dynamic financial plan based on a barbell model: adequate cash and liquidity for the short-term needs and emergency relief, combined with long-term investments to cover old age.

The chapters that follow will look at the development of personal financial planning and its six elements—cash management, income and insurance protection, investment strategies, retirement planning, estate planning, and tax planning. Then the focus will turn to equities, mutual funds, derivatives and specialty products, and real estate as part of your investment strategy. You will be presented with an extensive array of tax strategies to help reduce the tax burden, improve cash flow, and enhance returns on investments. Special attention will also be given to women's financial issues because there are unique savings and taxation issues involved here.

The central thesis of this book is that there is a need to act, utilizing a strategy integrating the six above-mentioned elements of financial planning. This should produce a synergistic return greater than that of just having an isolated investment or retirement strategy. Every decision will affect all six elements. The net result should be combined returns of 30% or more per annum, doubling your net worth every three years! This is not about getting rich slowly—it is about creating the ability to choose to be rich.

The Six Elements of Financial Planning

LEARNING HOW TO DOUBLE YOUR NET WORTH EVERY THREE YEARS

This is the most important chapter of this book. In this section, the essence of the elements of financial planning will be explained: how the six elements interrelate and how, by making proper asset allocation decisions when you establish your portfolio, you will over time learn to double your net worth on a regular basis.

The process is not overly complicated, excessively sophisticated, or unrealistically risk-oriented. By diversifying to create a broad-based bundle of asset holdings your risk is reduced and the potential for grabbing large upside returns is increased. By creating "portfolios of portfolios" in many of the categories, you further reduce risk and increase the potential for growth.

But before getting into asset allocation and core investment decisions, you must first learn about proper financial planning and how weighing decisions based on their impact on all the elements of financial planning is more likely to produce the wealth and financial security you seek.

The most frequent complaint I get from individuals who go to meet with a financial counsellor of some sort is that they are sat down in an office and an attempt is made immediately to sell them some mutual funds. Needless to say, this is not financial planning.

The essence of financial planning is understanding the relationship between the six elements in the process and making decisions based on the implications and interactions of these elements. No financial decision should be made in isolation from these six elements. All decisions must be regularly evaluated and updated.

The process of financial planning involves six dimensions:

- Cash Management
- Income and Insurance Protection
- Investment Strategies
- Retirement Planning
- Estate Planning
- Tax Planning

CASH MANAGEMENT

Where does your money come from and where does it go? How can you use your cash to maximize your returns? How do you increase your cash flow by using the other dimensions to enable you to have more to invest and, therefore, achieve higher returns on investment?

I regularly ask seminar audiences to keep a log or diary of every expenditure they make throughout the following 90 days. If you use this approach, right down to the last quarter you spend, you generally will observe that you are using 20% of your cash flow for impulse and non-essential purchases. As a result, by maintaining a log, you become sensitive to your cash outflow. You, therefore, reduce the impulse actions and conserve up to 20% more cash for investment purposes.

Most people are unaware that they can conserve cash by reducing cash deducted as income at their employment source. This can be done in several ways. Your entrepreneurial home business can create tax losses in the first year or two through direct expenses from an unincorporated business; these losses can be deducted from personal income. Advise your employer that you are in a different deduction category and ask to refile your deduction form for withholding tax. Some employers will say no, but you have the right to file.

Another way to free up cash is through RRSP contributions. If you contribute to your RRSP throughout the year, ask Revenue Canada to reduce withholding taxes under Section 53(1) of the Income Tax Act. If you can prove it is a legitimate deduction, Revenue Canada will approve it for you. This approach can also be used for those individuals making tax-deductible alimony or maintenance payments, tax-deductible investment expenses, or tax-reducing tax shelters. In most cases, a simple letter from you to the District Taxation Office will suffice. This sure beats waiting up to 16 months for a tax refund. Electronic filing of your tax return by one of the professional filing firms will reduce the waiting time for tax refunds from three months to three weeks.

Many individuals have a lot of dormant cash lying about in too many bank accounts, bonds, or GICs, rolling them over without thinking. Sell what you do not need and invest it correctly to profit at a maximum. Most tax-saving strategies will help you keep more cash in your hands rather than the government's.

The biggest cash repository is the home. Sitting there dormant, the home of late has been a poor performer except on the West Coast. More importantly for the older 50+ empty nester (whose children are grown up and have left), this is a terrible waste of cash that could be yielding higher returns for retirement. Leveraging up to 20% of the value of the property or selling it outright will give you two main options. You can move to a smaller centre, buy a cheaper smaller home with lower maintenance costs, and invest the difference. Kingston, Ontario, and Victoria, British Columbia, are hot in this area now. Or, you can rent in the same city and convert all real estate assets to cash. Your monthly costs of living will be lower and the investments will pay your rent as well.

Cash is king in the 1990s. How you utilize every dollar is critical to your financial planning. Proper financial planning will increase your flexibility to invest more money, more often, to generate even stronger after-tax cash flows. The result is obviously synergistic and self-enhancing.

Other Cash-Enhancing Strategies

1) Pay all credit card bills on time to avoid the interest expenses. If you do have trouble controlling impulse purchases, see if your bank has a debit card plan. If you need to borrow, use a home equity loan at prime.

2) Review all insurance for cost/benefit and coverage. There is almost always a better price.

3) Don't spread your cash among more accounts than you need. Amalgamate your cash into your minimum required number of high-yield accounts. Avoid chequing accounts that pay no interest.

4) Liquidate any non-performing assets. Clean out the garage and basement. Hold a sale and do it regularly.

5) Avoid all high-interest credit cards such as those from department stores and gasoline companies. You can negotiate any price if you can pay cash.

6) Shop at sales. Buy high-consumables (paper towels, soap, detergent) in bulk at a cheaper rate. Wait for sales and clearances if you can hold off buying an item.

7) Make your house and habits energy-efficient to reduce utility costs.

8) File your tax returns electronically to recover your refund in three weeks, not six months.

Remember Where Your Money Goes

- Housing
- Taxes
- Food
- Utilities
- Car/Transportation
- Insurance
- Impulse Buying

INCOME AND INSURANCE PROTECTION

Critical to any financial planning is a solid grasp of how you plan to protect your family's income and assets if you die unexpectedly or get sick and are unable to work. How do you protect assets such as your house, car, and jewellery from fire, theft, or flood? How do you protect your estate from capital gains taxes when you die? These are questions that will be dealt with in detail in Chapter 4, where insurance strategies will be discussed.

Proper insurance levels at the right price are critical to financial planning success. Your insurance decisions will affect your cash flow, income protection, investments, retirement, estate planning, and taxation. Many people who buy insurance only as a benefit from employers are seriously under-insured. A lot of self-employed individuals are also under-insured, and have no disability income protection. Often assets also are incorrectly insured and too many useless insurance products are regularly purchased.

Consumers usually fail to shop around and reassess the insurance requirements for their car, life, and home. As the most insured people on a per-capita basis in the Western world, Canadians have also bought too much insurance as an investment. Insurance should not be purchased as an investment.

Working with a financial planner, you can assess your insurance situation and look for ways to add more of the essentials and eliminate the high-cost, cash-consuming products.

INVESTMENT STRATEGIES

As you will read later in the chapters on equities, mutual funds, real estate, derivatives and collectibles, most Canadians have no investment strategy whatsoever. When there is one, it normally consists of following the crowd or doing the same old thing—acting as though we are living in the '60s, '70s or '80s, and not the 1990s.

Investment, as outlined later in this book, is a collection of strategies that involve your age, risk preference, knowledge, and experience.

Investment planning should always be tax-ameliorated not tax-driven. What I mean is that for any investment, the tax considerations should not be the deciding factor. Tax benefits such as capital gains exemptions, dividend tax credits, tax shelters, and retirement deductions should add value to an already strong investment.

The results of your investment success will have an impact on your estate and your beneficiaries. The more successful you are, the greater the value of your estate, and the happier your beneficiaries will be.

RETIREMENT PLANNING

Retirement planning starts the moment you begin to work as an adult. Ideally, this should be no later than at 30 years of age. As is the case with the other financial planning elements, retirement planning is related to the success of integrating the six elements.

Unfortunately, as you will read in the chapter on RRSPs and retirement, most Canadians still have chosen to do little or nothing. They are seriously under-invested for retirement, start planning too late, and fail to integrate investing or tax planning with retirement.

The experience of a number of representatives of Fortune Financial Management Inc., one of Canada's largest and most respected independent financial planning firms, has shown that there are six key reasons for personal financial failure.

1) *Procrastination*

    Do you remember the final scene in the movie classic Gone With the Wind, where Scarlett O'Hara stands, sobbing, "There will always be tomorrow," on the front steps of her mansion as Rhett Butler walks out of her life? In financial affairs, many Canadians suffer from the same delusion. Make today the first day of the rest of your life. Do not procrastinate with your financial future. Your ability to retire with financial security depends on your ability to take charge immediately.

2) *Failure to Establish Both a Goal and a Plan*

    Very few people become financially successful through pure luck. I do not want you to have to rely on luck. To successfully create wealth and manage your money, you must have a plan and stick to it.

3) *Failure to Learn and Understand Canadian Tax Laws*

The most important issue confronting Canadians managing their money is taxation. Therefore, failure to understand Canadian tax laws or failure to seek professional tax advice can ruin your financial plan. You are not a criminal for trying to minimize the impact of taxation on your hard-earned income. Every Canadian has the right to arrange his or her financial affairs in such a way as to pay the minimum tax required by law. You will be a big winner in the long run if you learn the rules of the tax game.

4) *Buying the Wrong Type of Life Insurance*

Unfortunately, many Canadians seem to believe that life insurance is a good investment. Nothing could be further from the truth. Although life insurance and investing are both integral parts of a complete financial plan, they have little in common. The only purpose of life insurance is to protect your family from financial ruin if you should die, while investing is designed to create wealth. Just remember the old expression, "Buy life insurance as if you are going to die tommorrow and invest as if you are going to live forever."

5) *Ignorance About Money Management*

Many Canadians do not understand how financial institutions work and what financial planning is all about. This often leads people to avoid confronting their lack of knowledge. Just trying to learn more about the financial-planning process is a big step toward developing a plan to become financially independent.

6) *Failure to Develop a Winning Attitude*

Strive to develop a winner's attitude. Believe in yourself and in what you can do. Without confidence in yourself, you are defeated before you start.

The purpose of retirement planning is to give you long-term peace of mind and financial security. Proper planning will enhance the last 30 years of your life to be the best you will ever experience. You should be at your richest and most independent at this stage.

ESTATE PLANNING

But what about the end result—the estate? Most people put off doing their estate planning until it is too late, perhaps believing they are immortal. If you never die, you do not need a plan, right? But this has been a reasonably rare occurrence. Once you have assets, you have an estate.

You could plan your estate at age 23, 33, or 43. The earlier, the better. Assume that you could be killed in an accident, get cancer, or die of a heart attack. This is not negative thinking, just pragmatic realism.

The estate plan will include a will, a listing of all assets with descriptions and valuations, and a financial plan that will probably contain insurance to pay capital gains taxes. Your RRSP will have a designated beneficiary and you will have a succession plan in place for your business. These are the basics. As your estate and asset base grow, so should your estate planning to mitigate tax and to ensure that the assets you have worked so hard to acquire will end up in the right hands and intact.

TAX PLANNING

Tax planning is a challenge for most Canadians. Not only have we had the continuous shock of tax increases, the introduction of the Goods and Services Tax, and losses in various capital gains allowances, but the provinces have often added to this misery by usually grabbing the tax reductions the federal government periodically offers. Many provincial governments, nearing insolvency as their debts become classified as being close to junk bond status, will continue to tax at aggressive rates. Municipalities are no better off. Some hold the line, but educational costs have pressured tax increases in most major cities.

Tax planning is not a felony, although many people perceive it as such. You have a right and a duty to minimize the tax impact in any investment strategy. If governments cannot look after you or your retirement, than you must do everything legally responsible and possible to take care of yourself. The chapter on tax planning outlines dozens of tax strategies and how they affect cash flow, investing, retirement, and estates.

I rarely worry over tax trivialities, but rather am more concerned with creating an appropriate overall strategy to maximize long-term tax savings. After all, this is a book about strategies, the most critical being the use of capital gains, dividends, RRSPs, and entrepreneurial ventures. If you follow through with careful planning for this core group, then your taxes will be greatly reduced and returns significantly enhanced.

It would be impossible to reach the 30% per annum returns you need without a tax plan in place as part of the overall financial plan.

The six financial planning elements combine and interact to heighten returns on investment, reduce taxes, and build wealth. This results in peace of mind, financial security, freedom, and flexibility. But remember, these goals are attained as a result of synergism (the whole being greater than the sum of the parts). All strategies and decisions are made on the basis of their interactions with and implications for each of the six categories. What sets the contents of this book apart from all other books is this synergistic approach to financial planning.

Cash Management and Family Finances

Over the years, I have learned that when Canadians think of the subject of personal finance, the most frequent questions they raise relate to cash management—what they do with the money they have in their possession at any particular time. Unfortunately, not all Canadians own portfolios of stocks, have adequate insurance coverage or prepare proper retirement and estate plans. But, regardless of whether we are millionaires or ordinary unemployed Canadians, each of us must somehow manage the cash we have in our pockets. Some of us do it better than others.

As you will recall, cash management is one of my "six pillars" of a proper overall financial plan. However, during the relatively prosperous years in Canada during the decades of the 1960s, 70s and 80s, cash management did not seem to be as important an issue for many Canadians as it has now become. Incomes seemed to be rising, personal debt was comparatively low, and the economy was growing. For the most part, Canadians generally felt pretty good.

In the 1990s, things are very different. Cash is once again recognized as a major asset and Canadians are now spending a lot more time worrying about how they manage the cash they have. High levels of personal debt, declining real incomes, high unemployment, and reduced savings mean that Canadians are are once again learning to maximize their use of available cash. This means speeding up inflows of revenue, maintaining strict control over the frequency, timing and amounts of cash disbursements, and insuring that cash reserves are generating the highest possible return.

To help you get started in developing your own cash management plan, there are a number of important "rules of thumb" which most financial planners believe you should follow.

1) Develop a system for monitoring your spending patterns (which should include every member of your family).

2) Keep track of all receipts for your purchases and document your family's spending on a regular basis every month.

3) Analyze your family's spending habits to try and find ways of reducing your total expenses or purchasing more carefully to get greater value for your hard earned money. Make sure you include every member of your family in these discussions.

4) Develop an annual forecast, or budget, for the upcoming year, which outlines expected family expenses. As part of this forecast, be careful to plan carefully any major purchases which you intend to make, and also prepare your family for any periods during the upcoming year when you expect income to drop by increasing cash reserves.

5) Consolidate your cash. Don't leave cash sitting around in too many different places. It makes it much more difficult and time consuming to manage and, in extreme cases, you may even forget where it all is. By keeping cash together it is easier to maximize returns to generate greater family income.

6) On the other hand, don't leave large amounts of cash sitting in the bank. The interest you earn is pitifully small. For most Canadians, it is generally between ½% and 3% depending on the type of account. As soon as you have accumulated enough cash to cover two months living expenses, work with your financial planner to move the excess into other types of short term, higher return investments which will still provide you with liquiditiy.

7) Time any payments on personal debt or liabilities to extend payment periods to the maximum or to capitalize on payment incentives or purchase discounts.

8) Always try to pay for purchases in cash. Buying on credit is expensive, especially with bank credit cards which charge high rates of interest. However, a better reason to pay in cash in the 1990s is that for the first time in their lives, many Canadians are actually learning to bargain. Remember, in the 1990s, the price of everything is negotiable—especially if you have cash to spend.

These are the basic "rules of thumb" on which to build your cash management plan. They are essential for every Canadian to understand. At present, there are a multitude of personal finance books on the shelves of bookstores all across Canada which explain the basic elements of proper cash management for individual Canadians in great detail including: ways of managing income and cash receipts, schedules for paying personal expenses, methods for monitoring personal spending habits, accounting formats for use in preparing cash flow statements, budgeting procedures, and various approaches for developing a savings plan. In addition, during the 1990s many Canadians have also learned that cash management now includes negotiating with creditors, dealing with bankers, and restructuring our personal debt payments. Most of the personal finance books currently in print cover these topics on a personal level very well.

Therefore, it is not my intention to simply regurgitate at length what other authors have already written on these matters. I do not think that serves any useful purpose. Proper cash management procedures are very important to your short term financial well-being, but they are also rather "mechanical" in nature. There are certain basic principles and guidelines to follow which very seldom change. Once you have learned and understand these basic practices for managing your cash, the key to success is primarily in having the self-discipline to follow through. To paraphrase the current Nike television commercial, "Just do it."

I do not think it is a useful exercise for me to repeat in detail what you can already find in many other personal finance books. My objective in this chapter is to present you with new ideas on how to generate income for you and your entire family by focusing on two topics which I believe have not been adequately explained in many other personal finance books. In these tough economic times, our financial success is not likely to come from frequent job promotions or regular wage increases. In a world of high unemployment and increasing job insecurity, most of us will not be so lucky. It is also not likely that Canadian families will be able to improve their cash flow by having a second member (or third or fourth member, for that matter) of the family going out to work. In most Canadian households, this is already the norm.

In my opinion, the future financial success of Canadians rests on our ability to understand how our financial world is changing and how to develop new ways of thinking which will allow each of us to recognize, and capitalize on, new opportunities to generate income for ourselves and our families. We have to make the money we have in our possession work harder and smarter.

The two specific areas that I see as being particularly important in the 1990s are how to manage total family income more effectively and how to help Canadian women prepare for the very unique financial needs which they have.

GAINS OF THE 1980s WIPED OUT

In many ways, Canadian families are worse off now than they were in 1980. Despite 80 months of growth in the 1980s, we have seen 72% of that rise in the standard of living wiped out in the most recent recession. Average real family income experienced year-over-year declines of 2.0% in 1992, 2.6% in 1991, and 2.2% in 1990. This left the average family with 4.3% less income than they had in 1980. Based on 1993 levels it will probably decline by a further 10% in aggregate by the year 2000. Furthermore, in 1992 income tax rose to 22% of the average family income as opposed to only 15.4% in 1980.

The National Forum on Income Security, a Canadian think tank, suggests that 2 million Canadians have been forced to go on welfare and that insecurity is spreading throughout the middle class. The decline is attributed to many things, including the following.

- the slowdown in labour productivity growth, which began in the 1970s

- the polarization in the labour market between low- and high-paying jobs

- marriage breakdown, which spreads personal income over more households (80% of all low-income Canadians are families led by a single parent)

- the massive increase in the public service at all levels of government

Canadians did not prepare themselves well for the 1980s, but neither have they properly planned for the years ahead.

A typical married couple, each spouse 45 years old, with joint income just under $100,000, will need $79,600 a year in inflation-adjusted dollars when they retire in the year 2014. If they are typical Canadians in this age category, saving 5% to 7% income, which they invest in the usual passive way, they will end up with only 60% of the income that they will need.

To generate the income that they will require in order to maintain the same standard of living during their retirement years, they should consider the following facts.

- If they bring their savings rate up to 12% of their annual income, they will increase their retirement income to 66% of their requirements.

- If, in addition to increasing the savings rate, they also double the proportion of their portfolio invested in equities from 20% (the typical Canadian amount for this age group) to 40%, especially using international, U.S., and domestic mutual funds, this couple will be able to generate 75% of their retirement requirements.

- If, in addition to the above strategies, these people are able to sell their current "empty-nest" house and move into smaller rental accommodations, then they should be able to obtain 90% of their requirements.

- Furthermore, most people will have to generate additional income in some form or other (e.g., part-time work, a home-based business, or an entrepreneurial venture) to fund the balance of their retirement requirements.

By following the concepts of the investment strategies in this book, these two people should be able not only to go over the top, but probably to have the highest standard of living they have ever had, after they reach age 65.

FINANCIAL ISSUES FOR WOMEN AND FAMILIES

Women comprise 52% of the Canadian population, live longer than men (81 versus 75 years), and Statistics Canada confirms that 74 to 91 out of every 100 women will eventually have to take control of their own financial affairs because they have never married, are widowed or divorced, or are the leading income earner in the family.

Women are different as investors. They tend to be more conservative and risk-averse than men, focusing too much on short-term issues such as paying bills and not enough on long-term planning. Many also lack financial knowledge. This is not meant to be patronizing to women. Women live longer and earn less; this is a statistical fact. Therefore, women need to save more and plan better than men.

This chapter will deal with a number of women's and family issues.

- Why women need to save more than men.

- What it costs to raise children.

- How couples can avoid money arguments.

- How the tax act treats women differently.

- How women are losing their jobs as fast as men in this downturn.

- Financial lessons you can give your children.

REASONS WHY WOMEN MUST SAVE MORE THAN MEN

- The annual retirement income and personal savings for men average $14,450—not that much at all. But women, by comparison, get only $8,020. Since women on average live six years longer than men, the females are more likely to run out of funds before they die.

- Women generally earn less than men throughout their careers and therefore have less to save. This is one reason why pay equity is such an issue now.

- This inequity can be explained by the fact that more women than men work in smaller businesses, which are less likely to offer pension plans. In our survey, 52% of men were covered by employer pension plans, compared with 39% of women.

- Women often must leave their jobs in order to have children, move with spouses, care for elderly parents, or handle other domestic problems. Because of the disruption, female employees may not have put in enough time to qualify for company plans or fail to build up much value in the plans because of lack of years on the job.

- If divorce or death of the husband occurs, women may lose part or all of the spouse's retirement income. Unfortunately, there is still the belief that a person can live off the spouse's savings.

To overcome these obstacles is not an easy task, but it is possible. Single women between the ages of 25 and 44, who earn $50,000 annually and have a company pension plan, should set aside more than 15% of after-tax income, which is double the amount suggested for men.

HOW MUCH DO CHILDREN COST TO RAISE?

This is a question I receive often from listeners and readers. It is relevant both for family budgeting purposes and in the case of matrimonial disputes.

Children are expensive to raise in Canada, as confirmed by the reliable sources of information to follow. The best is published by the home-economics section of the Manitoba Ministry of Agriculture.

The numbers, however, are based on the cost of raising a child in Winnipeg, so the figures will be higher for Toronto, Edmonton, or Vancouver—perhaps as much as 20% higher.

As the number of children in the family increases, there are synergies and economies of scale as costs are reduced because of factors including sharing and the re-use of clothing.

The following table is a most useful and valuable guide. It can also be used effectively to impress upon your children how hard you must work to support them. The costs include expenses for food, clothing, health care, personal care, recreation/school supplies, transportation, child care, and shelter.

THE 1993 COSTS OF RAISING A CHILD

Age	Total Cost	
	Boy	Girl
Infant	9,008	9,008
1	9,647	9,679
2	8,746	8,765
3	8,784	8,802
4	9,137	9,154
5	9,249	9,266
6	8,165	8,180
7	8,480	8,414
8	8,480	8,414
9	8,507	8,417
10	8,689	8,499
11	8,689	8,499
12	5,881	5,818
13	6,026	5,931
14	6,118	6,023
15	6,381	6,284
16	6,685	6,289
17	6,685	6,289
18	6,525	6,129

TABLE 3–1

HOW TO AVOID MONEY MISUNDERSTANDINGS WITH YOUR MATE

- Make a date with your spouse to discuss your financial situation.

- Start keeping a detailed log of how your money (every cent of it) is being spent. List the date, the type of expenditure, and the amount. After a month or two, this record might prove to be rather enlightening, especially in revealing discretionary spending.

- Set up a budget. If you have conflicting opinions, talk about them. Try to resolve them by attacking the issues at hand, not the person.

- Discuss your investment goals, whether that includes post-secondary education for your children or retirement plans for the two of you. Set up a portfolio based on your objectives.

- Always consult your partner before committing family funds to any investment or loan. A wife or husband can be held liable for the spouse's debts.

- Work out an investment plan that makes the more anxious spouse feel comfortable. If you have trouble coming to an agreement, consult an independent financial planner for objective advice.

TAX TREATMENT OF WOMEN

I recently read a report from the Canadian Advisory Council on the Status of Women, a group that gets federal funding to deal with women's issues. They have produced a booklet called *Tax Facts: What Every Woman Should Know* that points out how women are treated differently under the tax act in seven different areas. These are worthy of your attention and are interesting.

1) Homemakers are treated as dependents and the married tax credit goes to the income earning spouse. For lower income families the loss of this credit could be an important factor in the decision as to whether the women can work part-time or not.

2) Single mothers represent 80% of those at or below the poverty level. The GST as a regressive tax, despite the tax credit, has hurt them the most.

3) A high percentage (over 65%) of women have ended up poor in old age because of inadequate retirement savings.

4) Support payments are tax deductible for the payer and not taxable in the hands of the recipient. In addition, the child tax credit is lost to the recipient of the support payment.

5) The deduction of child care expenses such as babysitting or daycare has not been converted to a credit, benefiting higher income tax payers more. Many care givers do not provide receipts for the cash they receive, causing the loss of the deduction.

6) The universal family allowance for children under 18 has been replaced by a new income-tested benefit.

7) The $1,000 pension income credit does not apply to the old age pension or income supplement which is an important source of income for older women. Few women over 65 today have private pensions.

These points highlight the need to take charge of your finances today, to do proper retirement planning, and to learn not to rely on or trust the government to look after you.

New government austerity because of huge federal and provincial deficits means more bad news on the way. We can no longer afford our social safety net and there is an ever increasing need to save, tax plan and retirement plan while you are still young enough to do it.

While some of the inequities of the Income Tax Act will disappear over time, most benefits like indexing our family allowance plans are gone for good.

This is part of understanding economic realities of the 1990s. The government cheque is now bouncing!

WOMEN AND LAYOFFS

In 1983, women held only 27% of managerial and supervisory jobs in Canada. This rose to 47%—near job parity—in 1992. But the earnings gap is still there, with women on average earning only 75% of men's wages. This is the case despite the fact that since 1982 women have received 51% of all bachelors and masters degrees.

Women also represent a growing proportion of the unemployed. While men lost nine times as many jobs as women during the last five recessions, the current recession is proving different and is hitting hard in the white-collar sector. This time around, women are also experiencing a net job loss. In this recession, for the first time, the services sector of the economy has also been strongly affected. And as women dominate in services (80% of service workers are women), they have paid a high price.

As of August 1, 1993, of the 20% unemployed who were white-collar, nearly 40% were women. With the job situation the way it is, women are responding by choosing self-employment and small business, as you will read in the chapter on entrepreneurship. Women, who make up the fastest growing category in self-employment and home business, will represent 50% of small-business owners in less than five years.

Nearly one worker in five in Canada is now a part-time worker. Women represent nearly 80% of all part-time workers, which means that few have the full benefits, pensions, or adequate cash flow needed for a proper investment plan or tax plan.

FINANCIAL LESSONS FOR YOUR FAMILY

The latest survey of Canadian students aged 18 years and younger shows that they know less about finances than their parents did 35 years ago.

In addition, the group called "Generation X" (19- to 29-year-olds) has a whopping 43% of its members living at home with parents, and 17% unemployment. Most of these young adults recognize that they will never be as rich as their parents or ever earn as much in this new Canadian economy of the 1990s.

There are, however, some valuable lessons you can impart to your children, which will benefit them immensely in the difficult years ahead.

For parents of children aged 12 or younger:

1) Become a financial role model. Read books, take courses, go to seminars, and share knowledge with your family. Let your children see you budget, not conspicuously consume with your credit cards.

2) Give children an allowance. It will make them think about the value of money, how to buy things, how to budget, how to plan, and how to live within their means. A number of children's books on finance have appeared in the last few years. Buy them for your children and read the books with them. Some experts suggest giving the children one annual stipend and forcing them to live on it: don't give in and extend credit. I have one daughter who can live on $100 for a year and lend out half on interest. Another daughter needs $100 to survive a week and is always broke.

3) Encourage children to save all cash gifts from relatives and friends. Take children to the bank, open an account, and explain how interest works. Give your children a coin jar and wrappers and encourage them to save. That's how I started. By the time I was 21, I had saved enough coins to buy my wife a one-carat diamond ring (wholesale, mind you).

4) Let children buy one share of stock in a few special companies. Disney gives bonus coupons to stockholders, as do many toy manufacturers. There is also the magic of the dividend cheque on the share. Even a 12-cent cheque is a great and valuable lesson on the benefits of equities.

For the parents of children aged 13 to 19:

1) Provide a monthly allowance to cover all costs of movies, fast food, and nights out.

2) Encourage your children to get a part-time job. We often joke about McJobs, but one person in 10 probably got his or her first job at McDonald's and it was a great training ground and motivator. A friend of mine said his 17-year-old son was doing badly in school, so he made him get a job at McDonald's. He worked there for six months and his grades shot through the roof. He learned discipline, standards, self-esteem, teamwork, and of course the value of the dollar. The boy has now finished university.

For parents of children aged 20+:

1) Make sure your children work, but not in the first year of university, which is the most difficult transition year.

2) Make your children responsible for all their personal entertainment expenses.

3) Be a role model in terms of vices such as not smoking and drinking. You now know why they're called "sin" taxes.

4) Introduce your children to professionals so your kids can ask about career options.

5) Encourage your children to be entrepreneurial and help them if they ask for it.

6) If the children are stuck at home because of unemployment or poor cash flow, make sure they pay something. You might save it for them to help them out later.

7) Don't try to get your kids a job. Make sure they feel they either can get it on their own or can choose self-employment.

8) If your children want to return to school, do everything you can to make sure they do.

The purpose of these lessons is to teach your children the value of money by encouraging them to manage their own money. It is important to understand that you aren't doing your children any favours by giving them everything or sheltering them from financial matters. Rather, allow your children to participate in family discussions of financial matters. It will help them immensely later in life.

Insurance
Income and Asset Protection

Income, asset, and cash protection comprise a big element of personal financial planning. It is also the element most people hate the most—Insurance!

There are many horror tales of the poor airline passenger forced to sit next to an insurance salesman on a bi-coastal trip and listen to a sales pitch for five hours.

No one loves to buy insurance. Yet as a people, Canadians have the most insurance per capita of any Western nation. On a global basis, only the Japanese buy more. We all love those insurance commercials on TV—you know, the commercial where the guy is running on the tropical beach. Remember that the guy who is running and laughing is the insurance agent. Or how about another favorite, the commercial where you can buy $25,000 of life insurance with no medical exam regardless of your age? The elderly woman is bemoaning the fact her husband died without insurance, but now she has some. The commercial fails to mention that the most you can get back in the first two years is what you paid—about $500—and that the insurance is very expensive because of the high risk of the clients.

Bankers are not much help, either. They will ask you if you want life insurance for your loan, but neglect to tell you that you can say no! They also will not reveal that the bank-sponsored insurance is very expensive. And they will not admit that the bank makes a lot of money on the insurance.

You can buy the same type of insurance from an independent agent for about 40% cheaper if you really need it. Most people do not need it.

Credit insurance like this belongs to that category of products that are overpriced and generally totally unnecessary. Just increase your basic life and disability insurance for the term of the loan. The basic reason for insurance is to protect the dependants against an immediate loss of income and to protect assets.

Do not buy insurance to cover yourself against small losses that you could handle using your savings. And avoid policies that insure you for just one risk, such as a specific disease or plane crash. This is called narrow coverage and it's expensive and foolish.

Flight insurance, life insurance on children or a non-working spouse, cancer or AIDS insurance, and credit or loan insurance are all types of policies that simply conserve valuable cash flow but produce little benefit. Most credit card companies now provide flight life insurance if you book the trip with their card.

Product warranty insurance plans and contracts are also big profit centres for stores, but bad buys for consumers. Proper insurance is, however, an indispensable companion to your long-term financial planning. It lets you control how well you can cope financially if a major family catastrophe occurs. The worst situation financially is the loss of the principal wage earner. In addition, insurance should be in place as part of any portfolio or tax plan to protect your assets and your main wage earner.

In Canada, we do not have a death or estate tax. We eliminated them during tax reform between 1979 and 1981. But several provinces are now contemplating an estate tax, similar to that in the United States, on estates with assets worth more than $600,000.

We also have a capital gains tax in Canada. Under the tax act, Revenue Canada deems you to have sold your assets the day before you passed away, even though you did not. Capital gains on your assets are then subject to taxation: if your estate does not have the cash, the assets must be sold to pay the taxes. Now this assumes that you have died without estate planning and have not transferred or bequeathed assets to a spouse or child.

But there are also questions of liquidity to pay for the ongoing living expenses of survivors. The money has to come from somewhere. Employers do not do a great job here. Many, nearly 60% according to a William Mercer benefit survey in March 1993, are rationalizing benefits as part of cost-cutting measures.

Life insurance provided by employers is usually minimal. The first $25,000 is a non-taxable benefit, but most employers will offer you only three times salary. This is completely inadequate for any employee between 30 to 60 years of age with family members.

Outside of the traditional work environment, where people are self-employed or home workers, disability insurance is particularly rare. These individuals in many cases represent half of the family's income and most of the uninsured are women.

What happens if you get sick? Employer disability kicks in after 90 to 180 days and pays only 60% of earnings, although the benefit is non-taxable. This is not adequate, yet most employers are reducing this amount and passing costs on to employees. The self-employed, who rarely buy disability insurance, end up on welfare as a result.

As there are various trade groups, clubs, associations, and small-business groups offering disability coverage on a group basis, you should top up so that you have at least 67% or more coverage to ensure that the net cash flow covers your basics.

The following insurance worksheet will help you calculate what you need. This is based on a 40-year-old male earning $75,000 net income per year and his spouse, who is also 40, earning $20,000 net income from a home business. They have two children whom they wish to have attend university. The family has a house with a $150,000 mortgage, as well as $150,000 in insurance and $65,000 in income-producing assets. We might consider that the family actually needs insurance for 41 years if the adult male reaches the national average age of 81. There are no absolute rules of thumb. Some insurance experts suggest you need 80% of your income, others 67%.

SAMPLE INSURANCE WORKSHEET

FUNDS TO COVER		EXAMPLE
1. Funeral and other final expenses	_____	$10,000
2. Capital gains taxes	+ _____	+ N/A
3. Paying off mortgage (optional)	+ _____	+ 150,000
4. Paying off other family debts (optional)	+ _____	+ 10,000
5. University costs	+ _____	+ 50,000
6. Special needs	+ _____	+ N/A
7. **SUBTOTAL**	= _____	= 220,000

FUNDS FOR THE LOWER-INCOME SURVIVOR'S LIVING EXPENSES		
8. Current household expenses	_____	51,500
9. Target percentage	x _____	x 67%
10. Survivors' annual expenses	= _____	= 34,505
11. CPP benefits	− _____	− N/A
12. Survivor's take-home pay	− _____	− 20,000
13. Annual need	= _____	= 14,505
14. Number of years needed	x _____	x 25
15. **SUBTOTAL**	= _____	= 362,625

16. Total amount needed (Lines 7 + 15)	_____	582,625
17. Existing insurance	− _____	− 150,000
18. Income-producing assets	− _____	− 65,000
19. **ADDITIONAL INSURANCE NEEDED**	= _____	= $367,625

TABLE 4–1

The other question relates to how many times your income you need to have as protection. The old rule of thumb of 10 times earnings was based on investing the principal at 10% and living off the interest. But interest rates are now 4.2% on Treasury bills, so do you need 20 times earnings? No. First, it probably is too expensive for the family. Secondly, if the principal is properly invested as I suggest in the chapter on financial planning, the returns even in a good conservative portfolio should be around 20% per annum. More importantly, it is critical to shop aggressively for the best rate on term from the most reliable, well managed company with the best reputation for quality service and products.

In the table below are 10 suggestions for saving on insurance premiums. The dollar amount in the salary column represents the approximate amount you would save by following each guideline. Whole life insurance is expensive and performance yields are poor. I remember when, in 1948, my parents bought a whole life $1,000 policy for me to pay for my university education. One thousand dollars was a lot of money back then when my father was earning $50 a week. But when I reached age 18 in 1965, the policy had a value after all that time of $1,300, (enough for two years' tuition at the University of Toronto), essentially, only an annual yield of 1.5% compounded. Had my parents put the principal in Canada Savings Bonds, the portfolio would have been worth about $2,200, and had they bought shares in the Templeton Fund, the assets would have been worth nearly $7,500—enough for university, a car, and a trip to Florida.

WAYS TO SAVE ON INSURANCE

	Savings Net Salary
1) Keep reasonably fit with average blood pressure and heart beat	$ 75 to $100
2) Don't smoke; drink only in moderation	$100
3) Visit the doctor for a check-up every year	$50
4) Raise auto collision deductible from $100 to $500	$100
5) Raise comprehensive deductible from $50 to $250	$50
6) Raise house deductible from $250 to $500 and add smoke detectors and up-to-date wiring and burglar alarms	$100
7) Where possible, get one company to provide automotive, household, and even life insurance	$50
8) Shop around for your rates each year and get three bids	$100
9) Avoid bank insurance, flight coverage, single-factor policies, etc., and anything sold as a bargain on TV	$100–$250
10) Take the maximums provided by your employer's group plans for life, disability, dental, etc.	$100

Table 4–2

INSURANCE ISSUES BY AGE GROUP

Ages 19 to 39

1) Insurance is a major factor in the selection of a car. A sports car has insurance costs twice that of a family car.

2) A tenants' policy on apartment contents is a must to protect your assets. Make sure that the insurance covers: replacement costs, not cash cost, of your assets; provides payment for hotels if you are burned out of your apartment; and covers you if you damage the landlord's property or if someone is hurt on the property.

3) Make a detailed list of your key assets. You probably are computer-literate. Make a list on a disk and leave it in your safety deposit box. A video cassette of your assets is also valuable.

4) Buy term life insurance as soon as you are married and have dependants.

Ages 40 to 59

1) Establish specific floaters for all assets worth $5,000 or more.

2) Be sure to shop for car insurance discounts. This age group gets the cheapest rates.

3) Make sure you have an aggressive life insurance plan in place, following the guidelines in this chapter.

4) Don't convert your term life to whole life. Integrate the insurance plan with your financial planning program for tax, retirement, and estate planning, and make sure it's reviewed every three years.

Ages 60+

1) Use your insurance as part of your estate plan to pay your taxes.

2) Consider selling your house and becoming a renter.

3) Eliminate all unnecessary cars and assets that have specific policies that you don't use or need.

4) Keep fit and get regular check-ups to keep rates low.

5) Work with your financial planner to see that insurance is properly integrated into your total plan.

6) Consider how long you plan to work (if you are still working) and whether disability insurance is needed. Also consider expanding on health insurance not covered by government plans.

Equity and Mutual Fund Investment Strategy

Low interest rates, low inflation, slow economic growth, and high unemployment in Canada have generated the greatest focus on personal investments in nearly thirty years. The search for acceptable returns on invested capital has resulted in a steady flow of roughly $2 billion a month moving out of bank deposits and Guaranteed Investment Certificates into less traditional investments.

In spite of this trend, there is very little research into the subject of personal financial management in Canada. For example, personal finance is generally ignored in graduate business schools. In addition, training programs in large financial institutions rarely incorporate an understanding of the financial needs of their customers. Little, if any, quantitative market research is funded by these institutions.

THE MYTH OF LONG-TERM INVESTMENT STRATEGY

If clichés could kill, certainly one that has been both fatal and overused is the phrase "the importance of having a long-term investment strategy."

Clearly there is a lack of understanding of the concept of strategy and its application in the field of personal finance. Academics working in the field of finance suggest to us the need to document and codify a personal investment plan with a long-term vision expressed in clear and precise quantitative goals; however, this inflexible approach ignores the necessity of responding to the ever-changing realities of the economic landscape.

As for the conventional wisdom of large Canadian financial institutions and their perception of "strategy," John Kenneth Galbraith in his book, *A Short History of Financial Euphoria*, correctly points out that just because financial institutions are large does not mean that the people who are directing the affairs of these companies are smart. Amazingly, the expression "the importance of having a long-term strategy" is often used in public by major banking, insurance, and trust company officials who, in private, follow a long-term strategy of not training their own personnel properly. What is more, their long-term investment strategy of funding commercial real estate well after the end of its profitability cycle has proved disastrous to Canadian investors.

Strategy is supposed to be a set of specific actions to achieve clearly defined, measurable objectives. It is the "how" of the process. But, rigidly codified personal financial plans are a comfortable window dressing that ignores current reality, as the sheer rate of change within international financial markets increases at an incredible speed. Reality and contemporary experience suggest that the most efficient and effective route to investment success is the one being followed by many independent financial planners. It is built on two key elements, "flexibility, adaptability, and responsiveness" and "logical incrementalism."

The successful investor, from high-profile individuals like Warren Buffett and Peter Lynch on down, have extolled the importance of being flexible, adaptable, and responsive to the changing investment climate. This does not mean arbitrarily churning, but constantly adapting an investment portfolio to reflect changing interest rates, inflation expectations, business trends, globalization, and political and technological change. By incorporating this approach in the selection of my 1992 stock-pile list, the emphasis went from pharmaceutical, consumer goods, and resource stocks to gaming, discount retailers, and microchip producers. As a result, the portfolio growth over 12 months was 66% by 1993.

The practice of logical incrementalism suggests that success in personal financial planning is not based on a rigid or absolute long-term strategy, but a continuous process of constantly learning from our recent experiences. In effect, this is an enhanced version of "muddling through," constantly changing or letting the strategy evolve over time.

By following quarterly reviews of investment decisions by independent financial planners and applying constant tinkering, based on implementing past lessons for future profit, you can produce a dynamic portfolio that yields consistently above-average returns. The process of long-term wealth creation is not a rigid investment plan slavishly adhered to, but rather is based on an entrepreneurial vision that is constantly enhanced. If Voltaire were correct in asserting that the greatest enemy of good is better, then the proper method of investment management is one of continuous improvement to produce results that are more than just good.

Integrated with the six elements of financial planning, the results can result in doubling your net worth (30% returns per year) every three years.

BECOMING A SUCCESSFUL INVESTOR

There are three elements to making the investment process successful:

1) Decide how you are going to divide up your portfolio among broad categories of investments—stocks, bonds, and money instruments.

2) Decide how you want to diversify your investments within each category. For example, if you have some of your holdings in bonds, what percentage should be Canadian government bonds, foreign bonds, bond mutual funds, and corporate bonds.

3) You then should select optional products in each of the categories.

Your first step, deciding on how you will divide your portfolio among stocks, bonds, and money products, is the most crucial decision. Between 85% and 91.5% of the variance in performance of portfolios is based on this decision; only 15% of the variance in performance is based on individual products.

The process of deciding how to divide (or diversify) your investment portfolio among various kinds of investment vehicles and products is known as asset allocation.

The financial services industry is finally starting to recognize the importance of quantitative market research in helping investors to be successful. One of the first studies in this area, presented at the Canadian Association of Financial Planners' 1992 annual convention, was funded by the United Group of Funds. Two key issues were examined.

1) Do the services of an independent financial planner make a difference?

Interviews were conducted with 1,890 Canadian investors to determine their financial performance between 1989 and 1992. Those individuals who utilized the services of an independent financial adviser, realized net asset growth that was 34% higher than the financial returns achieved by investors who made their own investment decisions and did not receive outside professional advice during that three-year period.

These results should not be surprising, as this was one of the most volatile periods in modern investment history. The superior professionally advised return on invested capital was most often achieved by following advice to move assets out of real estate investments and fixed income securities into bond funds, international equities, and domestic mutual funds, as well as learning to time the interest-rate cycle.

2) Does asset allocation (or investment diversification) really work?

Canadians typically hold 85% of their investment assets in bank deposits, GICs, bonds, and other fixed income securities. Most portfolios have very little diversification. Essentially, we are a nation of vertical, not horizontal, investors.

Respondents in this survey were asked to outline in detail their investment holdings from 1981 to 1991. The study was limited to investors with a net worth in excess of $250,000, as we felt that members of this group would be more knowledgeable and organized in their investment holdings. Diversification was considered to mean holdings in a minimum of three categories of investment products, such as equities, bonds, and cash.

Throughout the ten years, investors who had developed and maintained an asset-allocation approach during the entire period had generated net asset growth 46% greater than those who had primarily vertically invested portfolios with limited diversification. A recently published *Wall Street Journal* study covering the twenty-year period from 1972 to 1992 produced corroborating results.

ASSET ALLOCATION

Whether you like it or not, you are constantly making asset-allocation decisions. Unfortunately, the typical investor waits until it is too late to give the decision proper consideration.

Asset-allocation decisions based on the investment strategies in this book are unique in that the decisions focus on many markets at once. In contrast, most other decisions deal with just one market at a time. Decisions such as when to move money into a market or what securities to buy are the ones on which the investor spends the most time. Most market timers devote their efforts to determining if a market is bullish or boorish. A security selector, on the other hand, tries to find the best security that has the most potential in a market. The asset-allocation decision is the one that considers the possibility that some entirely different market might have even more favourable risk/return characteristics altogether.

Numerous academic studies have concluded that the asset-allocation decision is by far the most important determinant of investment performance. A 1991 study in the *Journal of Financial Analysts* concluded that 90% of the difference in the long-term performance of 82 pension plans could be traced to these plans' original asset-allocation decisions, not to what the pension funds' managers did within each investment category.

In other words, there is a very high probability that you will produce dramatically better results from a superior initial decision on asset allocation than if you simply divided your asset portfolio into one-third stocks, one-third bonds, and one-third gold, for example.

The way most Canadians aged 40 and above decide to allocate assets, usually without much research or planning, typically results in: 80% bonds, GICs, and real estate; 10% equities and mutual funds; and 10% cash and miscellaneous holdings.

However, when 12 of the top investor asset-allocation advisory letters available in Canada and the United States (and their performance over the last four years) were analyzed, the top three performers with four-year gains between 58% and 92% had asset-allocation decisions as follows.

1) 65% stocks and equity mutual funds
   30% bonds, bond mutual funds, and GICs
   5% cash

2) 65% stocks and equity mutual funds
   35% bonds, bond mutual funds, and GICs

3) 55% stocks and equity mutual funds
   30% bonds, bond mutual funds, and GICs
   15% cash

None had many investments allocated to gold, but they did hold gold shares.

While the returns averaged about 15% to 23% per annum and not 30% or more, this does show that the overall asset-allocation decision can create, with greatly reduced risk, an annual threshold of 15% or more in these times. Then as you learn how to select equities and mutual funds, and then tax-plan your income stream, we can elevate your returns within the categories to more than 30% per annum, ensuring that your net worth doubles within three years.

Asset-allocation theory has produced annual returns that are up to 46% higher than typical portfolios in specific "vertical" investment categories. Diversification in stocks, bonds, and cash helps create less risk than investing in stocks alone.

The following table illustrates the value of diversification. For $100,000 invested in a diversified portfolio, the after-tax return is 38.5% (using the $100,000 capital gains exemption, $10,000 RRSP contribution, and dividend tax credit).

INVESTMENT RETURN PLAN
$100,000 INVESTED IN A DIVERSIFIED PORTFOLIO

Investment	Amount	$ Return	Return %	Return After Tax
Labour-Sponsored Venture	$5,000	$4,500	90%	$4,500
Capital Corporation				Grants and RRSP Eligible
RRSP Investment to maximum	10,000	5,000 refund plus 30% return	50%	RRSP tax recovery
Use Refund to pay off mortgage principal and save three times amount in interest expense	5,000	15,000 after-tax dollars saved		
Net return and savings are		$18,000	180%	
Equity Selections – Individual (assume 3% dividends and dividend tax credit)	$20,000	6,000	30%	5,800 tax-free capital gains
Mutual Fund– Equities	$30,000	9,000	30%	9,000 tax-free capital gains
Bond Funds	$15,000	1,200	8%	600 capital gains and interest
Bonds and GICs	$10,000	600	6%	300
Money Markets and Cash	$10,000	600	6%	300
TOTAL	$100,000	$39,900	39.9%	38.5%

TABLE 5–1

Even if the stock market goes through a 10% or greater "correction," those investors who properly allocated will find that they will be much less affected than those people who put all their eggs in one basket.

Arguments Against the Process of Asset Allocation

1) Complexity – It's a lot of work.

2) Monitoring – Constant updating is needed.

3) Interactions – Considering all six elements, financial planning is a lot of work.

4) Effort – To succeed at it requires effort.

5) Understanding – It is a demanding process to understand.

Arguments in Favour of Asset Allocation

1) Macro Decision – The impact changes your life, security, and future.

2) Diversity – It reduces risk and increases returns.

3) Globalization – You invest worldwide and reduce your risk.

4) Interaction and Synergy – The whole is greater than the sum of the parts.

5) Tax Amelioration – You keep more money and pay less tax.

Proper asset allocation increases returns and mitigates the impact of risk. A number of trust companies and mutual funds are offering asset-allocation services to clients. For instance, AGF Management's asset-allocation model might advocate putting 54% of investors' money in stocks, 42% in bonds, and 4% in the money market. The company reviews the model each Thursday to see whether an asset switch is needed. Other mutual funds create a balanced fund that puts money directly into the markets. Each of these funds has a fixed proportion of its portfolio allocated to stocks, bonds, and/or cash. Still, most of these funds are market-timing investment portfolios, not asset-allocation models.

The following table identifies some of the most common types of equity, bond and money market assets that make up a diversified portfolio.

TYPES OF INVESTMENTS IN A DIVERSIFIED PORTFOLIO

Equities	Bonds	Money Market
Canadian, U.S., Foreign, Small-Cap,	Canadian, Foreign,	Cash, GICs, CDs, T-bills
NASDAQ	Government, Corporate,	Mutual Fund—
Mutual Funds	Short, Medium, Long Term	Money Market
Growth, Value, Small-Cap	Bonds Funds—Domestic,	
Emerging, Asian	International	
European	Balanced	
Preferred High Yields	Stripped and Zero Coupon Bonds	
Limited Partnerships, Labour Pools		

TABLE 5–2

If we decide to allocate 60% of our overall portfolio to equities, we must then choose specific stocks from within that category. We are, therefore, selecting a "portfolio of portfolios." For example, our equity portfolio might look like this:

- Canadian TSE—10 to 12 stocks preferred and high yield
- Canadian Growth Mutual Fund
- U.S. Small-Cap Mutual Funds
- U.S. NYSE Equities—6 to 8 stocks
- Asian Market Mutual Fund
- Emerging Market Mutual Fund
- Labour Sponsored Fund

This sample equity portfolio includes stocks to create capital gains and dividends, and mutual funds to create capital gain and growth.

A portfolio of bonds might include bonds of different maturities as well as bond-based mutual funds for capital gains and income:

- Canadian Government—Long Term
- Canadian Corporate
- Stripped Bonds
- Bond Fund—International
- Balanced Mutual Funds

Following is a money market portfolio to maximize returns, liquidity, and flexibility:

- Bank Deposits
- CDs
- GICs
- T-bills
- Money Market Mutual Funds

When looking at the potential of an investment, you cannot judge the value just by the return percentage alone. Other factors should be examined too, including the tax implications for your particular financial situation.

Keeping all this in mind, here are some other tax-driven investment vehicles that you may also consider. You should understand that no more than 10% of the entire value of your portfolio should be comprised of these types of investments.

SAMPLE INVESTMENT PLANS

Below 40 Years of Age:

Equities (Canadian)	15%
Small-Cap Stocks (Canadian or U.S.)	10%
Growth Funds (Canadian)	10%
Equities (U.S.)	20%
Emerging Market Funds	5%
International Bonds	10%
Fixed Income Securities	10%
Cash	10%
Asian Market Funds	10%

Aged 40 to 60

Asian Market Funds	10%
Small-Cap Stocks (Canadian or U.S.)	5%
Equities (Canadian)	20%
Equities (U.S.)	10%
Emerging Market Funds	5%
International Bond Funds	10%
Long Bonds	10%
Fixed Income Securities	10%
Cash	10%

Aged 60+

Asian Market Funds	10%
Value Funds	10%
Equities (Canadian)	10%
Equities (U.S.)	20%
Long Bonds	10%
International Bonds	10%
Fixed Income Securities	15%
Cash	15%

TABLE 5–3

- high-yield equities paying dividends: $1 dividends = $1.25 interest income
- Limited partnerships in income ventures offering tax amelioration —particularly in active business income ventures, mutual fund limited partnerships, offshore real estate (especially China), multi-unit residential builings in the south eastern U.S., Caribbean hotel/ casino ventures, computer software, and management and education videos
- Junk bonds of quality in mutual funds

RISK MANAGEMENT

A profit is only taken when it is realized. That is, you have to sell the stocks or bonds before realizing the gain. People are always asking about when to sell an investment, especially if the price falls.

There are several views on this. As no one is right all of the time, the investor has to learn to cut losses. If the price falls, you must ask yourself if you should buy more or sell. Brokers call this process of buying more of a losing investment "averaging down," reducing the cost of an investment by purchasing more of it as the price falls so that your unit cost averages out lower. This is a foolish method. If the price falls 20%, you will have to realize a 25% gain to break even; if the price falls 25%, you will need a 33⅓% gain to break even.

In many mutual funds, to reduce risk, you just have to switch over to a better-performing category of fund in the same family of funds. You generally will not incur any transaction costs for the switch.

The rule of thumb is this: as the loss on an individual investment increases beyond 15%, the possibility of full recovery decreases to 50%. At 25% losses, the probability of breaking even drops to 25%.

Research on risk management indicates that there are a number of types of risk to avoid:

- loss of liquidity

- the non-systematic risk of the market created by buying an individual stock

- the general market risk created by overall upward and downward trends in the business cycle.

People buy mutual funds to reduce the first two classes of risk. You can get liquidity on your funds usually within five business days. Because funds are diversified into different companies, sectors, economies, and investment products (such as bonds and Treasury bills), they remove the impact of the lack of proper diversification.

An Investment's Potential for Profit in Different Economic Cycles

INVESTMENT	TYPE OF ASSET	REAL GROWTH	INFLATION	RECESSION
Real Estate	Real	Good	Good	Poor
Commodities (Gold, Silver)	Real	Getting Better	Good	Poor
T-Bills	Money Market	Poor	Poor	Good
Equities	Growth and Income	Good	Good	Poor
Bonds	Income	Declining	Poor	Good

TABLE 5–4

54

The risk of the market direction is reduced by market timing and following closely with your financial planner the general trends of interest rates and your local markets. You also reduce risk by diversifying globally to mitigate the impact of the Canadian market falling. If the Canadian market goes down, perhaps Europe, Southeast Asia, or South America will do better.

KEY INVESTMENT TERMS FOR THE 1990s

Diversification: If you have ever been told, "Don't put all your eggs in one basket," you have just received a lesson in the importance of diversifying your assets. If you own a number of different investments, you are less likely to suffer major losses than if you own a single stock or bond and it falls in value.

Asset Allocation: Asset allocation is the process of achieving diversification in your portfolio. The most important factor in determining how well your investment portfolio performs is how effectively you balance your assets within key broad categories—fixed income securities, stocks, bonds, and specialty products.

Compounding: This refers to the effect of accelerating income growth by earning interest on top of previously earned interest. For example, if you earn 10% interest on your savings account each year for four years (and you leave your money in the account), you will actually earn 46.4% interest in total. This is because in each successive year you are earning interest income on your original investment plus previously earned interest. The bad news is that with savings account interest rates as low as three-quarters of 1% in 1993, the benefits of compounding as an income source have been seriously eroded.

Growth: When investors or independent financial planners talk about "growth," they are really talking about a long-term investment strategy which emphasizes capital-gains earnings.

Risk: This term refers to the likelihood that you will lose money as a result of a short-term decline in value in your investments. Just remember, though, in our current economic situation, stocks are not nearly as risky as bonds or GICs if you are a long-term investor who is attempting to preserve the purchasing power of your money.

Total Return: This is the aggregate financial return earned by an investor over a defined period of time. Total return is specifically defined as the yield (dividends and earned interest) plus the net change in the price of the security.

Value: Investors or money managers whose investment strategy is based on a "value" philosophy purchase securities that they consider inexpensive relative to total corporate assets or current earnings. This philosophy is often contrasted with a "growth"-oriented philosophy.

—————— EQUITIES ——————

Canadians have had a long history of avoiding equities. Yet equities are at the core of this book's investment strategy for growth.

People always ask me about the "R" word, assuming it's RISK when in fact it is RETURN. They remember the crash of 1987, but ignore the 30 months of the bull market where investors had more than doubled their worth.

Since most Canadians in the 50+ age group without a corporate background have had little experience with equities, this chapter is devoted to explaining many of the basics of equity selection, including my 1993-1994 list of stock picks.

For most people, buying individual equities is a dangerous situation, as these individuals are not likely to monitor the stocks properly and tend to hang on too long. Mutual funds are more appropriate for most people because of the funds' breadth of investment and, therefore, their ability to remove the non-systematic risk of the market—a risk that is created by individuals when they buy too few stocks. You need approximately 15 to 20 stocks to remove the sector risk of an economic downturn.

Any successful long-term strategy for Canadians must utilize careful stock selection strategies.

Here are reasons why most people do poorly investing in stocks on their own.

1) They don't devote enough time to the process.

2) They don't have the necessary training and skills.

3) They take their cues from a broker, who is probably more interested in commissions than long-term results.

4) They let their emotions sway their judgement.

5) They hold onto losses in order to get even and they sell their winners too soon.

6) They trade too often because they like the action.

7) They have no system, discipline, or consistent approach.

SELECTING STOCKS

How do you choose which stocks to buy? How can you select the stocks with the greatest total potential return? I started selecting stocks in 1963 and only developed my current style in 1988, which is based on a combination of an analysis of certain industry sectors and a "value" orientation. There are several methods of selecting stocks and no one approach is absolutely guaranteed. Once you decide on the methodology that works for you, stick with it for the longer term, say four to five years to determine the results.

Sectoral Analysis

Analyzing industry sectors identifies those sectors of the economy that are most likely to experience growth in the years ahead. For example, semi-conductors and gold mining are hot. Many experts argue that telecommunications, consumer goods, and petroleum stocks will be solid in about a year.

Once you identify the sectors you feel confident in (by having done research such as reading investment publications and newsletters), you can then look for the front runners and leaders—those that have the best products, best cash flow, best management, and lowest costs. You can get this information by reviewing annual reports, press releases, and business and financial media reports; however, it is a lot of work. I like *Forbes*, *Barron's*, *Business Week*, *Fortune*, the *Financial Post*, the *Globe and Mail*, *Report on Business*, and the *Wall Street Journal* for this.

I tend to ignore all releases from stockbrokers, as many are trying to sell stocks held in inventory and few have ever given solid insight. It really worries me when many so-called "analysts" who work for large brokerage firms call me for my retail- or hospitality-industry stock analyses.

Most investment newsletters are poor performers over time as well, and only three or four have been reliable during the 1980s. I don't endorse any of them and most successful stock investors are amused by much of what they read in these letters.

Value Analysis

Although it sounds complicated, the process of value analysis for public companies is a relatively simple process that involves three specific steps.

The first step is to seek a P/E ratio lower than the market. The term "P/E ratio" refers to the relationship between the price per share of a company's stock and its corporate earnings per share. For example, if a company has earnings of $2 per share (calculated by dividing total corporate earnings by the number of outstanding shares) and the stock is selling at $20 per share, then the P/E ratio would be 10 (i.e., $20 divided by $2 = 10).

However, as an investor, it is important to understand that different industries or markets have different P/E ratios. For example, pharmaceutical companies generally have higher P/E ratios than retailers, and stocks traded on major stock exchanges (such as the Toronto Stock Exchange) tend to have lower P/E ratios than stocks traded in the over-the-counter (OTC) market.

Having completed this step, you have narrowed your list of stocks worth considering, but most likely there are still a lot of possible purchases. Some of the remaining stocks may still prove to be real "dogs" too.

The second step is to determine whether the dividend pay-out is higher than the market average. Different companies have different dividend policies. For example, some companies issue shares that pay a cash dividend while others do not. Shares that do not pay out cash dividends tend to be issued by younger, fast-growing firms. Other companies have dividend policies that pay shareholders in the form of additional shares instead of cash, while still others issue share splits to reward shareholders.

As a general rule, if the average Standard & Poor's 500 dividend pay-out is 3%, a value analysis indicates that you will want to invest in shares offering a minimum 30% premium. This would mean a dividend pay-out of at least 3.9% (130% x 3% = 3.9%). When you consider that money market mutual funds are paying about 4%, a common stock issue that pays an equivalent return but also has potential to grow substantially must be considered a fairly good investment.

So, after going through these first two steps, does that mean that the stocks that have passed these two tests are worth buying?

The third step is to determine whether the overall rate of growth of corporate earnings has been higher than the market average over the past five years.

It is always important to understand the past performance of a company in general. Its shares may be selling at 10 to 12 times earnings and be paying dividends of 3.9%, but you must determine whether these numbers are simply the result of an overall drop in corporate earnings leading to a decline in the price of its shares.

If you have determined that the company's general performance over the past five years has been satisfactory, it is time for the final test —investigating earnings prospects for the next five years.

Ask yourself some basic questions. Will corporate earnings continue to grow? Is the company developing new products or services? Is the company's consumer base expanding of shrinking? These are important questions, but they are also the most difficult to answer.

Once you have completed the first three steps, you will find that perhaps only 30% of the shares on your list are still attractive purchases. From the ones remaining, you will want to invest in the stock of five companies. Why five? Because it is still likely that one of the five you choose will be a mistake for reasons you did not expect. You still need to diversify your portfolio so that you can cover any mistake. The idea is to spread the risk.

BASIC MARKET STRATEGIES

1) There is, in the long term, a 100% correlation between the success of a company and its stock performance. The stock may be a short-term non-performer, but in the long term it will outperform the market if the company is successful.

2) Ignore companies with poor balance sheets or ones that are so complicated that you cannot understand them.

3) When buying small-cap stocks of firms that have less than $100 million in market value, make sure that they are at least profitable before you take the risk.

4) Ignore the economy to a large extent. The biggest fortunes are made in bad times. Many solid companies do great in bad times. If the company is a good investment, it will do well regardless of what is going on around it.

5) Do not get involved in too many stocks unless you have the time to devote to them. It's difficult even with on-line services to track more than 15% of the companies; that's why mutual funds were invented.

6) Warren Buffett, the billionaire American investor has said his long- term success can be traced to just a handful of key decisions. You should concentrate on a few really good opportunities. You can find them through careful study and long-term patience. This means avoiding churning (excessive transactions simply for the purpose of just doing something).

   Great long-term performance is either the result of luck or a great decision, but it is usually impossible to differentiate between them. Regardless of whether your success appears to be the result of luck or a crucial decision, there is usually a lot of research, preparation, and hard work. As the saying goes, "The harder I work, the luckier I get!" Too many investors are preoccupied with the short term. The difference between successful long-term investment results and churning is the difference between a long-term relationship and a series of one-night stands. Only now I have learned that the one-night stands can kill us!

7) Use the established MBA school approach. The currently accepted approach to determining superior investment return is based on the concept of "beta," which was first developed by Professors Fama and French. Beta was developed as a measure of a stock's volatility. It compares price movement of a specific stock relative to the overall movement of the entire market.

For example, if a stock is assigned a beta of 2, it means that research has indicated that for every 1% increase or decrease in the overall market, the stock will move 2%. In effect, the stock is twice as volatile as the market. Similarly, if a stock is assigned a beta of .5, it means that for every 1% increase or decrease in the overall market, the stock will move .5%. In effect, the stock is one-half as volatile as the market.

It is also possible for a stock to have a negative beta, which means the stock will move inversely to the market. The assumption has been that greater volatility leads to greater return over long terms. This means that a "high-beta" stock is expected to produce greater long-term returns than a "low-beta" stock.

However, this assumption has now been called into question by the same researchers who developed the beta principle. Fama and French conducted a new study that suggests you can still beat the market, but a new approach is required. They analyzed the performance of more than 2,000 stocks between 1940 and 1990 and discovered that volatility wasn't as important a factor in determining financial returns as originally thought. What they did discover was that the ratio between the stock price and the book value of the company on a per-share basis was the best indicator. Based on the results of this research, investors should focus on low price-to-book multiples.

8) "Contrarian Investment: Extrapolation on Risk," an academic study published in 1993 by three Illinois professors, concludes that value stocks (undervalued) outperformed glamour stocks (those that are currently the most popular) in every possible five-year period since 1963. The study says that the market is not as efficient at pricing stocks as academics suggest, but rather it habitually overreacts. The value stocks outperformed the glamour stocks even in the worst market conditions without incremental risk.

INVESTING CONSERVATIVELY FOR INCOME

With record-low interest rates, older and conservative investors should be actively seeking conservative high-yield (yield is the dividend as a percentage of share price) common stocks. To calculate the yield, divide the dividend by the share price.

A study reported in the *Financial Times of Canada* claimed that a mixed portfolio of 10 of the highest yielding Canadian stocks on the Toronto Stock Exchange did far better than the TSE index from 1981 to 1987.

These high-dividend stocks, usually in utilities, telephone companies, or banks, outperformed many equity-based mutual funds. Because the dividends are from Canadian sources, they qualify for the dividend tax credit, increasing the return by an additional 25% more than interest income.

If you combine the capital gains potential of these conservative companies and their average 7% to 8% dividend yields, the returns for many are close to 16% to 18% throughout the last 12 months. This is an excellent component of all portfolios, regardless of the age of the investor.

However, beware of "too high a yield," as it may foretell a drop in share price.

A MAJOR MARKET CORRECTION

One of the most frequent questions I have been asked is whether I think we will experience another stock-market crash in 1994 similar to what we experienced in 1987.

All I know is that some time in the future, there is a high statistical probability that there will be a decline. If people do not understand that, then they should not own stocks.

For example, in this century there have been 50 declines of 10% or more, or one every two years. Of these 50 declines, 15 have been 25% or more; that's once every six years.

The situation is clear, after the correction as well, that those who stay and hold for the long term and do not churn their stocks will dramatically outperform those who hold fixed income securities or those who run at the sight of a decline.

Rules of Thumb for Investing in Small Stocks

- Remember to diversify. No one is perfect. You should buy several stocks within any industry and not focus exclusively on one company.

- Ask questions. Call the companies you are investigating, identify knowledgeable analysts, and do some basic research. A second opinion is as important in investing as it is in medicine.

- Use "dollar-cost averaging." By purchasing stock gradually on a regular basis, you will ultimately buy fewer shares at higher prices and more shares at lower prices, which will improve your investment returns.

WHITE'S STOCK WINNERS

1992 Stocks	1993 Stocks	1994 Stocks
Rubbermaid	Intel	Compaq
Merrill Lynch	Compaq	Microsoft
WalMart	Sun Microsystems	Chrysler
Home Depot	Chrysler	International Gaming
Microsoft	International Gaming	Technology
The GAP	Technology	Citibank
Office Depot	Jackpot Enterprises	Chase Manhattan
Omnicare	Showboat	Cott Beverages
International Gaming	J.C. Penney	Weston-Loblaws
Technology	Home Depot	Bank of Montreal
American Barrick	Circuit City	Snapple
Chrysler	Burlington Coat Factory	AT&T
	Checkers Drive-In	J.P. Morgan
	Starbucks	J.C. Penney
	Outback Steakhouses	Chubb
	Learning Co.	Brookstone
		General Mills
		Procter & Gamble
		Rubbermaid
		Sara Lee
		Nike
		Pepsico
		Gillette
		Campbell Soup
		Intel
		CIBC
		Micron Technologies
		Motorola

TABLE 5–5

- Cut your losses. Always set "stop-loss" orders to minimize potential losses and always take into account the greater day-to-day volatility of small stocks.

- Compare apples with apples. When analyzing the performance of your portfolio, always use a relevant benchmark that has similar characteristics to your portfolio. For example, compare the performance of a bond fund with other bond funds, not equity funds.

- Avoid fads. If all your friends are talking about a "hot stock," you're too late.

- Avoid feeding frenzies. Minimize transactions during periods of high trading volume, sharp rallies, and corrections in the market.

- Consider mutual funds. Professional money managers have more time and knowledge to manage your money than you do, so let the experts do their job so you can sleep better.

A SAMPLING OF DISCOUNT BROKERS' FEES

	Canadian Stocks				Mutual Funds
	$1	$20	$40	Fees for trades less than $2,000	Front-end load
Marathon Brokerage	$35 and 0.5¢ a share	$35 and 0.5¢ a share	$35 and 0.6¢ a share	$43	Up to $25,000: 2% $25,000 and up: 1% Min. commission: $80
TD Bank's Green Line	$40 and 0.5¢	$40 and 0.5¢	$40 and 0.7¢	$45	$1,000–$4,999: 2.5% $5,000–$24,999: 2% $25,000 and up: 1%
CIBC's Investor's Edge	$40 and 0.5¢	$40 and 0.5¢	$40 and 0.7¢	$45	Up to $5,000: 2.5% $5,001–$24,999: 2% $25,000 and up: 1%
Royal Bank's Action Direct	$35 and 0.1¢	$35 and 0.5¢	$35 and 0.7¢	$40	$2,000–$24,999: 2% $25,000 and up: 1%
Bank of Montreal's Investor Line	$25 and 0.5¢	$25 and 0.4¢	$25 and 0.6¢	$25	Up to $25,000: 2% $25,000 and up: 1% Min. commission: $100
Scotiabank's Scotia Discount Brokerage	$25 and 0.5¢	$25 and 0.4¢	$25 and 0.6¢	$25	Up to $25,000: 2% $25,000 and up: 1% Min. commission: $50
Mouvement Desjardin's Disnat (Quebec only)	$35 and 0.5¢	$25 and 4.5¢	$35 and 6.5¢	$45	Up to $25,000: 2% $25,000 and up: Negotiable Min. commission: $45

TABLE 5–6

UNDERSTANDING DISCOUNT BROKERS

Find your comfort zone. If you have the time, interest, and confidence in your own ability to do the necessary research prior to making investment decisions, use a discount broker.

Shop around. Even within the "discount" industry, different firms offer different price structures and levels of service, so find the broker who best suits your needs. The table on the previous page provides examples of discount brokers' fees.

Seek independent assistance. Consider joining associations. A good start would be the Canadian Shareowners Association, which is a non-profit organization that offers educational services to investors. For an initiation fee of $24 plus an annual membership fee of $68, you can get a bi-monthly magazine, a stock-selection manual, access to investment securities, and telephone access to help if you need it. You can contact the association at P.O. Box 7337, Windsor, Ontario N9C 4E9, telephone 1-800-265-9543.

Educate yourself. Most local community colleges and universities offer investment courses on a "continuing education" basis. Most are open to anyone and do not require prerequisites. In addition, the Canadian Securities Institute, the Canadian Institute of Financial Planners, and the Investment Funds Institute also offer courses to the public.

Know yourself. Do not get in over your head and never invest in something you do not understand. If you use a discount broker, you are on your own.

LOOKING FOR BOTTOM DWELLERS AND VALUE STOCKS EVERYONE ELSE MISSED
Criteria

Profit Turn-arounds: Wall Street analysts cannot possibly monitor all companies all the time. Small firms are often ignored by Wall Street, and new company developments may often go undetected for relatively long periods of time—perhaps six months or more. Peter Lynch, the former manager of the Fidelity Magellan Fund, says that his experience showed him that Wall Street analysts typically recommended stocks only during the final 20% of their total gains.

Large Outstanding "Short" Positions: If you can identify companies out of favour with investors and with the potential for good news, you could profit handsomely. Good news will result in greater price acceleration, as all the short sellers move to cover their short positions.

Diamonds in the Rough: When entire industries go through hard times, many strong, profitable, and growing companies within the industry end up getting tarred with the same brush. Keep your eyes open for well-managed firms that will continue to perform well and will lead an industry recovery.

Low P/E Ratio: Stay away from declining P/E ratios. If a firm's stock price is falling due to a declining P/E ratio, it is most likely an adjustment to reality rather than representing a buying opportunity. Above-average multiples cannot be sustained forever, so the only question is figuring out when the multiple will get in line with the market. Look for a below-average, yet stable, P/E ratio and rising profits as the keys to a buying opportunity.

Stable Market and Economic Conditions: Seeking out bottom-dwelling stocks is a higher-risk approach, so you want as many factors in your favour as possible. Therefore, do not "bottom-fish" during periods of economic uncertainty or declining markets (which can send unpleasant surprises your way). On the other hand, stock markets are flat or rising roughly 80% of the time so if you are investigating options during the short periods of declining markets, just wait, look, listen. Do not do anything until the market re-establishes its upward movement.

Change in Management: Kicking out existing management and bringing in new faces is no guarantee that a struggling company will suddenly and magically start making money. Look at how much difficulty General Motors and IBM are having to staunch the flow of red ink regardless of how many staff they cut or how many times they rearrange the deck chairs of top management. In the case of a management shake-up, understand the talents and track record of the new group and the new members' relevance to the new situation.

New Product Development: There are a multitude of specific reasons why a company may rebound after going through an extended bout of red ink. Broadly speaking, however, they all fall into two general categories: doing the same thing better and doing something new. Unless a bottom-dweller is striving to do one or the other, it is likely to remain a bottom-dweller.

SPECIAL BENEFITS OF EQUITIES
Dividend Re-Investment Plans

Dividend re-investment plans, or DRIPs, are low-cost ways for a shareholder to re-invest dividend returns in more stock and at a bargain rate (normal discounts are about 5%).

Eighty-five Canadian listed companies offer DRIPs to existing shareholders. This 5% savings goes directly to your return on investment in reducing your cost of shares purchased. I have discovered 850 U.S. firms that do the same thing. You normally do plough back the dividends each quarter, which may not be the best time from a share-performance view, but more often than not it's a good deal.

Many DRIPs let you buy more shares for cash at the same time if you are a registered shareholder. You bypass the broker and save the commission as well. If you are interested in quick flips, the 5% discount also lets you get out fast with a quick gain.

SOME CANADIAN DRIPs THAT ALLOW ADDITIONAL CASH INVESTMENT

COMPANY	MIN./MAX. ANNUAL CASH CONTRIBUTION
Alberta Energy Co.	$50/$20,000
Bank of Nova Scotia	$50/$20,000
BCE Inc.	$50/$20,000
Dofasco Inc.	$50/$20,000
Imperial Oil Ltd.	$50/$20,000
Island Telephone Co.	none/$20,000
Northern Telecom Ltd.	$40/$20,000 (U.S.)
Nova Corp.	$50/$20,000

TABLE 5–7

Tax-Free Dividends

The level of Canadian dividends that can be received tax-free is in most provinces $23,754 annually. This figure applies to individuals with no other income. However, do assess income surtaxes on dividends in Saskatchewan, Quebec, Manitoba, and Alberta. Those individuals receiving less than their optimal dividend level are missing out on a great return.

Due to preferential tax treatment, dividend payments in Canada are subject to a gross-up and corresponding tax credit which, after tax, makes dividend income worth roughly 25% more than interest income. According to a publication entitled "Tax Facts," covering the 1992–93 tax year, KPMG Peat Marwick Thorne indicates that the actual factor to be applied is 1.28. In other words, if you know what your dividend rate is, multiply it by 1.28 to find out your required return on interest income.

For our purposes, the basic rule of thumb for an investor to remember when combining interest and dividend income is that you will need 25% more interest income than dividend income to net the same amount after tax. Thus, a 6% dividend is equal to an investment that provides you with 8% interest income. Therefore, in today's market, it is critical to "max-out" in Canadian dividends to get any sort of respectable returns.

———— MUTUAL FUNDS ————

If I have to start explaining the basics of mutual funds, then as investors you are in bad shape. Mutuals go back more than 40 years as an investment system for Canadians, yet the funds have only grown into being a major investment vehicle in the past four years. Holdings have increased by 400% in that period. There are 680 Canadian and 3,800 American and international funds from which to choose, the act of which involves an emotional element in any portfolio strategy regardless of the age of the individual.

The right portfolio mix in mutuals is very personal and subjective, but essential to success. One fund is probably inadequate, and on average I recommend four to five funds adjusted for risk preference, interest rates, and the age and income of the investor. For example, an average portfolio of funds would include an emerging market fund with South American stocks, an Asian market fund including Hong Kong, a Canadian small-cap stock fund, a Canadian resource or equity growth fund, and a balanced or asset-allocation fund. This would be ideal for a 40-year-old, with a $75,000+ annual income, whose goals are inclined towards growth. My selections given out at my many seminars would have produced about 38% to 45% returns for 1993.

Remember, though, that your mutual funds are only one element of a total portfolio strategy and therefore your portfolio of mutuals is part of your portfolio of portfolios strategy.

The high equity element is part of the portfolio weighting to equities. Your proportion of equities in your overall holdings including mutuals should be a product of deducting your age from 100. For instance, if you are 40 years old, you should have a 60% mix of various types of equities. If you are 60 years old, you should have a 40% equity mix. This mix is essential to ensuring that the aggregation of the portfolio returns will yield a return in the 30%+ range, which is necessary if you hope to attain the goal of doubling your net worth every three years.

HOW TO PICK A FUND OR SIX

If you read most texts on mutual funds, the first thing they tell you is to read the 40-page prospectus of each of the 680 Canadian funds. This, of course is nonsense.

The basics are simple. Check out the risk, and the cost, and performance history.

Risk is usually the deciding factor when selecting the type of fund to buy. The decision depends on your personal risk-tolerance level.

Your risk tolerance can be tested by using the check-list at the end of this chapter. The greater the risk, the more favourable the return in a growth market. More importantly, your risk orientation determines how you react to bad news if the short-term returns spike downward. Most people respond by selling out for big losses. Risk-takers hold on and do well on the upside.

Mutual funds are concerned with equity risk and interest-rate risk. Equity risk is the uncertainty of a return on a business activity. This is the principal hazard of a stock fund. If business does not meet expectations in earnings, the stock fund falls. Interest-rate risk is based on the uncertainty of rates and the volatility. If interest rates fall, bond funds soar. If inflation rises and rates follow, bonds suffer a great deal. Did you earn 20% or better in the last five years from your mutual funds? If the answer is no, you probably have been too risk-averse and misjudged or misunderstood the interest-rate risk.

CHOOSING MUTUAL FUNDS ACCORDING TO INTEREST RATES

The second element to consider when choosing a fund is the cost factor. You add together one-fifth of the load-sales commission and the expense ratio that includes management fees and overhead costs, deduct that from the return. You should always look for mutual funds with relatively low risk, low costs, and consistently solid performance. Our experience has shown that the most reliable database for this information is BellCharts Inc. This information can also be obtained through your financial planner.

Of the three criteria—risk, cost, and performance history—I consider performance history to be least relevant. With regard to performance, the important criterion in my opinion is what is expected in the future, not what has been done in the past.

When selecting mutual funds, remember these basics.

1) Never make a purchase decision based exclusively on past performance. Don't buy gold shares if the market has gone bust.

2) Be realistic. Don't expect all funds to perform equally well all the time. Mutual funds are for the long term. Don't worry about the three-month average. Funds are meant to be long-term holds. In our current slow economy, most North American equity funds will likely generate only a 6% to 8% return. Therefore, having Asian and emerging-market content is essential. Small-cap stocks (companies under $500 million in sales) will do even better; they have averaged about 14% above inflation.

HOW MANY FUNDS YOU SHOULD OWN

With approximately 680 Canadian and 3,800 American and international funds to choose from, how many should you hold? The answer is between three and ten, but the optimal number is five. The idea is to cover as broad a section of the market as you can afford without taking on more funds, expenses, and paperwork than you need. You spread your money among funds that figure to do well at different points in the economic cycle. If you have $10,000 or less to invest in a fund, choose one that is widely diversified—perhaps a balanced fund.

BUILDING A PORTFOLIO

Amount available to invest	Number of funds to purchase	Portfolio
$5,000 or less	One to two	One balanced fund and/or one stock fund blending growth and value investing styles.
$5,000 to $10,000	Three	One balanced, one growth, one value fund.
$10,000 to $20,000	Four	Add a small-company growth fund or Asian fund.
$20,000 to $50,000	Five to six	Add an international fund and/or an intermediate-term bond fund.
$50,000 to $100,000	Seven to eight	Add a small-company value fund and/or a short-term bond fund.
$100,000 or more	Nine to 10	Add a mid-cap stock fund and/or a world income fund or emerging market fund.

TABLE 5–8

Whatever the amount of money you have to invest, you should always try to get up the broadest portfolio that you can afford using the fewest number of funds possible. If you are working with less than $5,000, buy a balanced fund, which holds both stocks and bonds. As more money becomes available, you can add one or two more specialized funds. Even with $100,000 to invest, you do not need more than 10 funds. The portfolio suggestions above are for investors who are comfortable with moderate risk.

STYLE

Mutual funds can be profitably managed using one of any number of investment styles. The following table categorizes a number of leading mutual funds by specific investment styles.

EXAMPLES OF INVESTMENT STYLES

Value investors	Templeton Growth Fund Ltd. Cundill Value Fund Ltd.
Market timers	Guardian Timing Services Inc. Dynamic Strip Bond Fund
Theme investors	Ethical Growth Fund Investors Summa Fund Ltd.
Sector rotators	Altamira Equity Fund Mackenzie Equity Fund
Momentum players	AIM Weingarten Fund (U.S.) Twentieth Century Growth Fund (U.S.)
Asset allocators	AGF Asset Allocation Service Royal Trust Asset Allocation Service
Yield investors	Phillips, Hager & North Dividend Income Fund AGF High Income Fund
Small-cap investors	Bolton Tremblay Landmark Small-Cap Fund CIBC Capital Appreciation Fund

TABLE 5–9

AVOIDING THE FRONT RUNNERS

The easiest thing to do if you do not want to think is buy the front runner in the market or last year's best performers. These mutual funds get a lot of coverage in the business press and investor shows. I have cautioned against this for years, and now once again another major empirical study validates my position.

All types of funds have hot streaks. Small-cap funds were hot in the late 1970s into the 1980s and again since 1991. All funds go through similar cycles, just as gold was doing in 1993. Most investors generally get in toward the end of the cycle.

If a style of investing is hot, you are always better off picking the fund that has the best long-term performance with that particular style. More often than not, one year's best fund becomes next year's worst. A research paper published by the Brookings Institute concluded that one-year sprinters rarely go the distance. Good five- and ten-year performers do maintain their consistent results in the future. Someone who has been right more often than not for five to ten years will outperform a fund manager who is hot once.

However, a recent article in the *Wall Street Journal* made the catastrophic error of suggesting that you should buy last year's hot funds, as they are likely to do well again. Research, on the other hand, clearly shows that consistent long-term performance is the single most reliable factor. Investment styles and all the areas of popularity go in and out of vogue in different years: in 1993 Canadian resources were hot; in 1992, small caps were popular; and, for the past three years, Asian funds have garnered strong interest. You should pick the best long-term performance among the funds in a particular style group.

In general, I think that much of what you need to know about mutual fund sales can be summed up in these five basic principles.

1) As you work to build your portfolio, put as much of your money into equity funds as you can. The reason is that even if you discover in later years that you need income and have to redeem some part of your fund holdings, you are still better off to do this than to purposely keep money in a bank account or some other low-performing investment to cover incremental income requirements. Put the money in the fund and get the appreciation for as long as you can—you will be better off.

2) The principle of diversification applies to money within mutual funds as well. You should distribute your money among at least three different types of equity funds (e.g., growth, value, Canadian, foreign, etc.). This will increase the likelihood that you will always have at least some of your money invested in the most profitable sector of the market at any one time.

3) Understand the difference between various types of equity funds and know which ones you own. This is important so that you can correctly compare the performance of your assets. Always compare similar types of funds (i.e., value funds with other value funds) because if you do not, you will have difficulty making intelligent decisions regarding your money.

4) Every time you are planning to contribute more money to your equity fund portfolio, always put your money into the sector that has lagged the market for several years. Remember, everything is a cycle and you are likely buying in at the low.

5) Make your purchase decisions based on an expectation for the future, not on past performance. However, your expectations should be for the long term, not next week. Focus on solid performers only. Constantly moving money from one fund to another is not good investing and can be harmful to your net worth.

These are some general principles that I have always tried to follow. Now I will give you some more specific advice.

TWENTY-FIVE FACTS EVERY MUTUAL FUND INVESTOR SHOULD KNOW

Mutual funds are designed to provide an easy way for a small investor to buy into domestic and foreign stocks, bonds, and money market instruments. My goal is to provide you with information that will improve your investment strategies, therefore helping you to double your net worth every three years. Here are some basic facts.

1) Past performance is a poor guide to the future. Good historical numbers indicate that the fund did something good once or had a style that happened to be right for a particular time. The good past performance may be difficult to maintain because the fund manager may have quit or one or two great years just may never be able to be repeated. Or, the style may be out of favour. Think about the long term.

2) Everyone claims to be number one at one time or another. Every last-place fund in 1993 was probably number one five or seven years ago.

3) Even the best guys do badly. Because a fund usually follows a single style in a particular area—growth, small-cap, or emerging markets—if its style is out of vogue or its sector is performing poorly, it can underperform the rest of the market. Stick with the long-term track record of winners.

4) Equities get hit from time to time. Every time there is a major correction, good equity funds get hit hard. Do not avoid them if they have had just one bad year.

5) Most equity funds will slightly lag behind the market. As funds need to keep 10% or more cash for redemptions, they cannot be fully invested to maximize profits. Therefore, after expenses these funds will yield a return slightly behind market performance.

6) Buying the same securities independently from the mutual fund will not necessarily provide you with the same returns on your money because outside of the fund, you will not accumulate the benefits of the asset-allocation process. The timing of sales and purchases is also important to performance. If you want to get the fund's return, you had better buy the fund.

7) Understand the difference between a mutual fund's investment objectives and its investment style. Over time, many labels have become blurred because they mean different things to different funds. So when you hear a salesperson or planner talking, for

example, about growth funds or income funds, be sure you know whether it is used to refer to the overall fund objective or the fund's management style. Just because a company manages a growth fund does not mean that it invests specifically in growth stocks (young companies that have rapidly increasing earnings). Similarly, bond funds can use the term "government" in their name even if they have up to 35% of their assets invested in securities other than government bonds.

8) Watch the fund manager. Good fund managers are in high demand and some are lured away to greener pastures. The transition to a new manager is not always smooth and financial planners panic. When the fund managers went from United to set up the Ivy Fund for Mackenzie, financial planners called me in a panic. Soon, new and very competent managers were in place for United who are still doing just fine.

9) Over the first three years of a purchase, "load" equity funds typically generate a greater return than no-load equity funds. In addition, a *Money* magazine survey in 1992 showed that eight of the ten best performing equity funds over the past 15 years had loads. However, after 36 months, there is no appreciable difference in the performance of loads versus no-loads.

10) Money market funds do have risk. They hold commercial paper that can default on payment. They also are poor performers today because of record-low rates. Yet, about half of mutual fund buyers buy money market funds as a place to park their short-term money. This is a losing proposition.

11) Costs are a major factor in determining bond fund performance. Bond funds with low expenses generally do better than those with high expenses. The 25% of the funds with the lowest expenses were the best performers over the last five years.

12) Moving money around need not cost you money. As long as your transactions are within the same family of funds, you will probably incur no transaction costs. If you followed the research and moved your money from a money market fund to a bond fund as interest rates fell, as long as the funds belonged to the same family of funds, the move would be cost free. However, if you switched to a new company, you would pay.

13) The best way to buy funds is monthly. It is possible through electronic funds transfers to purchase a regular amount of mutual funds and place them in your RRSP. This is the fastest and best way to build growth and income protection.

14) A fund that does not charge a front-end sales commission is not necessarily a no-load fund. There may be a back-end sales commission or a distribution fee when you sell. Check first before you get in.

15) Never put all of your eggs in one funds basket. Many fund companies have products across all categories of investment options. Rarely do more than two within the same company perform well over time. Do not buy all one brand of fund, diversifying also means diversifying by brand.

16) There are ways around minimums. Many funds have a minimum amount, say $500 or $1,000 that you must invest. In reality, if you buy, say $100 a month, through a financial planner, the fund will waive the minimum.

17) You do not have to sell all of one fund at once. If you wish to get liquidity to buy something else, you can sell your shares in whatever amount needed. Liquidity is rarely a problem. Financial planners will do their best to get you a cheque in five business days. It's part of the service.

18) You should maximize the foreign content of your RRSP by using mutual funds. While your 1994 percentage of foreign content allowable is 20% for RRSPs, you can actually increase this to about 30% without penalty if you select Canadian mutual funds with high foreign content. Many foreign funds denominated in Canadian dollars or funds with 18% to 20% foreign content qualify as "Canadian." The higher the foreign content, the greater the RRSP return. Thirty percent foreign content created this way can affect RRSP yields by as much as 3% extra a year.

19) Most mutual fund buyers are wimps. Unfortunately, by making a decision to purchase a mutual fund, most Canadians do not change their overall investment style. Even in this era of record-low interest rates, most mutual fund purchases continue to be in bond funds and money-market funds. Less than 25% of all mutual fund assets are invested in equity funds where the returns are significantly higher.

20) Most Canadians ignore the world. In this environment where global markets are so important, not having 5% to 10% in Asian markets, 5% to 10% in emerging markets (South America), and 5% to 10% in U.S. equities—either value or small-cap stocks—is a serious investment error. These are the areas from which the double-digit returns are coming. Combining these global markets with your Canadian equity, Canadian small-cap, and Canadian

resources funds, you can have a dynamic portfolio (50% equities) that will yield the 30% you need to help you double your net worth in three years.

21) Most equity fund holders invest in the wrong mix of funds. Equity fund investors generally prefer funds that invest in blue-chip companies. The truth is that the best sector since 1957 has not been that of big business, but that of the small caps.

22) Even if you consider yourself a conservative investor, you do not have to restrict your fund holdings only to conservative stocks. You can minimize the risk of short-term price gyrations associated with emerging market funds and small-cap funds among others and still obtain some handsome gains over time by including them within a much larger portfolio of less risky stocks.

23) Do not own too many funds. Life is too complicated as it is, so do not make it worse. If you own more than a dozen funds, you probably own too many. This problem is most frequently seen in investors who do not have an overall strategy. They just buy funds willy-nilly and usually end up with funds that overlap each other and duplicate management styles or objectives. I recommend that you determine the types of funds you want to hold (e.g., foreign bond fund, blue-chip equity fund, etc.), then select at most two funds within each category.

24) If the stock market does experience a "correction" or even crashes, it's probably too late to sell your shares, so do not bother. Buy and sell orders are typically exercised at the end of the trading day, so the price reflects the day's trading activity. Except in the most dire personal circumstances, hold your assets for the long term.

LEVERAGING TO INCREASE YOUR MUTUAL FUND RETURNS

A key element to maximizing the potential returns on investment when interest rates are at a 29-year low is to leverage. That is, borrow against your net worth. For most people their after-tax cost of borrowing money will be about 3%, assuming a 6% prime rate and a 50% marginal tax rate.

It is reasonable to leverage between 20% and 25% of your net worth if you are secure about your cash flow and employment. This means that if you have a net worth of $200,000 it is reasonable to borrow up to $50,000 to invest.

1) If your money cost is a net of 3% and you get 20% return with your $50,000 in mutual funds, the net gain to you is $8,500—or 17% added to your other returns.

2) If your only asset is your house and you get a mortgage or home equity loan or line of credit for $50,000, the yield on the mutual funds will still pay your loan and leave you with 12% to 15% more cash flow.

3) Let's say you invest $200,000 in a house and $50,000 in a mutual fund plan by borrowing $150,000 and putting $100,000 equity in the house. With a 25-year amortization on an 8½% mortgage the house carries for about $1,150 per month. As for the mutual fund, after 15 years at an annual 12% net return, it will be worth about $126,000. At that point (after 15 years from the original investment), establish a systematic withdrawal plan with the mutual fund drawing $1,150 a month to pay off your mortgage. Twenty-five years after the original investment, you will be mortgage-free and still have more than $100,000 in mutual funds and you will have had 10 years of not having to worry about paying your mortgage. What peace of mind. Remember that the average rate of return on real estate from 1967 to 1992—25 years—was 9.9% in Toronto. The average return on a Canadian equity growth fund from 1967 to 1992 was 17.3%.

——— YOUR RISK PREFERENCE ———
A Quiz

This Risk Preference Quiz is to help you determine your tolerance level for equities and risk-taking in your investment strategies. The answers are often reflective of age and experience and should be a handy guide to decision-making on portfolio allocations. Take it before you act.

1) When it comes to investing, my luck has been ...
   a) rotten.
   b) average.
   c) better than average.
   d) terrific.

2) Most of the good things that have happened to me have been because ...
   a) I planned them.
   b) I was able to exploit the opportunities that arose.
   c) I was in the right place at the right time.
   d) God looks out for me.

3) If a stock doubled in price five months after I bought it, I would ...
   a) sell all my stock.
   b) sell half my stock.
   c) sit tight.
   d) buy more shares.

4) Making investment decisions on my own is something that I ...
   a) never do.
   b) do occasionally.
   c) often do.
   d) almost always do.

5) At work, when my boss tells me to do something that I know is a bad idea, I usually ...
   a) say directly that it is a mistake.
   b) get co-workers to join me in opposing the idea.
   c) do nothing unless the boss brings it up again.
   d) do it anyway.

6) For me to invest 10% of my current net worth in a venture that has at least 75% chance of success, the potential value would have to be at least ...
   a) the same as the amount invested.
   b) three times the amount invested.
   c) five times the amount invested.
   d) no amount would be worth the risk.

7) When I watch TV and see people involved in such sports as hang-gliding and bungee jumping ...
   a) I think they are idiots.
   b) I admire them but would never participate.
   c) I wish I could try such sports just once to see what they are like.
   d) I seriously consider participating myself.

8) If I held a finalist ticket in a lottery with a one-in-three chance of winning a $50,000 prize, the smallest amount I would be willing to sell my ticket for is ...
   a) $30,000.
   b) $17,000.
   c) $13,000.
   d) $10,000.

9) In the past, I have spent $100 on one or more of either gambling in a casino, betting on recreational activities (golf or friendly poker), or betting on professional sports.
   a) I have done two or more of these in the past year.
   b) I have done one of these in the past year.
   c) I have done one of these a few times in my life.
   d) I have never done any of these.

10) If I had to make a critical decision that involved a large amount of money, I would probably do one or more of the following (circle if more than one).
   a) Delay the decision.
   b) Delegate the decision to someone else.
   c) Ask others to share the decision.
   d) Plan strategies that would minimize any loss.

Scoring

For questions 1, 3, and 4: if you answered (a), give yourself one point; (b), two points; (c), three points; and (d), four points.

For questions 2, 6, 8, and 9: if you answered (a), give yourself four points; (b), three points; (c), two points; and (d), one point.

For questions 5 and 7: no matter what you chose, don't give yourself any points; moral courage and physical bravery have nothing to do with your tolerance for, or abilities at, investment risk.

For question 10: subtract from five the number of answers you circled and give yourself the rest.

If You Scored ...

8 to 16: Conservative investor; you are willing to take few risks.

17 to 24: Average investor; you'll take a moderate risk.

25 to 32: Aggressive investor; you are willing to take greater-than-average risks.

Specialty Investment Products

With the movement out of fixed income securities starting in 1990, the growth in mutual fund sales is not over yet.

Specialty investment products, collectibles, limited partnerships, precious metals, commodities, and derivatives are all getting much more attention. Most of these items are for speculators and for the serious, experienced, highly knowledgeable investors, which means that these products are wrong for the majority of the population. For example, gold spiked upward to around $410 (U.S.) an ounce in July 1993, only to fall below $368 (U.S.) six weeks later.

Specialty products can be fun and interesting, but need special attention and close monitoring. Many of these items, such as baseball cards, become fads with entrepreneurs milking the market for all it's worth. The concept is built on a single incident of a very rare Honus Wagner card purchased by Wayne Gretzky and Bruce McNall for $450,000. Suddenly everyone was buying boxes of cards, going to card shows, and buying autographs. Retail card shops opened everywhere.

Many individuals who bought some of the billions of cards now realize that they were foolish lemmings for lining up at the same time as everyone else and will have to face enormous losses. Collecting cards is a hobby, not an investment.

A NO-BRAINER

Two years ago, the federal government created labour union investment funds sponsored by unions as a means of raising equity/venture capital to fund dynamic young high-technology industries. This was built on the model established in Quebec a decade ago, which raised large sums of money that greatly stimulated an economic boom in new ventures in that province.

Even though Canadians are very conservative as individual investors, the funds attracted large amounts of money from the public. After all, Canadians, being equity-averse, need massive inducements to invest in their own economy. The goal is to create high-tech jobs and make Canada more competitive.

Working Ventures was the first of these national funds established with the Canadian Labour Congress. Ontario, British Columbia, and Prince Edward Island provide marketing grants if the investment is in their province, and more provinces will join over the next year. The program works as follows.

1) You invest $5,000 into Working Ventures.

2) You receive a federal tax credit of $1,000.

3) You receive a provincial credit of $1,000.

The only problem with this is that Working Ventures has attracted $160 million but has invested only $4.5 million; the rest is in fixed income securities producing a 5% return.

There is also a better way to handle the investment.

1) Put the $5,000 Working Ventures investment in your RRSP; get $2,500 back from Revenue Canada.

2) Add this $2,500 to the $2,000 in tax credit you receive for investing in Working Ventures. This will give you a total of $4,500, leaving only $500 at risk.

3) Re-invest the total $4,500 back into your mutual fund portfolio, giving you a total of $9,500 invested.

4) Depending on your cash flow and risk orientation, you may borrow the initial $5,000. At today's rates, the after-tax annual cost of funds is $150 to have $9,500 working for you—a rather exciting return on investment.

A new fund, The Integrated Growth Fund, expected in 1993–94, will be sponsored by the Canadian Union of Food and Commercial Workers. It promises to be a more aggressive investor and hopefully will produce yields greater than money markets. The excitement of the deal is that this is one of the few federal/provincial grant programs still available to the consumer. Use it, it will not last long, as Ottawa is very tight for funds.

SYSTEMATIC WITHDRAWAL PLANS

When most people retire, they are frequently advised to put their money into a term deposit or a guaranteed investment certificate and live off the interest. At first glance, this may seem to be a wise decision because their income from the interest initially appears to be sufficient to meet their needs. However, over the years, this money decreases in real value due to inflation and taxes on interest income.

Systematic withdrawal plans, which are available from many mutual fund organizations, are an alternative that can outstrip inflation and provide an opportunity to increase the size of the original invested capital. To open a systematic withdrawal plan, you must determine how much money should be withdrawn from your account monthly, bimonthly, or quarterly to provide the money you will need on a regular, systematic basis. This amount will be transferred directly to the bank, trust company, or credit union of your choice or to any person you designate. One obvious advantage is that by receiving a regular payment, the investor can budget and plan for expenses, while leaving the remaining capital free to enjoy the benefit of long-term growth.

A second and equally important advantage—although greatly misunderstood—is the tax treatment that the withdrawals receive. The tax treatment of the income from a systematic withdrawal plan will be favourable because the income consists of and is treated as interest, dividends, capital gains, and return of your own capital. To examine the tax advantage, consider the two alternatives outlined, where the investor is in a 50% tax bracket and has $100,000 to invest.

Alternative A shows the purchase of a GIC yielding 12%. Alternative B illustrates a systematic withdrawal plan in a fund having a 12% growth rate, a year-end distribution of $1 per unit, and investor withdrawals of $1,000 a month (12% annually).

THE TAX ADVANTAGE OF A SYSTEMATIC WITHDRAWAL PLAN vs. A GIC

Alternative A: GIC		Alternative B: Systematic Withdrawal Plan	
	Year 1		Year 1
Investment	$100,000	Investment	$100,000
Annual Interest	12,000	Annual Withdrawals	12,000
Tax (50%)*	6,000	Tax (50%)*	666
After-Tax Return	$6,000	After-Tax Return	$11,334

* The marginal tax rate of 50% in this case applies to the entire $12,000 of interest income, as it is fully taxable.

* Although the marginal rate is still 50%, only $1,332 of the $12,000 income in this case is taxable. The rest is principal tax-reduced capital gain (eligible for $100,000 lifetime capital gains exemption) or dividends (subject to the dividend tax credit).

TABLE 6–1

LIMITED PARTNERSHIPS

Limited partnerships can play a useful role in many diversified investment portfolios. They can be good investments, excellent tax shelters, and an interesting and exciting way to participate in ventures as varied as oil and gas exploration, hotels, apartments, retail stores, restaurants, film, and new business ventures.

For limited partnerships (LPs) to be of value, first they must be good investments that are highly likely to succeed, have good management, and offer a realistic potential for capital gains. Secondly, the LP must have some potential for liquidity—a way out if you need to get your money back or your loan paid off, as many LPs are purchased on a leverage basis. And last of all, any tax benefit must be considered as a bonus. Tax-driven deals produce short-term benefits and generally are poor investments.

It is important to know who the LP's developer or promoter is and the track record of the management team. Critical, too, is the mark-up the promoter is making on the deal. Deals with mark-ups above 30% are usually poor investments. Find out who has done the evaluation of the deal. Who is the law firm and accounting firm and how was the due diligence done by the firm selling the unit to you?

Be sure not to put all your eggs into one basket. Be certain that you can afford it, that your liability is limited only to your investment, and that the tax benefits are clearly of benefit to you. Many limited partnerships offer little value to those not in the top-margin tax bracket. Generally you would have to be in this bracket to afford and/or qualify for a loan for one.

Since 1990, Canadian real estate, hotels, and some nursing/retirement homes have done poorly. Areas that have done well include: flow through shares; many oil and gas exploration offerings; and multi-unit residential developments in Texas, Florida, and Georgia. New film and video prospects for instruction films, training, and personal development have also prospered, but not Canadian feature films.

GOLD

Gold offers special fun and excitement. I always said that I love gold in watches, teeth, or earrings, but not as an investment.

The lemmings bought in en masse in 1979 at $860 (U.S.) an ounce, only to see it fall to $540 (U.S.) within a few months. Everyone was lining up to buy it. Therefore, there was no opportunity for profit except for the bank vendor.

Gold coins are attractive and fun to collect if you are a numismatist, but they are expensive and dependent on market fluctuations. Armagedonists always bought a money belt filled with gold coins in case of an atomic holocaust; they didn't realize that the gold would melt anyway.

Shares in gold-producing companies, which have the lowest cost of production per ounce extracted are always the more favourable of the gold stocks. However, the key determinant of the price of shares in gold companies is the open-market price of gold bullion.

Canadian gold- and resource-based mutual funds were strong performers throughout the first three quarters of 1993. Increased demand in Asia and a strong Chinese economy should ensure that gold shares will continue holding their position into 1994.

OTHER DERIVATIVES

There are many equity-related specialty products for sophisticated investors. One type of product is derived from a stock index such as Standard & Poor's 500 Index or the Toronto Stock Exchange 35 Index or even a specific stock. Some are even good for RRSPs.

Another type of derivative is a stock option. Options are not for everyone, yet many serious equity investors say that stock options can enhance returns and add stability to the prices. As a speculative tool to control larger blocks of stock, options can result in huge losses if you are forced to buy stocks above the market price or sell below. But a few investors to whom I spoke told of 8% and 12% returns this year from option trading. By writing or selling "calls," investors collect a premium and agree to sell their shares, on demand, at the agreed-to option price. If the price of the shares does rise and the options are exercised, the call options writers who own the shares are covered before they can sell the shares from their portfolio. At the strike price, their gains can be larger or losses lower because of the option premium. However, they have given up their chance for larger returns if the stock's price continues to rise.

Some investors of substance and experience sell call options on stocks they do not own. This is called being "uncovered" or "naked." They may have to buy the stock at a higher market price or sell at a lower one.

"Puts" are the exact opposite of a call option, giving the holder of the put the right to sell while obligating writers to buy shares. If shares rise, the holder will not exercise the put because better results are available by selling in the market. If the stock price falls, put holders can sell shares at above-market prices.

The protective put is designed to provide insurance to the investor who is concerned about prices going down and who is willing to pay to get protection if the price goes down in exchange for a lower upside.

Options reflect the market. The healthier the market, the better the reason to use options. You can know in advance the most you can lose.

MAKE MONEY IN LEAPS—OR TIPs, PINs, PEACS, OR SPECS

There are a number of more innovative types of derivative products that are worth mentioning briefly. Although it is always good to have a broad understanding of new types of financial products, I certainly would not recommend investing in any of these products without the advice and assistance of a professional adviser or an independent financial planner.

Toronto 35 Index Participation Units (TIPs): This product was introduced in 1990 for the purpose of allowing investors to purchase units of shares in the 35 blue-chip companies that comprise the TSE 35 Index. Investors receive a quarterly dividend. Unfortunately, there is no opportunity to automatically re-invest your dividend income. The advantage of purchasing TIPs units is that they offer diversification at a lower overall cost than buying shares in each of the TSE 35 companies directly. Unlike mutual funds, TIPs units have no annual administration costs or management fees to be paid when the units are bought or sold. However, the downside is that this investment will not perform any better than the TSE 35 Index itself. You do not get the benefit of expert stock selection, which you do with mutual funds, and you restrict yourself to one narrow segment of the overall market. In effect, you are buying equivalent performance of the TSE at a lower cost.

Standard & Poor's 500 Protected Index Notes (PINs): Similar to TIPs, this is a TSE-listed investment that tracks the performance of New York's S & P 500 Index. PINs provide returns based on their January 3, 1997, redemption value. Unlike TIPs units, investors are assured of a guaranteed minimum value and can always redeem their units for the $10 issue price. Interestingly, PINs are RRSP-eligible and are not subject to foreign-content RRSP regulations even though they are derivatives linked to foreign stocks.

Payment Enhanced Capital Securities (PEACS): This product is a brand-new equity option that was first issued in November 1992. The financial returns of PEACS are based primarily on dividends issued by selected TSE-listed shares and, to a limited extent, capital appreciation. PEACS are subject to a five-year expiry date, which may restrict their appeal among some investors.

Special Equity Claim Securities (SPECS): SPECS were launched simultaneously with PEACS. In contrast, however, the returns of SPECS emphasize capital appreciation. In effect, SPECS are similar to a long-term call option with a single exercise date. They represent the right to purchase shares at a pre-determined price. Generally speaking, they are too speculative for most RRSP investors and are only appropriate for an individual who would purchase equity warrants. SPECS also have five-year expiry dates.

Long-Term Equity Anticipation Securities (LEAPS): LEAPS are available in two forms: "calls" or "puts." If you hold LEAPS in the form of put options, they are not RRSP-eligible investments, whereas call-options LEAPS are eligible. This differing treatment reflects the treatment accorded to standard call and put options on individual stocks. LEAPS in either form can be held for up to two years, they have regular expiry cycles, and they also have a range of exercise prices. These features make LEAPS an attractive investment for a sophisticated investor when compared with standard three-, six-, and nine-month expiry-date cycles for normal options on individual stocks.

Tax Planning
That Really Works

This chapter on tax planning is not a unit on tax minutiae. We will not consider tax trivia that has minimal if any benefit to the majority of taxpayers.

Tax planning is not an isolated or independent function that you do as an afterthought. Rather, it is a cohesive plan of cash retention, investment strategy, and financial planning, which relates to retirement, estates, and overall return on investment.

The essence or core of the process is built on:

1) entrepreneurship and tax amelioration through deductions and income-splitting;

2) RRSP and retirement planning; and

3) investment strategy and tax reduction.

If we do these basics together, with the other five dimensions of financial planning, we should go far in achieving our objectives. In fact, given the massive tax assault on the average Canadian over the past dozen years, it is irresponsible for any Canadian not to do tax planning.

Most individuals choose not to do anything except file a tax return each year and perhaps make a small RRSP contribution. Few wish to be aggressive in their planning, either out of ignorance or a fear of government, which is unfounded and baseless.

What annoys me the most is that:

1) the people who pay too much tax are middle-income Canadians who can least afford it;

2) most people show up to tax seminars only in February or March;

3) most Canadians I surveyed overpaid their taxes through ignorance or laziness; and

4) the average overpayment was between 10% and 20%, depending on income source.

This is no exaggeration. I estimate that in April 1993, Canadians overpaid their taxes by at least $400 million.

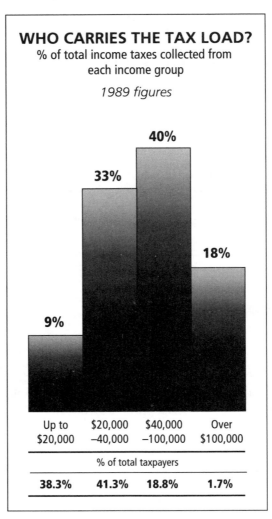

WHO CARRIES THE TAX LOAD?
% of total income taxes collected from each income group

1989 figures

Up to $20,000	$20,000 –40,000	$40,000 –100,000	Over $100,000
9%	33%	40%	18%

% of total taxpayers			
38.3%	41.3%	18.8%	1.7%

FIGURE 7–1

A classic case for me is the proverbial senior citizen who comes up to me at the end of an evening seminar. The individual usually has about $300,000 in Canada Savings Bonds and is too old for an RRSP. The person had about $18,000 in income from bond interest and paid about $7,200 in taxes, leaving about $10,800 before pension income. If a diversified portfolio had been created using the investment strategies we discussed earlier, the results would have been different.

A Diversified Portfolio			
With Returns Based on 1993 Average Performance			
TYPE OF INVESTMENT	INVESTMENT AMOUNT	RETURN	TAX
1) Money Market Mutual Funds – Interest	$90,000	$5,400	$2,160
2) European Bond Fund – Capital Gain and Interest	30,000	2,700	720
3) Bank Cash – T-Bill Account Interest	30,000	1,200	480
4) Canadian Equities – Capital Gain and Dividend	30,000	6,000	420
5) Equity Mutual Fund – Capital Gain and Dividend	60,000	12,000	840
6) Preferred Share in Public Companies – Capital Gain and Dividend	30,000	3,000	480
7) Equity Mutual Fund – Capital Gain	30,000	9,000	0
8) Entrepreneurial Home Business – $2,000 in house expenses	0		(800)
Utilizing the dividend tax credit, the capital gains $100,000 exemption, and better return vehicles – assuming a 40% tax rate for this individual.			
Total –	$300,000	$39,300	$4,300
The net return after tax is $35,000, which is more than three times the after-tax return of the			

TABLE 7–1

Tax planning protected the capital gains and dividends. The home business created a $2,000 deduction simply by utilizing existing cash expenses and without incurring any more costs. It reduced taxes by $800. To further add to this, I created a more aggressive diversification plan to improve returns.

Utilizing only the average performance of categories, a 300% increase in net cash flow to the individual was produced. The increase in risk is more than offset by the returns. But is there not a greater risk in living on $10,800 a year instead of $35,000 and suffering the humiliation of poverty? Is there not greater risk in paying 40% tax versus only about 11% tax?

Tax-based decisions maximized the after-tax returns to the individual. Working with financial planners, I have done this for individuals from age 25 to 91 with similar results and consistently superior returns after tax.

This chapter has more than 100 tax strategies and tactics that will have an impact on the family, investments, cash flow, and your overall costs. Remember, though, the chapters on investing and RRSPs are all tax-interrelated. This chapter should not be read in isolation as a collection of last-minute acts.

The reason I have chosen to be so adversarial toward tax is related to massive tax increases, especially the subtle ones that Ottawa slips over us. A number of good Canadian tax writers have taken notice of these issues.

Here are the worst elements of which you may not be aware.

TAX CHANGES

Inflation: Prior to 1986, Canadian tax rates were indexed to account for the effects of inflation. Tax brackets were automatically adjusted each year to compensate for the first 3 percentage points of inflation. However, after 1986, this indexing was ended. This means that Canadians are now subject to "hidden" tax increases. In these recessionary times, if your take-home pay simply keeps pace with inflation, does not increase at all, or actually declines (e.g., as Ontario residents subject to the NDP government's "social-contract" legislation discovered), you still end up potentially paying higher taxes. In addition, not all tax deductions are indexed to inflation. For example, employee-benefit term-insurance limits, which are fixed at $25,000, have not changed in 20 years.

Interest Deductions: Interest charges on loans you receive and use to finance the purchase of a business are deductible. However, if you either sell the business or subsequently declare bankruptcy, you lose the deduction, even if you are still paying off the loan. In the case of buying a business, one option to use to circumvent this inequity is to charge the business a loan guarantee fee. Depending on your circumstances, this approach may preserve your deductions.

Equivalent to Married Exemption: If you are a single parent, you are entitled to a tax exemption for any children you have until they reach age 18. However, on the child's 18th birthday, you lose the exemption, even if the child is still fully supported by you and attends school.

Free Loans to Government: Get this one! If you over-pay your tax, no interest is earned on your account until 45 days after the April 30 tax filing deadline, even if you paid early. But you guessed it:

Revenue Canada charges interest on any unpaid taxes you owe starting immediately from the first day that they are owed.

Instalment Payments: Let's say you are a professional (e.g., a doctor or dentist) or you pay your income taxes in quarterly or monthly instalments based on estimates of your full-year annual income. If you suddenly receive some unexpected taxable income such as a capital gain on a sale of some assets, you are charged late-payment interest charges from the start of the year. This is regardless of the date when the income is received.

Timing of Tax: If you own investments that are paying you interest income (e.g., government or corporate bonds), you must declare the income annually and pay taxes on that income annually. This is regardless of when you actually receive your interest income. In addition, if you receive an unexpected lump-sum payment for previous work, it is fully taxable in the year it is received. You are not allowed to spread the income back over the years in which it was earned to reduce your tax bill.

Averaging: Revenue Canada has ended the practice of income-averaging. This was a common practice for many professional athletes and other high-income earners who experienced significant fluctuations in income from year to year. Ostensibly, this action was justified on the basis of removing an inequity of tax law that favoured these individuals relative to the majority of Canadians who receive more consistent income from year to year.

Company Car: Strangely, the concept of automobile depreciation escapes Revenue Canada. For example, an employee who takes home a five-year-old company car is assessed a taxable benefit as though the car is still worth its original price.

Bad Advice: If you approach Revenue Canada for answers on a particular tax matter and you receive incorrect advice (which incidentally happens more often that you would care to know) that you follow, you still can be pursued by Revenue Canada for unpaid taxes plus interest.

Paid Advice: It is no secret that Canadian tax laws are incomprehensible to the majority of Canadians. But, if you are an independent business owner or professional, you are allowed to deduct the fees you are charged by your accountant or tax adviser. However, if you are a salaried employee or wage earner and you seek and receive professional tax advice, you are not permitted to deduct this expense.

COMMON LAW IS OUT

In 1993, there were approximately 800,000 common-law couples living in Canada. Prior to that year, these individuals could obtain a substantial tax benefit by filing separate tax returns with each partner claiming full personal tax credits. Married couples, however, were not able to do this, and the overall benefit to common-law couples could amount to as much as $4,000 per year.

However, in 1993, Revenue Canada developed a new definition for common-law couples. The tax rules would affect two people of the opposite sex who are, or have been, involved in a conjugal relationship during the preceding 12 months or are the parents of the same child. The result: no more separate tax filing.

Here are some important implications of this change in the tax treatment of common-law couples.

- The loss of the tax exemption for children under 18. (Single parents, on the other hand, can claim this exemption.)

- The loss of the right to claim GST tax credits, child care, or other allowable amounts against separate incomes to maximize refunds. Now each partner must report the other's income.

- No more avoiding attribution rules. Common-law partners are no longer able to transfer funds to lower-income partners in order to minimize taxable income by using the lower-income bracket.

- The loss of the right of maintaining capital gains exemptions on two principal residences.

However, as a result of this new definition of common-law couples, there are now some benefits, too, to common-law families.

- The higher-income partner is now able to establish and contribute to a spousal RRSP in the lower-income spouse's name.

- Family medical expenses and charitable donations can now be claimed by either of the partners. Allowing the combined family expenses to be handed over to the one partner who can gain the most from such claims will help couples to maximize available tax credits.

- If one partner's transfer to a new job in a new location requires moving the family and the other partner finds new work as well, both partners are able to split moving expenses.

- One partner may transfer to the other any unused tax credits for such claims as education, and tuition, pension income, disability amounts, or dividend income.

- RRSPs, properties, business, stocks, etc. may be willed and rolled over to the surviving partner on the death of the other.

STRATEGIC TAX TIPS
Investment Income

You should review your investment strategies, taking note of your preference for interest, dividends, or capital gains. The effective tax rates for these sources of income for an individual in the highest marginal tax bracket are as follows:

Interest	53%
Dividends	35%
Capital Gains	38%

Consider electing to include your spouse's dividend income on your tax return and claiming the related dividend tax credit. This is usually beneficial where it increases your married credit and your spouse cannot utilize the entire dividend tax credit.

Capital Gains

Seventy-five percent of capital gains is taxable. Rumours persist that the $100,000 capital gains exemption will be eliminated. It has been so for real estate that is not a principal residence. If your exemption has not been fully used, review your portfolio to determine if there is an opportunity to trigger capital gains in 1994.

Use your capital gains exemption before using capital losses to offset capital gains.

Consider selling or transferring assets with accrued gains to your RRSP or family members to take advantage of the exemption. Remember, only certain assets are eligible RRSP investments.

Cumulative Net Investment Losses (CNIL)

You may be surprised to discover that you cannot use your capital gains exemption to shelter your capital gains because you have a cumulative net investment loss (CNIL). Simply stated, your CNIL is the amount of investment expenses you have accumulated. The net effect is that you will be blocked from using your capital gains exemption if you have high investment expenses with little or no investment income.

There are some methods to reduce your CNIL and restore your capital gains exemption, including the following:

1) If you own your own business, pay yourself a dividend instead of a salary since the dividend will reduce your CNIL.

2) If you made an interest-free loan to your company, start charging interest so that you can use the interest income to reduce your CNIL.

3) If desirable, sell your investment early in the calendar year and repay the associated loans. By doing so, you can reduce your CNIL, thereby re-establishing your eligibility for a capital gain exemption.

4) Use borrowed funds to acquire a business or professional interest rather than for investing, wherever possible, since interest expenses on business loans are not included when calculating your CNIL balance.

Automobiles

This is a major cost area and the tax rules are complex.

1) Any automobile purchased after September 1, 1989, is subject to a maximum cost of $24,000 for capital cost allowance (depreciation) purposes. The $24,000 excludes both the goods and services tax (GST) and provincial taxes, including the Quebec sales tax (QST).

2) A similar restriction applies to lease costs. Leases entered into, or renewed after September 1, 1989, are subject to the maximum tax deduction for lease costs which is $650 a month. However, this does not mean that if lease costs are $650 a month the full amount will be deductible. The law contains a complicated formula that limits the deductibility of lease costs to the equivalent lease for a $24,000 car. The formula utilizes the manufacturer's list price as well as any refundable deposits to determine what portion of actual leasing costs will be deductible. For example, if you rent a $72,000 car for $650 a month, approximately ⅓ of $650 will be deductible (i.e., $24,000 is ⅓ of $72,000).

3) Financing costs on automobiles purchased after September 1, 1989, are limited to a maximum of $300 per month.

4) All costs associated with owning or leasing an automobile (subject to the above limitations) are deductible based on the portion of business use.

5) For employees who have personal use of a company car, the standby charge is 2% per month times the original cost of the car,

or ⅔ of the total lease cost (not including any insurance costs) for the year. GST of 7% must be added to the standby charge. For Quebec income tax purposes a QST benefit of 8% of the standby charge including GST, will be added. A reduction of the standby charge is possible if you use the car 90% or more for business purposes and you drive less than 12,000 personal kilometres a year, or you pay an amount to your employer to cover the personal use of the car.

6) In addition to the standby charge, an employee with a company car will be taxed on an operating benefit equal to the personal use portion of operating expenses paid for by the company. GST of 7% (plus 8% QST for Quebec income tax purposes) will be added to the operating benefit. Any amounts paid by an employee to an employer to cover operating costs will reduce the operating benefit. If you use the car 50% or more for business purposes and you notify your employer in writing before the end of the year, the operating benefit can be computed as ½ of the standby charge. This option should only be considered if ½ of the standby charge is less than the operating benefit.

7) A "reasonable" allowance received (i.e., one based solely on business kilometres driven) is not included in income for an employee. If the allowance is received in addition to other reimbursements of auto costs, other than reimbursements of supplementary business insurance, parking, or tolls that are not already reflected in the determination of the allowance, then the allowance is included in income.

Tax Tips for Automobiles

1) Keep track of your automobile usage by maintaining a diary that includes mileage, maintenance record, dates, names of people and places visited, and the reasons for the appointments.

2) To avoid paying business-related operating expenses out of personal funds, be sure your allowance is fair and it is not based solely on business mileage driven.

3) Since the stand-by charge is based on the original cost of the car, to reduce the stand-by charge investigate the savings from buying an older company car from your employer—it must be purchased at fair market value.

4) If you want to minimize the amount of personal use and therefore the standby charge and deemed operating benefit, try leaving the car at work every night rather than driving it home.

5) If your lease was executed prior to September 1, 1989, it may be worthwhile to renew or extend your lease to obtain an increased deduction for lease costs.

6) The more expensive the company-owned vehicles are, the more important it is for the company to determine the relative costs and benefits from owning rather than leasing the vehicle. Over $24,000, the deductibility formula kicks in and the amounts you can write off decline proportionately as the manufacturer's original list price increases.

7) If the car is going to be purchased, make as large a down payment as possible so that monthly interest expense is less than the maximum limit of $330 per month.

8) As cars age, consider the tax benefits of refurbishing rather than purchasing new ones. Refurbishment is justifiably considered a "repair and maintenance" expense and as a result is tax-deductible as an operating expense.

Donations and Medical Expenses

As always, keeping complete records of charitable donations and medical expenses is important.

Charitable donations can be claimed by either spouse. Under the new rules, it will never be beneficial to split charitable donations, so one spouse should claim all donations to maximize the tax credit. Since a tax credit is of equal value, regardless of which spouse claims it, the lower-income spouse should claim it so that he or she will have more after-tax funds available for investment.

You may claim your own medical expenses as well as those of a spouse or dependents. Because the claim is limited by the taxpayer's net income, it may be beneficial for the lower-income spouse to claim the credit to the extent that he or she has taxes payable. Medical expenses are eligible if paid in any 12-month period ending in the taxation year.

Home Office

To qualify for this expense, the home office must be your principal place of business or be used on a regular basis for meeting clients or customers. Keep a record of their visits to your office. Ensure that the space you set aside for your home office is used exclusively for business.

Borrowing Costs

Interest on loans to acquire most income-producing investment continues to be deductible.

If you sell an investment and do not replace it, the related interest expense will no longer be deductible. Consequently, it may be prudent to hold the investment until the loan can be repaid.

Where possible, convert your non-deductible interest to a deductible expense by using available cash or selling investments to retire non-deductible debt and then, after a reasonable time lapse, borrowing for investments.

Income Splitting for Investment

Giving your spouse money for investing usually causes the return on investment to be attributed back to you. Keep in mind the awful attribution rules. However, if you exchange assets with a spouse, trading cash for a bond or swapping jewellery of fair and equal value for equities, you avoid direct attribution. Remember, too, that attribution works in mysterious ways. If you give a child a 6% bond, the 6% income is attributed to you and the compounding in subsequent years is attributed to the child. This is called "second-generation income."

To avoid attribution, arrange for a demand loan agreement with your spouse. The agreement should document the amount of the loan, the fair market interest rate, and the repayment terms. The interest must be paid within 30 days of year-end at a rate prescribed by Revenue Canada or at the commercial market rate. The interest received by you should be evidenced by its inclusion on your tax return.

If you lend or give money to a spouse for a small business, home business, or self-employment venture, there is no attribution on the income earned.

Income attribution applies to all children under age 18, grandchildren, great-grandchildren, nieces, and nephews.

However, consider the following.

1) For gifts of money or assets to a child, attribution stops the year the child turns 18.

2) There is no attribution on capital gains. Instead of a bond or bank deposit account, consider buying the child an equity-based mutual fund. Capital gains—either the annual distribution or on redemption—are only taxable for the child. Dividends, however, are subject to attribution.

3) Parents can provide mortgage loans at zero or low interest to children without attribution. You might consider borrowing from a grandparent who has a lot of bonds and GICs with low returns.

The loan would provide the lender with a better return than if the money sat at the bank, be fully secured by the house, and cost the borrower less than a mortgage from a traditional lender.

4) Income-splitting loans for children age 18 and above from in-laws and grandparents are covered under attribution rules if the money is given as a loan. Gifts are exempt.

5) The child tax credit can be invested in the child's name without attribution.

6) Gifts from relatives outside of Canada are exempt from attribution rules. If your parents retire to Florida and send your child a gift, the returns on the funds are attributed to the child.

7) If the lower-income spouse receives an inheritance or gift, invest it in that spouse's name and be taxed at a lower rate.

8) In a two-income family needing one income to cover costs, invest one income and pay all costs from the higher income. This means having separate bank accounts for each spouse. The income accrues to the lower-income spouse and the higher-income one gets more deductions to reduce tax liability.

9) If you elect to pay a spouse and children reasonable salaries and dividends from a small business, there is no attribution. The first $23,750 of annual dividend income is non-taxable for those with no other source of income. A spouse with no other income will need salary from the small business to be eligible to make RRSP contributions.

10) Elect to split Canada Pension Plan benefits received. There will be no attribution on such income.

The Clawback

If your net income exceeds the prescribed limit, you will be forced to repay some or all of your Old Age Security (OAS) benefits.

By income splitting and shifting some income to your spouse, you may be able to minimize the impact of the clawback. If you can regulate your income, you may be able to avoid the clawback. For example, if your average net income is $60,000, you could take $50,000 one year and $70,000 the next. In this way, the clawback would only apply in the second year.

Tax Instalments

Ensure that you pay your quarterly tax instalments on time because you will be charged interest at the prescribed rate plus 2% on any deficiency. This interest is compounded daily and is not deductible. On top of this, there is an additional penalty on deficient instalment interest above a threshold level.

Unincorporated Business

If your business is not incorporated, this could be a good time to incorporate. Not only will there be lower corporate tax rates and the opportunity for significant tax deferral, but you could set the stage for ultimately getting the benefit of an additional $400,000 in tax-free capital gains. This additional exemption is only available if you incorporate.

Owner-Manager

If you have a private corporation involved in an active business, ensure that it will meet the necessary conditions to qualify for the additional $400,000 capital gains exemption.

Consider having your company accrue a bonus. Your company can deduct the bonus in one fiscal year and you can defer paying tax on it until the following year, provided the bonus is paid within 180 days of the company's year-end.

Whether you withdraw funds from your company as salary or as dividends can make a difference. You should determine your optimal salary/dividend mix. Here are some guidelines.

1) If the company's profits exceed $200,000, a much higher corporate rate will apply on the excess. By paying salary or bonus, you can reduce the amount of corporate profits that are taxed at the higher rate.

2) If the large salary is putting a drain on the company, you can loan funds back to the company. The company can repay the loan to you at any time on a tax-free basis.

3) Ensure that you receive enough salary to maximize your RRSP and CPP contributions. Remember, your 1994 RRSP contribution will be based on 1993 earned income.

4) Unlike salary or bonuses, dividends do not reduce your company's taxable income. However, due to the dividend tax credit, they receive preferential tax treatment in your hands. In fact, if you or a family member have no other source of income, the first $23,750 of dividend income for the year is tax-free.

5) The CNIL rules (discussed previously) may also favour dividends because they may restore your ability to claim the capital gains exemption.

6) Consider taking dividends to avoid taxes based on payroll (e.g., Ontario Health Tax) which can be as high as 2% of salary, depending on the company's total payroll.

7) Remember, if you do not require funds for personal living expenses, you may want to simply retain profits in the company to obtain a tax deferral. This is particularly worthwhile if your company is still eligible for the small-business deduction.

Reimbursements Instead of Salary or Bonuses are Non-Taxable

Reimbursements are one way of getting a break on certain expenses that might not otherwise be deductible. The following items, assuming they are not claimed as separate deductions by the employee, could be reimbursed by an employer without triggering a taxable benefit to the employee.

1) Moving expenses, including those which may not be acceptable for ordinary deductions, such as reimbursement for the loss on a sale of your old home.

2) Dues (professional, social, athletic).

3) Convention and seminar expenses.

4) Tuition fees for job training.

5) Job-related books and equipment.

6) Trips for business purposes.

7) Up to $25,000 worth of group life insurance (term).

INVESTMENT-RELATED TAX STRATEGIES

Some of the best overall investment strategies are the ones that have strong tax components.

1) Dividends from Canadian corporations. With a tax credit of 16⅔% of the dividend, this form of income provides a significant benefit for most Canadians. The maximum tax rate is approximately 35% and, of course, if you have no other income except dividends from a Canadian source, the first $23,750 of dividend income is tax-free. Therefore, $1 dividend equals $1.25 interest income.

More Canadians should be looking into dividends as a part of an overall portfolio strategy if they are to be successful.

2) Capital gains. We all have a $100,000 lifetime capital gains exemption with the exclusion of an investment in real estate. Our principal residence is tax-free, but any other investment in real estate, such as a cottage, second home, or rental property, is no longer exempt from the lifetime capital gains protection. In addition, we are allowed $400,000 more from the sale of Canadian-controlled private corporations. This is a major plus. If you happen to own a business for two or more years and 50% or more of your assets are operating in Canada (excluding real estate), there is potential here for $500,000 cumulative capital gains exemption when you sell your small business. This is one of the great remaining tax shelters open to Canadians. Seventy-five percent of the residual of capital gains are taxed, and the maximum tax rate normally averages about 38%.

3) Deductible expenses. In the 1990s, the emphasis will be less on the so-called "tax overdose." You should be focusing on building stability, preserving wealth, and protecting your investments against downturns in the Canadian economy. Fixation on excessive deductions and trying to deduct everything will only send out red lights on your file to Revenue Canada, making you subject to financial scrutiny.

The Best Options

1) The stock market over time. Despite the 1989 to 1992 shortcomings of the Toronto Stock Exchange, international markets such as the New York Stock Exchange between 1956 and 1992 have produced substantial gains. For example, $100 invested in 1956 is worth about $2,300 today.

2) Mutual funds over time. Equity-based mutual funds would have produced a 2,400% return over the last 30 years. If you invested in fixed income securities, based on the peak prime rate available each and every year, that would have only produced a 1,200% return.

3) Universal life policies. Many insurance people would argue that universal life insurance is not the ideal instrument for all Canadians and they are right. It is ideal for those who have fluctuating incomes—a very good year and then a very bad year. If you can make a maximum investment in the universal life policy over a three-year period, there will normally be enough earnings

in that policy to pay your term life insurance cost for the balance of the term of the policy.

Term insurance policies for people with less volatile income are ideal. Always avoid the insurance offered to you by a bank, especially as it relates to loans because it is overpriced. Acquire the policy from a totally independent agent who will search out the best rate that is geared to your individual circumstances. Having quality term insurance of about 12 to 14 times your current earnings if you have a family to support is now a basic rule of thumb for the 1990s, as it is real income and lifestyle protection.

4) The RRSP. It is the cornerstone for all Canadians, whether you are one of the 37% who is pensioned or not. The dollar-amount growth potential has an enormous impact. The RRSP's tax-deferral potential is also substantial. Invest $12,500 in an RRSP at 12% over a 40-year period and you will have more than $10,000,000 in your RRSP. Think about its potential in terms of becoming a millionaire.

5) Quality entrepreneurial business. This allows you incredible flexibility from a tax-planning perspective. It allows you substantial deductions and the one-time opportunity for realizing on that $500,000 capital gain. It is one of the greatest opportunities for self-sufficiency and independence for Canadians.

6) Quality, investment-directed limited partnerships. I am often critical of limited partnerships that are highly speculative and tax-driven. If the limited partnership is investment-driven— where there is a quality investment, positive cash flow, and some liquidity potential down the road—then unquestionably, some limited partnerships can provide good returns.

TAX SHELTERS

Who buys tax shelters? Interestingly, most people who buy limited partnerships have taxable income normally between $40,000 and $100,000. In addition to that, very few people who have taxable income beyond that actually buy them. Approximately 135,500 Canadians have purchased limited partnerships and another 72,000 have purchased investments of the development type (oil and gas).

The best performers over time have been oil and gas, representing 50% of the top-performing investments. In addition, real estate development properties in the southern United States have done extremely well. These are primarily in rental/residential properties—multi-unit buildings in places such as Texas, Florida, Arizona, and Georgia.

Film tax shelters have rarely performed well because Canadian films have not sold well unless there are strong presales—video and TV deals already in place. Nowadays, there are management and training videos that are good deals and might be worth a look.

Here is a summary of the current tax treatment of a number of popular specialty products. Always remember, however, that any investment decision must be made on the basis of its merit as an investment and not primarily on the basis of tax benefits flowing from the deal. Tax benefits ultimately dry up and you do not want to be left with a "stinker" on your hands. Besides, an investor in the 50% tax bracket still risks 50 cents of his or her own money for every $1 invested, even with a 100% tax deduction.

- New mutual fund limited partnerships are gaining wide appeal. However, Revenue Canada has reduced the tax relief associated with these investments. Write-off provisions have been restricted to three years and carry tax deductions of 50% in the first year, and 25% in each of the subsequent two years.

- With regard to resource properties, investors may deduct 100% of their pro rata share of Canadian exploration expenses. If at some time the properties begin production, those same investors are currently able to deduct 30% of their pro rata share of Canadian development expenses. For oil and gas properties, the tax deduction is 10% of the pro rata share of ongoing operating expenses. In the case of both development and operating expenses, these deductions are calculated on a diminishing-balance basis.

    In order to provide additional investment incentives in Ontario, the provincial government offers any investor an incremental cash grant that equals 25% of eligible exploration expenses. Quebec has gone even further. It has offered tax deductions on both underground and open-pit mine exploration costs, equivalent to 133⅓% and 166⅔% respectively, if the costs were incurred before January 1, 1994.

- Investors who participated in the purchase of multiple-unit residential buildings, usually referred to as MURB, are entitled to deduct their pro rata share of full depreciations and related losses from other personal income until 1993. Unfortunately, rental losses flowing from the capital cost allowances are not deductible.

- Tax deductions relating to construction soft costs have been severely restricted, but some peripheral expenses such as landscaping continue to be deductible.

TAX-PLANNING OPTIONS

As part of your overall planning exercise, you should look at the best tax-planning options open to you. The best options are neat, clean, and simple. You should not have to pay $10 to save $9. Here are the top 10 strategies.

1) Use income splitting as a strategy. Particularly if you have self-employed earnings, it is smart to put money in the hands of another family member who is at a lower tax bracket.

2) Set up a spousal RRSP. Put money in the hands of the lower-income spouse. On retirement this person will be able to take out income at a lower tax rate.

3) Use all available non-taxable benefits, such as the $25,000 life insurance that your employer may offer you, which is not taxable.

4) Taking advantage of any income deferrals. These income deferrals are things such as RRSPs.

5) Use tax shelters that are investments, not just tax shelters. Make sure that they are not just tax-driven investments, but have significant upside potential as well as liquidity.

6) Utilize all available legal deductions, such as charitable donations and medical expenses that are well documented.

7) Make sure that the debts you have are all deductible. Interest expense incurred for the purpose of earning income, whether investment income or business income, is deductible, but interest expense from credit cards or your home mortgage is not deductible and, therefore, offers no tax advantage.

8) Make use of capital gains. Not only are they taxed at a lower rate, but you do have that lifetime capital gains exemption.

9) Tax avoidance is not tax evasion. Your primary strategy should be to reduce your tax liability. This is not avoiding taxes in terms of legislation that says that most tax-avoidance schemes are no longer accepted. Doing proper tax planning for the purpose of not incurring substantial tax is not illegal.

10) Aim for dividend income, not just because dividends are a representation of entrepreneurial investment, but also because they are subject to the dividend tax credit. The more dividend income you incur, the less proportionate tax liability you create.

LOANS TO CHILDREN

If you have a child who's in the mid-teens, you should consider a number of tax-advantageous ways of transferring funds into your child's name.

For example, if you have set aside money for your child's university education or wedding, you may consider giving it to the child at age 17 by placing the funds into a one-year investment certificate that will mature some time after your child's 18th birthday. The reason for this recommendation is to ensure that no interest is earned until after your child reaches age 18. Earnings would then become taxable in the child's name at a much lower tax rate and only after the parent has lost the dependent child tax credit.

Another approach is to lend your child money through an interest-free loan. The rationale is to provide for your child's living expenses and spending money on the condition that he or she invest any money earned through summer or part-time jobs. Any interest income or dividends from these investments then accrue to your child and are taxable at the child's lower tax rate. Once the child begins working full time, he or she can begin to repay the loan.

Remember these two points. First, if you collect interest on the loan to your child, it becomes taxable for the parent and it must be declared. Secondly, if you lend money to your child to be invested, rather than spent, the earnings from the investment are attributable to the parent and are taxable at the parent's higher tax rate.

One final point. If you or your spouse have claimed a child under 19 years of age as a dependent and the child was not married or a parent, or still lived at home as of December 31, 1993, you may claim the GST tax credit for that child.

SUMMER CAMP FEES CAN BE DEDUCTIBLE!

The Income Tax Act actually allows parents to deduct the cost of camp fees for children, including fees paid for sports and hockey schools. Fees paid for attendance at a day camp, sports camp, hockey school, or a camp where your child stays overnight is acceptable as a child care expense.

The maximum claim per week is $150 for a child under age seven and $120 for a child aged seven to fourteen. The claim must be made by the lower-income spouse and must be made against earned income. This includes income from home businesses, self-employment, and director's fees.

A stay-at-home spouse with no earned income cannot use this deduction.

The higher income spouse can use the claim only if the other spouse is infirmed for two consecutive weeks or more, disabled, separated for at least 90 days ending in the tax year, or attending an education program on a full-time basis.

SPECIAL TAX AND INVESTMENT TIPS FOR 1993/94

Moving costs can be deducted. Canadians are very mobile people and change jobs and residences an average of six times during their careers.

Here is a list of expenses that can be deducted on tax returns for those who move to start a new job, business, or courses as a full-time student. You must be moving to a place at least 40 kilometres closer than the previous home to the new school or workplace. The deductions apply to income earned at the new home. You may deduct the following expenses.

1) The cost of selling your old home, including real estate commissions and legal fees.

2) Travel expenses such as car and meal costs to move you and your family to your new home.

3) Expenses for packing, handling, storage, and insurance for your personal property that is moved from your former residence to your new home.

4) Legal fees for the purchase of a new residence if the former house is being sold as a result of the move.

Non-deductible expenses:

1) Connect and reconnect fees for utilities.

2) The value of items that movers will not carry, such as perishables.

3) Costs for house-hunting trips.

4) A loss on the sale of your former house.

Unused portions of deductions can be carried forward to the next year. Reimbursed expenses from your employer cannot be claimed. If you have to move more than once in a year, those expenses can also be claimed.

For 1993/94:

Some provinces have increased their top marginal tax bracket to levels above their corporate rates. For example, in Ontario in 1994, the top marginal rate will be nearly 53%, but the corporate rate will be 44%.

If you have a substantial investment portfolio, incorporate a personal investment holding company to receive your investment income and pay tax at a rate 9% lower.

In order to increase revenue, provinces may have made 1993 tax increases retroactive to July 1, 1993. In Ontario, this rate is 62% for 6 months before falling to 58% in January. Try to defer income until January 1, 1994, and pay at the lower rate.

The Tax Nightmare for Cottagers

In February 1992, the government restricted the use of the $100,000 capital gains exemption on second properties. This includes any capital gains on cottage property after March 1, 1992.

The good news is that there has been little or no gain in real estate value and in most cases prices have fallen.

But, if you do have a cottage and expect to hold it for some time, there may be a need to tax-plan around this issue.

If you and your spouse both pass away, the cottage would be deemed to have been sold for tax purposes, passing on a potential tax liability to your estate.

Here are a few options to consider.

1) Buy insurance to cover the liability, including a "last to die" policy that pays only when you and your spouse are dead. It covers the tax liability.

2) Establish a cottage property trust, an inter-vivos trust, where you relinquish ownership of the property to the trust on behalf of your children, but you can still control your assets, which may be distributed to them at a later date.

3) Transfer ownership of the cottage to your children now and avoid the tax problem. It must be done at current market value.

4) Make the cottage your principal residence if it is more valuable than your city residence.

Labour-Sponsored Equity Pools

Labour pools were established to provide venture capital to Canadian entrepreneurial business. Successfully pioneered in Quebec, these pools have had great sales success. Here is a simple illustration of the tax and investment benefits.

Assume that the maximum investment permitted per year is $5,000. The taxpayer borrows $5,000 from the bank. The after-tax cash cost of the borrowing will be approximately $150 if the prime rate is 6%.

Invest $5,000. You receive $1,000 from the federal government and an additional $1,000 if you reside in a province that participates in this program.

You then place the $5,000 unit in your RRSP and claim a $2,500 deduction (assuming you are in the 50%+ tax bracket).

You have recovered $4,500 of your $5,000 and now you reinvest the $4,500 recovery. It, too, perhaps can go into your RRSP, producing a further $2,250 tax recovery.

At worst, you recoup $4,500; at best, you have as much as $11,750 invested, earning substantial tax-free income at a cash cost of $150. Not bad, even in these difficult times.

If you are interested in the benefits of this type of investment, investigate the Integrated Growth Fund or Working Ventures. Both are labour-sponsored venture capital corporations.

PERSONAL TAX FILING TIPS TO SAVE CASH

1) File. Even if you don't owe any money or have no taxable income, you may be cutting yourself out of some refundable tax credits. For example, you have to file the 1993 tax form to get the child tax credit and the goods and services tax credit. Children 19 and over should file whether or not they have income in order to receive the GST credit.

2) Claim medical expenses. Remember that medical expenses above 3% of your net income can be claimed. Uninsured dental expenses such as capping teeth or braces for yourself or your dependents can easily push you over the limit.

   Expenses claimed can be for any 12-month period that ends in 1993. So you could combine two major expenses even if one occurred in 1992.

   Then once you are over the limit, it pays to include even small eligible medical expenses. It is easy to forget that payments to private medical insurance plans, especially those made by payroll deduction, are allowable medical expenses.

3) Deduct investment expenses. Don't forget that investment counsel fees and safety deposit fees can be deducted from investment income as well as interest paid on money borrowed to make the investment.

   If you have income denominated in a foreign currency, you can use either the rate you actually converted at or the average rate for the year, whichever is to your advantage.

4) Watch out for double taxation on reinvested dividends. If you have cashed in a mutual fund into which you reinvested dividends over the years, be careful not to pay capital gains tax on dividends you reinvested. You have already paid income tax on those dividends. You have to calculate the average price you paid

for your units and compare that to the price per unit you received when you sold.

5) Reassess tax strategies if the high income earner changes. Married couples should reassess who is the higher earner. With many people losing jobs or earning less, the balance often shifts these days. The more highly paid person should consider using the other spouse's deductions for such things as moving expenses, medical expenses, charitable donations and political contributions.

6) Couples can pool some deductions. Pool charitable donations with your spouse. In this way you can claim 29% as a tax credit for donations over $250 rather than for donations over $500 between the two of you.

7) Transfer education amounts. Parents or grandparents (including in-laws) can claim any of a child's educational expenses (maximum of $4,000) the child cannot use.

8) Past errors often can be rectified. If you remember that you missed major deductions like the equivalent-to-married amount for any year back to 1987, you can resubmit your income tax return to get back refunds for such a claim.

ELECTRONIC TAX FILING TO IMPROVE CASH FLOW

Electronic filing, or E-file, is now available nationally. Introduced four years ago as a pilot project in Manitoba, it has gradually spread across the country, with Ontario and the Atlantic provinces logging on this year.

"It's fast, it's accurate, it's paperless," Revenue Canada boasts, adding that most taxpayers who file electronically should receive their refunds within two weeks. Former Revenue Minister, Otto Jelinek, goes one better. "The maximum is going to be two weeks," and if things go smoothly, it'll be "a matter of days," he vowed. Despite its optimistic projections, Revenue Canada still asks filers to wait four weeks before contacting their district tax office about their refunds.

There are about 4,500 agents—from big accounting firms to one-person operations—registered for E-file in Canada. Check your local tax office for the one nearest you. Transmission prices vary. Some firms include it in the cost of preparing your return. If you prepare your own return, the cost is between $15 and $25.

Confirmation that the return has been accepted used to take as little as two or three hours, but now that all 10 provinces and two territories are on-line, it sometimes takes 12 hours or more.

There's no question E-file is paperless, but you'll still need receipts. The taxman plans to do random audits of returns filed electronically just to make sure you're honest.

It greatly improves cash flow, beats discounting your refund and gets your money back three months faster.

MOVING TO THE UNITED STATES: LOOK BEFORE YOU LEAP

Contrary to a recent Gallup poll suggesting that more than 55% of Canadians are content to remain in Canada, we are inundated with reports of businesses and individuals moving to the United States.

Visions of expanding markets, lower costs, and larger profits are luring many small businesses south of the border. Are these relocations planned and based on an in-depth comprehensive evaluation of all the factors (personal as well as business) that influence a decision of that magnitude? Or are they initiated by a more emotional response to our current Canadian woes? Before you throw up your hands in despair and join the growing exodus to the United States, you should examine some of the non-business differences between living in Canada and the United States.

The biggest bone of contention for Canadians, and clearly the most publicized, is the tax-rate differential between the two countries. Most Canadians do not realize that the top 1993 U.S. federal personal tax rate of 39% is more than the top Canadian federal rate of about 32%. The main variance in tax rates on both sides of the border is due to the differences between the various state tax rates and those of the provinces. The U.S. state tax rates vary from as low as 0% to as high as about 10% in Utah, Idaho, and Nevada, while a high-income resident in Ontario would pay about 53%. As U.S. state taxes are deductible for U.S. federal purposes, the highest combined marginal tax rate would be about 43% in the United States, compared with 53% in Ontario.

The cost of health insurance is one of the main reasons why Ontario's tax rate is much higher than the highest U.S. state rate. Health insurance for most American families is a significant expenditure (it could be in excess of $4,000 per year) while all Ontario residents are covered by OHIP (Ontario Health Insurance Plan) with no cost to the individual resident (above that which is raised through the tax system).

The other highly publicized difference between the two tax systems is the fact that Americans can deduct home mortgage interest. This is clearly a major advantage to the U.S. taxpayers and goes a long way in reducing the tax bill. However, what about the home itself? How do the two countries differ in the treatment of gains on the sale of the principal residence? Most Canadians realize that any gains realized from the sale of the principal residence are free of tax. In the United States, if you replace your family home within two years and the cost of the new home exceeds the net sale price of your old home, then the gain is deferred. As long as you continually trade up in family homes, the tax is deferred. But what happens when you sell your last family home? Well, as long as you're aged 55 or older, $125,000 of the deferred gain is tax-free; the rest is subject to normal tax rates.

The costs of a Canadian university education are increasing every year, and there is little solace in the fact that the student can claim a credit for the tuition paid or that a limited tax credit is potentially available to the parent. At a comparable institution in the United States, the tuition can be four or five times the Canadian cost and the tuition is not generally deductible. To take the comparison one step further, Canadians attending university in the United States can claim tax relief for U.S. tuition, while the American students at the same institution cannot.

The RRSP continues to be the best tax shelter available to Canadians. The maximum contribution limit in 1994 is $13,500, rising to $15,500 in 1995. With about 30 years of contributions, a significant nest egg can be hatched on retirement. In addition, the only penalty for withdrawing funds from your RRSP prior to maturity is that the proceeds have to be included in your tax return in the year of withdrawal and are subjected to normal marginal rates. The U.S. equivalent to the RRSP is the Individual Retirement Account (IRA). However, that is where the similarity ends. With a maximum annual contribution of only $2,000, there is no way that the funds in an IRA on retirement will remotely approach those accumulated in an RRSP. If IRA funds are withdrawn before age 59½, not only are the proceeds included in the recipient's tax return and subjected to the U.S. marginal tax rates, but an additional 10% penalty for early withdrawal is assessed.

Still on the issue of retirement funding, the U.S. social security system costs far more than the Canada Pension Plan. Annual employee contributions in the United States exceed $4,000, while the corresponding CPP maximum is approximately one-quarter of this amount. The U.S. employee's contribution is not deductible, while the Canadian counterpart obtains a tax credit for the contribution. U.S. social security pays about twice the amount of CPP benefits received by retirees. However, when Canadian old age security is considered, the retirement benefits in Canada and the U.S. are approximately the same.

Finally, when a Canadian dies, this person is deemed to have disposed of his or her assets at their fair market value on the date of death. Seventy-five percent of any resulting capital gains is included in calculating the income in the final tax return of the deceased and is subject to the marginal tax rates. Americans are not taxed on the increase in value of an asset at the date of death; they are taxed on the value of their worldwide estate (including life insurance) in excess of $600,000. For those Americans who have accumulated substantial property and wealth over their lifetime, the estate is a significant tax levy to swallow. While it may be financially more attractive for well-to-do individuals to accumulate wealth in the United States, Canada is generally a better place to die when it is time to pass on that wealth unless you establish a trust in a tax-free zone such as Bermuda or the Cayman Islands. K.C. Irving did just that and required that at least three of his survivors establish offshore residences as well so that Canada cannot touch his immense wealth.

While conventional wisdom suggests that you can save a significant amount of taxes if you move south of the border, it is dangerous to just assume that you will be better off in the United States. The question of whether someone is better off in the United States or Canada can be answered only after an examination of how the two systems affect an individual's particular circumstances.

RRSP: DEATH AND TAXES

RRSPs are deemed to be cashed in immediately upon death. The RRSP proceeds are included in the deceased's income and are taxed at the deceased's tax rate.

RRSPs left to a spouse (legal or common-law) or to a disabled or dependent child continue to be sheltered from tax by virtue of a tax-free roll over. Where the funds are left to a spouse above the age of 71, a grace period of 60 days is given to convert the amount into a registered retirement income fund or an annuity.

It is important that intended beneficiaries be named as beneficiaries in the RRSP and not just in the will. If they are named in the will only, the transfer of funds between RRSPs still takes place. However, income earned on the plan proceeds from the date of death to the date the will is probated and is taxed at the beneficiary's rate. Depending on the size of the estate, this may result in a significant amount of tax to the beneficiary of the estate.

Where no specific beneficiary of the RRSP is intended, the estate should be named as beneficiary in the RRSP. Then, as designated in the will, the funds will be distributed after the estate taxes and fees are paid.

Naming specific beneficiaries in the RRSP may also reduce probate fees payable by the estate in certain circumstances. Usually, insurance companies and financial institutions process RRSP transfers without probate if there is a named beneficiary (check first). Alberta charges probate fees starting at $25 for the first $5,000 in value of the estate and increasing to $1,000 for estates in excess of $500,000.

As part of your overall estate planning, you should consider reviewing all your RRSPs to ensure that you have named beneficiaries in the RRSPs themselves, not just in your will.

Retirement and Estate Planning

Statistics indicate that once a Canadian reaches the age of 65, the individual can expect to have another 16 to 25 good years left. Unfortunately, most Canadians do not have enough savings to last for their longer lives. Even though the average Canadian saves nearly 10% of his or her disposable income, which is twice the average savings rate of our friends in the United States, Americans are more financially secure because of their more aggressive, equity-based investment style.

It would be safe to say that more than half of all Canadians above the age of 30 have no retirement plan at all, never mind an early retirement strategy. But with corporate downsizing being a permanent feature of the 1990s, many more Canadians must look ahead and contemplate their expected financial situation for the time that they turn 55. Remember, your goal is to live the last 30 years of your life in style and comfort. Yet, the majority of Canadians will not. Most Canadians grossly underestimate their financial needs when they retire.

Most Canadians are capable of saving twice as much money if they put their minds to it. Instead, they use their RRSP, if they have one, to store cash for a year or two and they use tax refunds for vacations. The end result is that many baby boomers who are now 45 years of age will ultimately become a financial burden on their children and society.

Many corporate pension plans are under-financed and the Canada Pension Plan is within a decade of becoming insolvent. Governments do not seem to be able to raise adequate net tax revenue to fund our retirement care. Financial planning for retirement by both individuals and government officials seems to be viewed as an extra rather than as an absolute necessity of life.

The purpose of this chapter is to look at Registered Retirement Savings Plans as a set of strategies that will allow you to retire early and live well. I do not want to review dozens of pages of clichés drawn from more than 30 books that have been written on the subject of RRSPs over the last 10 years. I want to provide you with specific action plans and effective investment strategies to follow, which will ensure that your RRSP generates maximum investment, tax-planning, and retirement-planning potential.

If you are following the investment strategies in this book, you will probably be working with a financial planner. Planning for early retirement at age 55 requires careful analysis, planning, and investment wisdom. This is especially true now as we try to cope with the effects of dismal job prospects, minimal increases in wages and incomes, more restrictive benefit plans, and the likelihood of actual reductions in pension-plan pay-outs.

Two separate studies, one by the CIBC and Angus Reid and the other by Royal Trust and Decima Research, each published similar findings—that more Canadians than ever before are concerned about planning for retirement, but only 35% plan to contribute to their RRSPs. These studies also found that only 29% of those interviewed felt that the Canada Pension Plan will be available to everyone on retirement; almost 60% believed that they will have to rely on government or company pension plans; and more than 70% worried about the effect of taxation on their future pension income. For 1993, on average they each planned to contribute $2,911 to an RRSP, which is the same as in 1992. But that is a 15% decrease from the $3,441 average that Canadians said they would invest in 1991.

Even Statistics Canada and the federal government's chief statistician admit that in fiscal 1991-92, the Quebec Pension Plan paid out more than it took in. They report that by 2026, 23.2% of the population will qualify for pensions under the current system. Ottawa's last actuarial report stated bluntly that CPP contributions will have to rise from their current level of 2.5% of income to 12% of income if the CPP is to be properly funded.

Several important changes have been made recently to RRSP rules. They include the following:

1) The maximum RRSP contribution for the 1993 tax year is 18% of earned income or $12,500, whichever is less. This goes up to $13,500 in 1994.

2) Up to 18% of the book value (defined as the price you originally paid for the investments) of your RRSP may be held as foreign content in 1993. This will increase to 20% in 1994.

3) Beginning in 1993, common-law couples were allowed to set up spousal RRSPs, which would allow them to split income with each other after retirement.

4) Disability pensions from the Canada and Quebec Pension Plans may now be included as earned income for the purpose of calculating RRSP contribution limits.

5) Until March 1, 1993, married couples were allowed to borrow up to $20,000 each, interest-free, from their RRSPs to buy a home. The deal must have closed by September 30, 1993. This loan may be repaid over 15 years, starting in 1994.

THE $100,000 RRSP ERROR

The following actions will *reduce* the value of an RRSP by approximately $100,000 during its potential 30- to 35-year lifetime.

1) Contributing late in the year. Making a single lump-sum contribution at the last possible date will reduce the ultimate value of the plan by as much as 10 percent when compared with the effect of a regular contribution plan.

2) Under-contributions or deferrals. If the average contribution is $2,500 per person and the potential contribution is $3,500 or more, the loss in value of the RRSP is at least $100,000.

3) Withdrawals. The foolhardy 1992 plan that allowed plan holders to withdraw up to $20,000 from the plan for use as a down payment on a house ultimately reduces the value of the plan by roughly $86,000 when considering the maximum-allowed 15-year payback period.

OTHER RRSP TIPS AND STRATEGIES

1) Be sure to name the beneficiaries of your RRSPs. That way, the RRSP money can be rolled over to the beneficiary's RRSP without being taxed. Otherwise, the money would go to your estate and would be subject to probate fees and income tax.

2) During a time of grief when a family member dies, many investment issues are overlooked. However, do not forget that in the case of the death of the family's principal wage earner, funds from the deceased can be used toward a tax-deductible contribution to a spousal RRSP for the surviving spouse.

3) Most people do not understand how being laid off can affect RRSP decisions. Most importantly, you can make a contribution

to your RRSP of $2,000 for each year of service to your employer. Use your severance pay and do it. Secondly, you can make an additional contribution of $1,500 per year, for each year prior to 1989 that you did not have a registered pension plan or deferred profit-sharing plan in place. This is a key issue because Revenue Canada taxes your severance package as if it is earned income—except the amount that goes into your RRSP. Some employers will make these payments on your behalf at the time of termination and adjust your severance accordingly. Be sure to ask your employer whether the company will do it or not. If your employer will not do it, you can do so at any time up to the end of February following the year in which you lose your job.

4) Many people focus exclusively on the tax benefits of an RRSP. You should remember that the same asset allocation principles apply to your RRSP as to any other asset portfolio. Balance your holdings—always maintain a diversified portfolio.

5) Maximize your eligible foreign content, but do not exceed it. The cap is set at 18% for 1993 and 20% for 1994. Revenue Canada charges a penalty of 1% monthly interest on the excess.

6) A key consideration is the status of your $100,000 lifetime capital gains exemption. If it remains largely unused, you are better off to keep any equity investments outside your RRSP and shelter income-bearing investments such as GICs and Treasury bills (which are normally fully taxable) inside your RRSP.

7) Make a contribution to a spousal plan, particularly if your spouse has no income or is in a lower tax bracket. This is a common income-splitting strategy. Then if you wait at least three years before withdrawing money from the spousal RRSP, the withdrawn funds will be taxed in the lower-income spouse's tax bracket instead of at the higher-income contributor's higher rate. The other advantage is that the money can stay sheltered longer if the spouse for whom the spousal RRSP is set up is younger than the contributing spouse.

8) During an era of low interest rates, make the effort to learn about RRSP-eligible investments other than simple savings accounts or GICs. Mutual funds and self-administered plans are two other possibilities.

9) Review your investments regularly and do not accept poor performance. If your returns are less than satisfactory, do something to improve them.

10) Keep capital losses outside your RRSP.

11) Try to put the maximum allowable contribution into your RRSP every year and avoid relying on the carry-forward allowance that lets you make up unused RRSP deductions at a future date. By making the maximum annual contributions, you will get the maximum possible tax deduction and at the same time also maximize the ultimate future value of your plan.

12) Set up a regular monthly contribution plan to your RRSP. By doing so, you avoid scrambling for a whopping lump sum in February and you end up increasing the value of your RRSP by earning tax-sheltered income sooner. This strategy will add roughly 10% to the ultimate value of the RRSP over its life.

13) Do not delay. The younger you are when you start making contributions to an RRSP, the longer your money compounds interest-free. A few years' delay can cost you tens of thousands of dollars in the final value of your RRSP.

14) Make a contribution. Only one-third of Canadians are likely to do so for 1994.

15) Do not make RRSP decisions based exclusively on administration costs. You should always investigate the overall costs of maintaining your RRSP, such as administration fees and loads, but the key consideration is the long-term potential return. For example, a mediocre, no-load fund may be a poorer value than a high-return fund with a load.

16) For a self-administered plan, pay your fees personally to ensure that they are tax-deductible.

17) Understand that you are allowed a one-time $8,000 over-contribution, even if you are covered by a company pension plan. This will add dramatically to long-term earnings within the plan.

18) To make a self-administered plan worthwhile, you need a minimum of $25,000 to $50,000 in your plan because of the fees normally assessed against these plans.

19) Consolidate your holdings. Fewer plans result in lower costs.

20) Remember that 1994 is the last year for the $6,000 tax-free rollover (that is, you can roll over up to $6,000 from your pension plan to your spouse's RRSP tax-free, to increase the value of the spouse's retirement plan).

21) You can withdraw part of an RRSP without collapsing it, but don't draw down to buy a house or cash out to pay for a holiday.

22) Borrow if necessary to maximize your contribution and use your tax refund to pay down the loan.

23) Remember that interest expense on RRSP borrowing is non-deductible and an RRSP usually cannot be pledged as collateral.

24) Remember the benefits of a spousal plan when you want to have a sabbatical or take maternity leave. Plan three years in advance and avoid the attribution rules.

25) The minimum withholding tax is 10% on $5,000 or less. Therefore, as an example, if you have to borrow $15,000 from your plan, make separate withdrawals of $5,000 each day for three consecutive days rather than a single lump-sum withdrawal.

SELF-DIRECTED PLANS

I assume that you have heard of the benefits of RRSPs and especially of a self-directed plan if you have a minimum of $25,000 to $50,000 under administration. It is ideal to consolidate the number of plans you have to reduce administrative and transfer fees. It is also a flexible approach that allows you to hold a large number of different investment products such as stocks, bonds, rights, warrants, and options. Work with your financial planner to set up a self-directed plan to help you attain maximum flexibility and make sure that all administrative fees are paid personally, outside of the RRSP, to ensure tax deductibility.

MORTGAGE WITHIN YOUR RRSP

This much-talked-about idea was based on the premise that you had a large mortgage and $50,000 or more in cash or liquid securities in your RRSP and interest rates were 10% or higher. After fees and expenses, you would get a nice 8% yield in tax-deferred income within an RRSP. But interest rates and mortgage rates are low, and in order to qualify, your mortgage must be at market rate. Therefore, at the current time, placing your mortgage within your RRSP is a poor and expensive strategy and is not worth considering until mortgage rates exceed a threshold level of 10%.

OVER-CONTRIBUTIONS

Every Canadian is allowed a lifetime $8,000 RRSP over-contribution that is not subject to penalty. It is not deductible from taxable income like your normal annual RRSP contribution, but it still can accumulate income interest-free for the lifetime of the plan.

Even if you have made the maximum allowable tax-deductible RRSP contribution and are covered by a company pension, you are still eligible to make this over-contribution. Both you and your spouse can each have an $8,000 over-contribution. My suggestion is to do what you can to find an extra $1,000 per year for 8 years to take advantage of this opportunity; it will pay off in the long run.

REGISTERED RETIREMENT INCOME FUNDS (RRIFs)

At some point, you will have to decide how to collapse your RRSP to provide income in your later years. A common strategy is to purchase an annuity or a Registered Retirement Income Fund (RRIF), which will provide you with a regular monthly income to cover your living expenses. This can be done at any time up until age 71, at which point in time it is mandatory. The only other age-related consideration is whether you are covered by a corporate pension plan. If this is the case, you are required to convert the corporate pension plan to an annuity or a RRIF no later than 10 years following the date of your retirement. Ontario residents can use this corporate pension plan to buy a Life Income Fund (LIF). Just like a RRIF, there is a minimum annual payment scale, but unlike a RRIF, you must buy an annuity by the time you are 80 years of age.

These are tough times for RRIFs and annuities because of the low rates of interest. Therefore, within your portfolio you must still have assets other than an RRIF, LIF, or annuity if you are to maintain your current lifestyle.

This means that the old ways of planning for retirement are no longer reliable. The following guidelines indicate what you should be saving as a percentage of your after-tax household income, beyond any pension plans that you may have.

PERCENTAGE OF AFTER-TAX HOUSEHOLD INCOME TO SAVE FOR RETIREMENT

HOUSEHOLD	AGES			
	25-34	35-44	45-54	55-64
Single woman earning $30,000	11.4%	9.6%	10.6%	8.9%
Single woman earning $50,000	10.0%	10.0%	11.8%	15.7%
Single man earning $50,000	1.3%	7.5%	13.3%	18.2%
Married couple earning $50,000	1.9%	5.2%	11.7%	17.2%
Married couple earning $100,000	4.7%	9.3%	16.6%	22.6%

TABLE 8–1

As you can see, this table indicates that women must save much more money during their early years. This is because, on average, women live longer than men and tend not to earn as much money later in their careers.

Approximately 50% of Canadians in 1993 wanted to be able to retire between the ages of 50 and 64. Of course, many may have developed outside interests, home businesses, alternative sources of income, as well as the temperament and talents to do so. They are not tied to their careers.

After you retire, your cost of living can be expected to drop to about 80% of what you spend on day-to-day living today, after considering the effects of inflation. For example, taxes, clothing expenses, and transportation costs will decline once you stop working. Also remember that once you reach the age of 60, a major focus of your investment strategy is wealth and capital preservation. This strategy is essential to ensuring a stable cash flow and a consistent style of living.

It is interesting to note that in a recent issue of *Fortune* magazine, a survey of the wealthiest 1% of U.S. citizens indicated that the single most important objective for these people was to keep the money they had accumulated intact—wealth preservation. However, in my opinion, it is important to understand that wealth preservation must, of necessity, include equity investments. Capital growth is required to maintain the performance of your investment portfolio. To not include it is a fatal long-term error.

Dozens of times during the last few years, older Canadians have approached me after an evening seminar and lamented that their $500,000 in Canada Savings Bonds have ensured their poverty. Their cash flow continues to decline while their tax burden increases. They have never established a diversified portfolio or considered the tax consequences of their holdings. Instead, they buy 11-year compound interest bonds and pay tax annually on interest income they cannot expect to receive until many years in the future. With the lowest interest rates in 29 years, cash flow for these Canadians has been reduced by 57%. But their capital is intact! This is called poverty through capital preservation.

After investing for growth during their twenties and thirties, then working to accumulate assets during their high-income middle years, sixties-plus investors who are on the verge of retirement must structure their portfolio of assets and investments to provide optimal cash flow as well. They will need income to cover day-to-day expenses plus an additional cushion of 2% to 4% per year to cover the effects of inflation over the next 10 years. Equities can provide that protection, but stocks and stock funds are more volatile than bond funds. Therefore, retirees must balance conflicting financial goals: sufficient income, reasonable growth, and low risk and volatility.

However, you must understand that in the 1990s, there is no such thing as a "risk-free 10% investment" anymore. The 14% to 19% interest rate returns of the 1980s were an anomaly of the 20th century and will not return again in my lifetime. The worst mistake is to invest too conservatively in GICs and bonds. You must gradually shift the balance of your portfolio as you grow older, based on the following investment guidelines.

- At age 55, put 45% of your portfolio into equities.

- At age 65, put 35% of your portfolio into equities.

- At age 75, put 25% of your portfolio into equities.

Note: As a rule of thumb to follow for any situation, deduct your current age from 100 and the remainder represents the percentage of your portfolio that should be invested in equities.

To reduce stock volatility, eliminate aggressive growth funds and stay with balanced and blue chip income funds. High-dividend stocks and high-yield funds are another safe bet for early retirees.

I often get asked how much a person should save each month to be able to retire at age 55 and still live comfortably. If you think in "current 1993 dollars," the following table will give you some guidelines as to how much money you will have to save each month.

HOW MUCH TO SAVE EACH MONTH TO RETIRE AT 55

CURRENT AGE	CURRENT GROSS INCOME					
	$25,000	$40,000	$60,000	$75,000	$100,000	$125,000
50	0	833	3,875	6,333	10,333	12,583
45	0	533	2,183	3,317	5,250	6,417
40	225	625	1,375	2,000	3,042	3,583
35	192	417	875	1,258	1,892	2,208
30	175	317	625	883	1,300	1,500

TABLE 8–2

This saving strategy will yield roughly 80% of your pre-retirement net income, assuming, you have a 20-year corporate pension; your Canada Pension Plan kicks in at age 65; and your savings will earn a net yield of 8% after tax.

Here's how to figure out your "earned income" for RRSP purposes. Remember that earned income does not currently include pension benefits or interest, dividend, or capital gains. To calculate your tax-deductible RRSP contribution limit for 1993, take 18% of 1992's earned income to a maximum of $12,500 and subtract your pension adjustment. Do the same for 1994, but use 1993's earned income and pension adjustment.

RECENT CHANGES IN LEGISLATION ON RRIFs

Recent changes in the legislation governing Registered Retirement Income Funds now allow:

- increased minimum payments to RRIF holders between the ages of 71 and 77;

- decreased minimum payments to RRIF holders between the ages of 78 and 90; and

- RRIF holders to continue to draw income from their plans after the age of 90.

The effect of these changes is that by allowing plan holders to increase the minimum income they receive on a monthly basis out of their plan, the government has limited the flexibility of plan holders to manage their assets. Individuals are being forced to take greater income and thereby limit the assets which could potentially be saved for estate-planning purposes. In other words, the ability to reduce income and preserve capital, which the old rules allowed, has been restricted.

However, there is another important investment consideration resulting from this change in rules. Using 71-year-olds as an example, the minimum annual withdrawal guideline has been raised to 7.38% from 5.26% of the "beginning of year" asset base. Research has shown that this increase has meant that if a RRIF plan holder is not generating a "real rate of return"* of at least 6%, then the individual forced to withdraw higher minimum monthly instalments will experience a "real"* decline in both assets and income over time. This means that a 71-year-old who is not earning at least 7.38% on his or her assets is suffering an immediate erosion of capital.

The following table demonstrates the effects of inflation on an individual who gets RRIF minimum payments at the end of each year. Note that at the current rates of inflation (2%), the investor can no longer accept the modest returns of 6% or less from fixed income securities and still maintain a constant standard of living. A more aggressive approach is needed to reflect the new tax and withdrawal rates, as Ottawa proceeds to increase its tax grab and get as much back from you as soon as it can to improve Revenue Canada's cash flow.

---

* "Real rate of return" and "real income" are defined as rate of return on assets and purchasing power available from income respectively, after inflation has been taken into consideration.

RRIF INCOME

Age	RRIF min	RRIF Balance at beginning of year	Int 8%	RRIF min	Inflation Adjusted Income 2.00%
71	7.38%	$100,000	$8,000	$7,380	$7,380
72	7.48%	100,620	8,050	7,526	7,379
73	7.59%	101,143	8,091	7,677	7,379
74	7.71%	101,558	8,125	7,830	7,378
75	7.85%	101,852	8,148	7,995	7,387
76	7.99%	102,005	8,160	8,150	7,382
77	8.25%	102,015	8,161	8,314	7,383
78	8.33%	101,862	8,149	8,485	7,387
79	8.53%	101,526	8,122	8,660	7,391
80	8.75%	100,988	8,079	8,836	7,394
81	8.99%	100,231	8,018	9,011	7,392
82	9.27%	99,238	7,939	9,199	7,399
83	9.58%	97,978	7,838	9,386	7,401
84	9.93%	96,430	7,714	9,576	7,402
85	10.33%	94,569	7,566	9,769	7,404
86	10.79%	92,366	7,389	9,966	7,405
87	11.33%	89,789	7,183	10,173	7,411
88	11.96%	86,799	6,944	10,381	7,414
89	12.71%	83,361	6,669	10,595	7,418
90	13.62%	79,435	6,355	10,819	7,427
91	14.73%	74,971	5,998	11,043	7,432
92	16.12%	69,925	5,594	11,272	7,437
93	17.92%	64,247	5,140	11,513	7,447
94	20.00%	57,874	4,630	11,575	7,340
95	20.00%	50,929	4,074	10,186	6,333
96	20.00%	44,818	3,585	8,964	5,464
97	20.00%	39,439	3,155	7,888	4,714
98	20.00%	34,707	2,777	6,941	4,067
99	20.00%	30,542	2,443	6,108	3,509
100	20.00%	26,877	2,150	5,375	3,027
101	20.00%	23,652	1,892	4,730	2,611
102	20.00%	20,813	1,665	4,163	2,253

TABLE 8–3

EARLY-RETIREMENT TEST

The change from a working life to a sudden retirement situation is one of the most difficult transitions you will ever make in your life. How you deal with it is important to your financial health. Everybody reacts differently. However, to the best of your ability, you must prepare yourself as much as you can beforehand. I have included a simple little test that will help you start thinking about your situation and an early retirement strategy. You may circle more than one answer for each question.

1. Which of the following actions have you taken to determine if you can afford to retire right now?
   a) You have calculated the income and benefits you will receive from your company pension plan and the Canada Pension Plan.
   b) You have calculated the anticipated income you will be receiving from other sources.
   c) You have calculated your family's anticipated retirement expenses.
   d) You have not done any of the above.

2. To build up income for your retirement, which of the following investments have you regularly purchased?
   a) RRSPs.
   b) Mutual funds.
   c) Stocks or bonds.
   d) Investment-grade real estate.
   e) None of the above.

3. If you stopped working today, how would you feel?
   a) You would feel financially secure.
   b) You would enjoy not having to report for work.
   c) You would worry about what others thought about you.

4. To earn income during your retirement years, what would you do?
   a) You would immediately start developing new skills before you retire.
   b) You would try to turn a hobby into a source of income.
   c) You would continue doing the same type of work you are doing now, but on a freelance basis.
   d) You do not know what you would do.

5. When you take time off from work, what do you do?
   a) You stay at home and have fun.
   b) You prefer to travel.
   c) You get restless and look forward to getting back to work.

6. At present, what activities are you involved in outside of work?
   a) You are a volunteer worker.
   b) You are a member of a club, society, or organization.
   c) You are a regular participant in group activities outside of work.
   d) You do none of the above.

7. What do you do to stay healthy?
   a) You exercise regularly.
   b) You follow a healthy diet.
   c) You manage your exposure to stress.
   d) You do none of the above.

8. What have you done in preparation for possible early retirement?
   a) You have recently talked to at least two early retirees who have been retired for five years or more.
   b) You have not talked to anyone who has retired early.

9. How does your spouse or partner feel about your early retirement?
   a) Your mate thinks that early retirement would be good for you.
   b) Your mate is looking forward to spending more time with you.
   c) Your mate would find it difficult with you at home all the time.

10. How do you plan to keep your family insured against medical expenses until you reach age 65?
    a) You plan to extend your current insurance policy from your employer through to age 65.
    b) You plan to purchase incremental health coverage on your own through Blue Cross or some other private insurance company.
    c) You do not know.

Scoring

The most important factor affecting the quality of your life following early retirement is the state of your personal finances. Without enough money to live comfortably on, you are in trouble. For the first two questions in this quiz, give yourself two (2) points for every circled answer except the last one in each question, which gets zero. For each of the other questions, give yourself one (1) point for each of your answers except the last one in each question, which gets zero.

Results

1 to 13 points: You either will have difficulty adapting to early retirement—financially or psychologically— or you need to start preparing yourself immediately.

14 to 22 points: Although early retirement is not your preference, you would probably adapt relatively well to it. The best strategy is to keep doing what you are currently doing and try to preserve your health.

23 or more points: Go for it. You are probably financially and psychologically prepared already.

ESTATE-PLANNING CHECKLIST FOR CANADIANS

Name: _____

Date: _____

(Keep an updated copy of these pages at all times to function as a complete listing of your personal wealth. Update every three years or after a major change in assets.)

Personal Information

Name: _____

Soc. Ins. No.: _____

Home address and telephone: _____

Business address and telephone:

_____

_____

_____

Date and place of birth:

_____

_____

Is evidence of birth available?   _____ yes   _____ no

Residence: _____

Citizenship: _____

Domicile: _____

Marital status: _____

Spouse's name: _____

Spouse's Soc. Ins. No.: _____

Spouse's date and place of birth: _____

Spouse's residence, if different from above: _____

_____

_____

Spouse's Citizenship: _____

Marriage contract: _____

Jurisdiction of marriage: _____

If previous marriages, terms of divorce settlements, if any:

_____

_____

Terms of any separation agreement:

_____

_____

_____

Parents' names, date of birth, residence, domicile, and whether dependent:

_____

_____

_____

_____

_____

_____

_____

_____

Children's names, date of birth, residence, domicile, and whether dependent:

_____

_____

_____

_____

_____

_____

_____

_____

Grandchildren's names, date of birth, residence, and domicile:

_____
_____
_____
_____
_____
_____
_____
_____
_____
_____
_____
_____
_____
_____
_____
_____

Other beneficiaries' names, date of birth, residence, and domicile:

_____
_____
_____
_____
_____
_____
_____
_____
_____
_____
_____
_____
_____
_____

ADVISERS

Lawyer

Name: _____

Address: _____

Tel. no.: _____

Accountant

Name: _____

Address: _____

Tel. no.: _____

Bank

Name: _____

Address: _____

Tel. no.: _____

Life underwriter

Name: _____

Address: _____

Tel. no.: _____

Financial planner

Name: _____

Address: _____

Tel. no.: _____

Trust company

Name: _____

Address: _____

Tel. no.: _____

ASSETS

1) Cash accounts: _____

    Banks: _____

2) Short-term notes/Guaranteed Investment Certificates

    Issuer: _____

Face amount: _____

Interest rate: _____

Expiry date: _____

3) Accounts receivable

Debtor: _____

Face amount: _____

Outstanding amount: _____

Cost: _____

Fair market value: _____

Interest rate: _____

Date due: _____

Terms of repayment: _____

Collectibility: _____

4) Loans receivable

Debtor: _____

Face amount: _____

Outstanding amount: _____

Cost: _____

Fair market value: _____

Interest rate: _____

Date due: _____

Terms of repayment: _____

Collectibility: _____

5) Marketable securities, commodities, and futures

Name: _____

Cost: _____

Valuation day: _____

Fair market value: _____

Pledged or margined: _____

Control block: _____

Large minority shareholding: _____

6) Bonds and debentures

Issuer: _____

Face value: _____

Cost: _____

Valuation day: _____

Fair market value: _____

Interest rate: _____

Date due: _____

Special terms: _____

Pledged or margined: _____

7) Mortgages receivable

Mortgager: _____

Name of property: _____

Cost: _____

Outstanding amount: _____

Valuation day: _____

Fair market value: _____

Interest rate: _____

Date due: _____

Terms of repayment: _____

Collectibility: _____

8) Private corporations

Name: _____

Percentage of ownership of each class of share: _____

Attributes of shares: _____

Cost: _____

Valuation day: _____

Fair market value: _____

Underlying assets: _____

If real estate, capital, or inventory: _____

Types of surpluses: _____

Adjusted cost base reduced by dividends: _____

Shareholder's agreement: _____

Location of share register: _____

Jurisdiction of incorporation: _____

Year-end: _____

9) Investments in real estate

Location of property: _____

Capital or inventory: _____

Percentage of ownership: _____

Nature of ownership: _____

Cost: _____

Undepreciated capital cost: _____

Valuation day: _____

Fair market value: _____

Details of mortgage(s): _____

Gross annual income: _____

Net annual income: _____

Year-end: _____

10) Personal real estate

Location of property: _____

Nature of title: _____

Date acquired: _____

Cost: _____

Valuation day: _____

Fair market value: _____

Principal residence status: _____

Source of funds for acquisition: _____

Details of mortgage(s): _____

11) Partnership interest—professional

Name: _____

Percentage of ownership: _____

Cost: _____

Valuation day: _____

Adjusted cost base: _____

Fair market value: _____

Goodwill: _____

Provisions for disability, retirement, death: _____

_____

_____

_____

Partnership agreement: _____

Buy/sell agreement: _____

1994 Accounts receivable: _____

Year-end: _____

12) Unincorporated joint ventures

Name: _____

Percentage of ownership: _____

Cost: _____

Valuation day: _____

Fair market value: _____

Nature of assets: _____

Nature of enterprise: _____

Location of assets: _____

Buy/sell agreement: _____

Year-end: _____

13) Options to purchase assets

Property: _____

Cost: _____

Fair market value: _____

Expiry day: _____

Contingent liability: _____

Exclusivity: _____

14) Insurance

Insurer: _____

Life insured: _____

Beneficiary: _____

Owner: _____

Premium payor: _____

Nature of insurance(term or not): _____

Face value: _____

Cash surrender value: _____

Loans outstanding (convertible): _____

Interest rate on loans: _____

15) Special products

Limited partnership names: _____

Amount: _____

16) Mutual funds

Amount: _____

Company: _____

17) Registered pension plan

Amount: _____

Beneficiary: _____

Details of benefits: _____

18) Employee profit sharing plan

Amount: _____

Beneficiary: _____

Details of benefits: _____

19) Deferred profit sharing plan

Amount: _____

Beneficiary: _____

Details of benefits: _____

20) Registered retirement savings plans

Self-directed or not?   ____ yes   ____ no

Amount: _____

Company: _____

Beneficiary: _____

Details of plan: _____

Rate of interest: _____

21) Canada Pension Plan

Amount (payable on death): _____

22) Other assets (articles of personal, domestic, and household use or ornaments including artwork, jewellery, antiques, furniture, cars, boats, etc.)

— Description: _____

Cost: _____

Valuation day: _____

Fair market value: _____

— Description: _____

Cost: _____

Valuation day: _____

Fair market value: _____

— Description: _____

Cost: _____

Valuation day: _____

Fair market value: _____

— Description: _____

Cost: _____

Valuation day: _____

Fair market value: _____

23) Interest in estates or trusts

Income: _____

Capital: _____

Terms: _____

24) Expected Inheritances

_____

_____

_____

_____

_____

_____

_____

LIABILITIES

1) Loans and Notes Payable
   Creditor: _____
   Amount: _____
   Interest rate: _____
   Date due: _____
   Collateral: _____
   Terms: _____

2) Mortgages Payable
   Creditor: _____
   Amount: _____
   Interest rate: _____
   Date due: _____
   Collateral: _____
   Terms: _____

3) Margin Accounts
   Creditor: _____
   Amount: _____
   Interest rate: _____
   Security: _____
   Terms: _____

4) Guarantees
   Amount: _____
   On whose behalf: _____
   To whom: _____
   Terms: _____

5) Charitable or Non-Charitable Pledges
   Amount: _____
   Name: _____
   Specific purposes: _____

6) Miscellaneous
   Charge accounts, etc.: _____

   _____

   _____

7) Will
   Location: _____

8) Safety Deposit Box
   Location: _____

WILL PROVISIONS

1) Is the will being made in contemplation of marriage?
2) Executors and trustees.
3) Guardians of minors.
4) Registered retirement savings plan, deferred profit-sharing plan, and registered home ownership savings plan designations.
5) Insurance declaration.
6) Specific disposition of articles or ornaments of personal, domestic, and household use.
7) Specific disposition of any other assets.
8) If spouse survives, specific provisions for children.
9) If spouse survives, specific provisions for grandchildren.
10) If spouse survives, specific provisions for parents/parents-in-law.
11) If spouse survives, specific provisions for other beneficiaries, including charities.
12) Provisions for spouse.
13) If trust for spouse, disposition of balance of property on death of spouse, or if spouse predeceases.
14) Disposition on common disaster or failure of trust(s).
15) Circumstances requiring special consideration (e.g., physical or mental disability of a beneficiary).
16) Bequests to charities on subsequent death of spouse or in event of common disaster or failure of trust(s).
17) Are any adopted children to be treated the same as natural children?
18) Dower provision.

19) Should the will contain different dispositive provisions depending on whether testator has received a capital interest in an estate or trust or an expected inheritance?

20) Does testator wish to exercise any power of appointment granted to him under any will or trust agreement? If so, obtain a copy of the document granting the power.

21) Should the succession-duty exoneration clause apply to all beneficiaries? Is the buy/sell agreement exclusion required?

22) Special instructions concerning burial, organ transplants, etc. Note that executors, next of kin, and physician should be made aware of these provisions.

23) Does testator wish to grant any powers of appointment?

24) Does testator wish to prepare any memoranda for the guidance of the trustees?

25) Consider inclusion of the following trustee powers:
    a) to retain infants' shares;
    b) to make payments on behalf of infants;
    c) to convert or retain original assets;
    d) to divide in specie;
    e) to invest in trustee or unrestricted investments;
    f) to deal with real estate (maintenance, management, repair, disposal, options, etc.);
    g) to deal with share in corporations (same powers as testator when alive: voting, exercise of options, direction of management, etc.);
    h) to incorporate corporations;
    i) to carry on a business or partnership;
    j) to create separate trusts for business income for benefit of non-residents;
    k) to renew notes and guarantees, and to distinguish between capital and income receipts;
    l) to borrow;
    m) to buy estate assets, take remuneration, pass accounts, etc.;
    n) to make all advantageous elections under the Income Tax Act and (if relevant) The Succession Duty Act.

ESTATE-PLANNING CONSIDERATIONS

1) Consider advisability of freezing part or whole of estate.
2) Estimate liabilities and consider method of payment.
3) Consider ownership and premium payer of life insurance.
4) Ascertain amount of income available to maintain the family after death.

5) Consider ownership of personal real estate.

6) Consider creation of charitable foundation.

7) Consider advisability of trusts for the children, either as estate-freezing devices or as income-splitting strategy.

8) Consider advisability of agreements such as buy/sell agreements, voting trust agreements, etc.

9) If client should have any foreign-source income, consider whether any tax planning in Canada would be advantageous.

10) Consider purchase of an annuity for a charity.

11) Consider creation of holding corporation to defer income tax, change situs of assets, etc.

DOCUMENTS REGISTRY

List all documents and location of originals. Make copies of all relevant documentation.

_____

The Expert Adviser

Your Financial Planner

Many people ask me why I have a bias in favour of independent financial planners. After all, why not work with insurance agents, stockbrokers, or bankers? I always reply that I am without a doubt biased in favour of anyone who has the following qualifications.

1) The adviser has been trained and is certified as a financial-planning professional.

2) The adviser has gained significant experience in the financial services industry.

3) The adviser's compensation is closely tied to the success of the client's investments.

4) The adviser will openly provide references from satisfied clients.

5) The adviser is truly independent and is capable of sourcing all available funds, annuities, and financial products rather than a fixed and limited range of products offered by a single financial institution.

A salaried worker has little motivation for excellence because of the lack of commission earnings. A person tied to one institution is limited to perhaps six or eight mutual fund products instead of the 680 Canadian and 3,800 American and international funds.

I have met many excellent stockbrokers who sell quality equities, limited partnerships, bonds, and mutual funds. However, the difficulty I see is that these individuals deal only with the "investment" aspect of your financial plan and not all the other five elements of a complete plan. Also, I have little confidence or respect for the so-called research and information newsletters they generate. There is too much potential conflict of interest and self-promotion for this "service" to be truly beneficial.

Many good insurance agents are now calling themselves financial planners as if they were embarrassed to be known as insurance salespeople offering expertise in income and cash-flow protection. In fact, they are not financial planners.

Many banks and trust companies are expanding their business into the financial planning field because of its rapid growth in the past several years. My feeling is that the consumer would ultimately be better served by someone who could review the 60 different annuity rates available each day instead of the *one* posted in the bank. The variance of annuity and GIC rates on any given day may be as much as one-half of a percentage point or more. With today's low interest rates, such a variance will make a substantial difference.

Thus the difference between true independence and "tied relationships." Independence directs the financial-planning professional toward optimizing the return on investment in all product categories in the context of a total and complete financial plan. This optimizing process, combined with careful supervision, regular communication, and strategic updating is essential to long-term appreciation of your personal net worth. If you are to achieve your goal of doubling your net worth every three years, then your professional adviser must play a key role.

So how do you identify the appropriate adviser to work with you? The following steps will help you focus your search.

1) Identify and locate several reputable independent financial-planning firms or individuals in your area. The best sources or references are relatives, friends, and business associates with similar incomes and financial goals as yours. Once you have chosen three individuals, telephone each of them to set up an introductory meeting—which should be free of charge.

2) Subject the candidate to a tough interview. Make use of the introductory session to find out how the adviser gets compensated and whether this person has any potential conflicts of interest. Use this time to assess the financial planner's expertise and to see how well you get along. From the point of view of compensation, there are three kinds of planners.
   a) Fee-Only Planner—you will pay roughly $100 to $150 per hour plus an annual fee of 1% to 2% of the value of your portfolio.
   b) Fee-Based (fee and commission) Planner—you will pay similar fees in addition to commissions on investments and in

surance policies he or she sells, which should roughly cost 3% to 5% of the value of your portfolio on an annual basis.

c) Commission-Only Planner—you will pay a commission only, which is payable at the time of each transaction, typically costing, on an annual basis, 3% to 5% of the total value of your portfolio.

I do not believe that one method of compensation is particularly better than another. However, if the adviser accepts commissions, ask about the investments that this person tends to sell. If the person is only pitching one brand or product, you are likely dealing with a salesman rather than a financial planner. Find out about this person's experience and the types of clients he or she has. Hire someone who has more than three years' experience. Ask for a description of other clients' income levels, portfolio sizes, and occupations. You will want to work with an adviser who tends to deal with clients whose finances are similar to yours, since the financial planner will already be familiar with the same issues you face. Also ask for a sample of one of the adviser's financial plans (obviously with the client's name deleted for privacy) and read it when you get home to check that it is easy to understand and that its suggestions are precise and workable.

3) Verify that the planner has a good record with the regulators and has positive recommendations. Call your provincial securities commission to see if the financial adviser has ever been subject to disciplinary action or judgement. Also be sure to contact client references that the planner provides in order to verify that these people have been satisfied with the services they have received.

My recommendation is to ask the planner the following questions as part of the interview because these points cover most of the key issues you should discuss.

1) What is this person's educational background and experience?

2) Does this adviser have a "Registered Financial Planner" designation? If not, why not?

3) What are this person's areas of particular expertise?

4) What products is this planner licensed to sell?

5) What is the fee structure? Annual retainer?

6) Does this adviser charge for every telephone call you make and how available is this person to answer your questions?

7) What is the process of building a financial plan? Who will create the plan—the adviser or an assistant? How much involvement will the adviser have or is all the work done by assistants?

8) Does this planner have any "tied relationships" and, if not, which institutions does he or she generally prefer to work with?

9) How often will this person be able to meet with you and review your plan? How much feedback and advice will the planner regularly provide?

10) Has this adviser ever been sued by a client?

11) How does this planner keep up to date on the industry and the laws governing the business?

CHAPTER 10

Entrepreneurship

People often ask me why I add entrepreneurship to a book about investment strategy. Perhaps, they surmise, I was first a professor of entrepreneurship at the University of Toronto and many of my earlier books were about success in entrepreneurship. Or they suggest that many of the world's richest people today originally built their fortunes, not from stock trades, but rather from launching successful entrepreneurial ventures. After all, Bill Gates of Microsoft and the late Sam Walton of Wal-Mart both became billionaires who made their money from entrepreneurship. In Canada, we all have heard the family names of Weston, Thomson, Bronfman, Irving, and McCain.

Entrepreneurship is nothing more than finding a market opportunity, and meeting the needs of it successfully is a key element in the process of wealth creation. Entrepreneurship also has a direct tie-in to your investment strategy. Taking an entrepreneurial approach to investing—seeking new opportunities and new methods—is the core concept of what this book is all about. As Canadians struggling to cope with new economic realities, we must learn to say "yes" to new ideas and new investment strategies.

Being an entrepreneur and starting a home business, becoming self-employed, or buying a business or franchise will significantly alter your tax-planning position and could improve your overall cash flow. Home businesses now employ 1.5 million Canadians and this number includes a 14% increase in 1992. The average business costs $1,000 to start and 50% of the businesses started in 1992 were owned by women.

The impact of this choice of career on personal taxation is substantial. Consider the following.

1) If you have a six-room house, you could deduct one-sixth of the household costs—including mortgage interest, heat, light, telephone, and insurance—from income realized from the business. In many cases, this could create a loss, which is deductible from personal income. This will further reduce personal taxable income and enhance personal cash flow.

2) Should you reach a level of business income that makes it worthwhile to incorporate (say, $54,000) and have other family members as shareholders, it is possible to pay out dividends of up to $23,500 to each family member if there is a profit. Because of the dividend tax credit, this $23,500 per person would be non-taxable if the recipient had no other income.

3) If the venture is a Canadian-controlled private corporation that has been incorporated for two or more years and whose assets are other than real estate (with the exception of working farms), the business could be sold at some future date, largely tax-exempt. In addition to the lifetime $100,000 capital gains exemption, there is also an additional $400,000 tax exemption which could produce an aggregate of $500,000 in potential tax-free capital gains.

People often tell me they are not entrepreneurial and are all risk-averse. A small home venture (such as knitting clothing for sale at a fair, providing word processing, doing woodworking, making handicrafts, or canning home preserves) is hardly risky or capital-intensive. It just involves work, which means extra effort.

Entrepreneurship has no age limit or sex barrier. Forty-three percent of all small businesses and 50% of all home businesses are owned by women. Colonel Harland Sanders was 65 years of age when he started Kentucky Fried Chicken. The only requirement for an entrepreneur is the desire to act, save tax, and make money. Entrepreneurship can save up to one-sixth of your total personal tax liability if structured properly and can add thousands of dollars to your household cash flow, thereby increasing the amount of money you have to invest.

Just as reasonable leveraging adds to your financial returns when interest rates are low, good entrepreneurial financial planning creates even greater financial opportunities to increase your chance of producing a 30% per year return on investment. You have more to invest and therefore a higher, less-taxed cash yield.

If I had to summarize what I have learned over the years about the personal characteristics of a successful entrepreneur, I would say that you need the following traits.

- Stamina: the ability to work long hours

- Realism: the ability to make rational decisions when the pressure is on

- Self-motivation: the desire for independence and freedom to control your own destiny

- Self-confidence: success is built on a belief in yourself and your abilities

Entrepreneurship is about calculated risk-taking, not about beating the odds on unreasonable risks.

DISPELLING THE MYTHS OF ENTREPRENEURIAL FAILURE AND RISK

The claim for the past 30 years by so-called "experts" and business lenders is that 80% of all small businesses fail within the first five years of operation. This high attrition rate is used as the basis for rejecting small businesses as too risky for credit, loans, or even equity investments. After all, who would take such a high risk? The situation is regarded as so dangerous that governments have created special vehicles to induce lenders and investors to take these risks.

All levels of government across Canada have, since 1968, offered innumerable courses and seminars in small-business management to assist in reducing this perceived high mortality rate of new ventures.

From where did this mythology of small-business failure come and what are the facts? A thorough review of the literature draws us back to studies in the early 1970s that measured the number of incorporated smaller businesses (less than $5 million in sales) that were no longer in business after five years. Included in the calculation of the 80% "death ratio" were companies that never operated, those that voluntarily gave up their charter, and those that were sold or merged. Excluded were sole proprietorships and partnerships (which as a group account for more than 60% of all owner-managed businesses).

A more definitive long-term view was the pleasant-sounding *Canadian Business Failure Record*, which was published by Dun & Bradstreet and covered the time period up to 1990. It listed the number of failures and reported that the highest failure rates were in retailing and construction. At best, this data indicates that failure rates rise and fall with changing economic conditions and certain business sectors are more precarious than others. When the number of failures is actually compared with aggregate start-ups, the "death ratio" is actually quite low. However, once a myth starts, it is hard to correct.

In 1984, I participated in a six-year study entitled "The Rise of

Female Capitalism," which was published in the University of Western Ontario's *Business Quarterly*. The study showed that women had a business failure rate of less than one-third of the reported national average when failure is defined as closing down and leaving unpaid liabilities. The actual rate identified in this study was less than 20%, and after six years, 46% of the companies were still in the hands of the original founders and in full-scale operation.

In 1990, American Express, in its U.S. study of the status of small business, reported a failure rate (once again defined as closing down and leaving unpaid liabilities) of roughly 20% in a major internationally reported research program.

Most recently, we have a massive piece of corroborating evidence that small-business owners and entrepreneurs are not stupid and can see the high ratio of success that has been consistently denied by our so-called experts—most of whom have never operated a business. Professor Bruce Kirchoff of the New Jersey Institute of Technology has recently published the results of an eight-year study of small-business mortality. The study, based on a sample of 814,000 businesses in the United States, discovered that 54% of the companies survived in some form or another, 28% shut down voluntarily with no liabilities to any creditors, and only 18% actually failed in that they left outstanding liabilities.

The actual failure rate of small businesses should be more realistically pegged at 18% to 20%— one-fourth of the mythological total traditionally expounded. The excuse for not lending to, investing in, or starting a small business has no basis in fact and the practice of segregating small businesses into some form of financial leper colony must end.

Some small steps have been taken toward rectifying this. In December 1992, the federal government altered the RRSP rules to permit arm's length investors to place up to 100% of their investment in small business investment shares into their self-directed plans. The program permitted no more than 50% of any RRSP to be invested in a small business.

The Small Business Loans Act has been recently amended again to provide credit insurance at 90% coverage to lenders for loans to small businesses. Not only has the threshold been lifted from 85% coverage, but the process has also been extensively promoted to encourage small businesses to apply.

Over the last 10 years, small businesses in North America have created 20 million new jobs while large corporations have eliminated four million positions. The need is not for lower interest rates to assist entrepreneurs—we already have rates as low as ever. The need is for fair treatment based on fact, properly trained lenders schooled in entrepreneurship, and a society that supports entrepreneurship, as a legitimate means of wealth creation.

The Best New Business Opportunities of the 1990s

1) Personal security (home, car, etc.). The population is older and less secure.

2) Environment-related businesses. The rise of "reduce, re-use, and recycle)."

3) Software and CD ROM technology.

4) Handicrafts from craftsmen and artisans. Canadians want better made goods.

5) Home-office equipment. This sector is experiencing 14% to 15% growth annually.

6) Conversion franchising of established businesses. This strategy reduces business risk.

7) Independent financial planning. This industry will continue to grow as financial services and products become increasingly complex.

8) Contract employment. As businesses continue to downsize, they will make increasing use of highly skilled contract workers.

9) Catalogue marketing and direct selling. Consumer markets can be segmented more accurately and successfully.

10) Traditional family services. Weddings, flowers, photography, and banquets will grow in importance as society is returning to traditional values.

EDUCATION OR ENTREPRENEURSHIP: WHICH PROVIDES A BETTER RETURN?

Based on widely quoted statistics indicating that 30% of the total number of currently unemployed people in Canada are white-collar workers and professionals, the current recession may be appropriately designated as a "service-industry" recession. This leads to the important question as to what choices represent the optimal career investment options open to these newly unemployed individuals (as well as thousands of other Canadians who are either classified, or consider themselves, under-employed).

With nearly 2.7 million unemployed middle-management workers across North America discovering that re-employment opportunities are almost non-existent within corporate ranks, many are realizing that their two best investment options are either re-educating themselves to develop new skills or pursuing entrepreneurial self-employment opportunities. So what are the financial benefits of each option and which one provides the greatest personal financial return for Canadians?

Let's tackle re-education first. Re-education, not education, is a serious option for most unemployed middle managers. They desperately need new skills relevant to a restructured Canadian economy. Similarly, the magic of an MBA degree seems to be lost. With 77,000 graduates this year from North American business schools trying to integrate themselves with roughly 1 million MBA graduates already in the workforce from the past 40 years, many companies are now seriously questioning the benefits, validity, and cost associated with this type of training.

Corporate recruitment on campus at North American business schools is down sharply and registrations for MBA programs are also suffering. This illustrates that this degree increasingly lacks relevance in today's business world because the MBA training does not adequately prepare graduates for the realities of the new work environment. It fails to teach important entrepreneurial abilities, consulting skills, leadership expertise, communication skills, and innovative management techniques.

If you could obtain the five above-mentioned talents and combine them with a higher level of computer proficiency, then it would be safe to forecast that for each year of post-secondary incremental education, you could add approximately $16,000 *per year* to your earning potential. Even Employment and Immigration Canada is now funding 7,000 UIC recipients, through a new pilot program, to be re-educated in entrepreneurship and self-employment. "Enterprise Development Centres" are being established in several cities to re-train, support, and re-educate unemployed workers. These centres are teaching skills that definitely will provide an above-average return on investment in the 1990s.

But, now that re-education has been discussed, what about self-employment as another option? More than 1.5 million Canadians are now self-employed in various types of home businesses. These numbers are growing by an overall rate of 14% per year. Even more amazingly, the number of home-based women entrepreneurs is growing by 29% per annum.

Self-employment is producing dramatic financial benefits, even when self-employment is only a part-time activity. Part-time home-based ventures as unincorporated businesses generate tax deductions that can include up to one-sixth of all household expenses (such as mortgage interest, heating, and telephone) which reduce personal taxable income and even deductions at the source by employers. The financial flexibility for tax-planning purposes, the ability to capitalize on income-splitting strategies in an incorporated small business by paying dividends to family members, and the incremental $400,000 capital gains exemption for a Canadian-controlled private company at the time a business is sold (over and above the basic $100,000 lifetime capital gains deduction) all add to the value and return on investment associated with pursuing an entrepreneurial venture.

While banks and accountants love to point out the higher rates of failure of entrepreneurs and small-business ventures, this perception, as we have seen, is often exaggerated. The actual documented statistics relating to failure rates of start-up and growth-stage ventures within the small-business sector of the Canadian economy are far lower than commonly thought, especially in the area of home businesses.

Clearly, the two best career investment options in the 1990s are effective re-education and entrepreneurship. As to which one produces the best rewards, perhaps the best answer is to increase your chances of financial security by tenaciously combining both options into a single plan.

Real Estate

THE "INFALLIBILITY OF REAL ESTATE" SYNDROME

The essence of investment strategy of the 1980s was inflation and real estate: prices would continue to rise forever and real estate could never fall. The actual collapse of 50% in value was first predicted in 1983 by Robert Beckman in his book *The Downwave: Surviving the Second Great Depression.* He correctly predicted the sharp decline in both commercial and residential markets, but was publicly vilified for even suggesting the market would go down.

I remember in 1988 when a high-profile Toronto economist predicted that real estate would fall by 30%. He was nearly lynched and he received many death threats. Banks and insurance companies were still lending aggressively into 1989 to real estate developers and speculators, only to be caught at the end of the cycle.

Nowadays, my radio listeners tell me they are having a hard time getting house mortgages renewed. Commercial property owners who borrowed five years ago at 11¾% and met every payment are finding it difficult to get a renewal even at 9%. No one wants to finance real estate. We all remember when it was about the only collateral a bank would accept. Today we are in a long-term phase of depressed housing prices and the upturn will not occur until 1997 at the earliest and perhaps as late as 2005.

WHO IS BUYING HOUSES AND WHERE?

In 1992, first-time home buyers accounted for approximately 37% of all homes purchased in Canada. This was the highest proportion of first-time buyers since 1986 and was primarily the result of declining house prices and very low mortgage rates.

Of all the homes that were purchased in 1992, 23% were bought by singles (i.e., unmarried individuals) and within this group approximately 48% of homes were purchased by single women. In Vancouver, Calgary, Toronto, and Ottawa, single female buyers actually outnumber single male buyers and the overall percentage of single female buyers is continuing to rise.

Interestingly, in 1992, Vancouver was both the hottest condominium market (where they account for 40% of housing sales) and the city in Canada with the highest percentage of home buyers above the age of 50 (23%).

Despite all the criticism we have placed on real estate, there is a basis to conclude that certain categories of real estate will outperform others over time if you look at the market strategically. There is a cycle of real estate investment.

REAL ESTATE: HOW GOOD AN INVESTMENT?

This table represents the return on a $100,000 house after five or 10 years of ownership. The figures reflect payment of 6% of purchase price in closing costs and a brokerage fee of 6% of sale price upon sale of your house.

	ANNUAL RATE OF APPRECIATION			
	Cash After 5 Years	**Annual Rate of Return**	**Cash After 10 Years**	**Annual Rate of Return**
0%	−$12,000	−11.6%	−$12,000	−6.0%
1%	−$7,200	−5.0%	−$2,200	−0.9%
2%	−$2,200	−1.6%	$8,600	2.9%
3%	$3,000	2.2%	$20,300	5.9%
4%	$12,000	5.8%	$33,100	8.6%
5%	$14,000	9.0%	$47,100	10.9%
6%	$19,800	12.0%	$62,300	13.0%
7%	$25,800	14.8%	$78,900	15.0%
8%	$32,100	17.4%	$96,900	16.8%
9%	$38,600	20.0%	$116,500	18.5%
10%	$45,400	22.4%	$137,800	20.2%

TABLE 11–1

YOUR MORTGAGE CHECKLIST

If the thought of shopping around for a mortgage causes you to break out in a cold sweat, you are not alone. For many Canadians, it is a very confusing experience.

Most people make the mistake of considering only the actual mortgage rates they will have to pay. However, mortgages come in many different shapes and sizes, so you must consider all the features before you sign on the dotted line. For example, if you find a mortgage that offers flexibility to pay down your principal faster, you may have greater peace of mind and save thousands of dollars in interest as well.

Because dealing with mortgage lenders can be a complicated and frustrating experience, think about the questions you want to ask beforehand. In fact, make a list. It will simplify the process and reduce your stress.

Here are some important questions you should ask.

1) What are the current mortgage rates?

2) How many types of mortgage plans does the lender have and how do the terms differ?

3) What are the prepayment options (e.g., monthly, annually, etc.), if any?

4) If you take advantage of prepayment options, do you suffer a penalty in any way?

5) What happens if you miss a payment?

6) Can you renew your mortgage early or do you have to wait until the end of your term?

7) Do you have an option to increase your existing mortgage if necessary, at your current rate?

8) Are the terms of your mortgage transferable, or portable if you move to a new property?

9) If you sell your current home, can the new owner assume the existing mortgage?

10) What are the administration or set-up fees that you will be charged?

11) Does the lender offer low-cost mortgage life insurance or job-loss insurance?

12) What is the reputation of the lender in general?

SHOULD YOU SELL YOUR HOUSE?

If you are relocating or if you are an empty-nester thinking about unloading the old homestead for a smaller space, consider moving into rental accommodations rather than buying another house. There are two main reasons why selling your current home would be a good alternative.

- Home prices are not even keeping up with inflation. In 1992, house prices nationally rose less than 2% against a 2% inflation rate. When looking at the long term, real housing prices can fall by a total of 47% by the year 2007.

- As home prices are slipping, so are rents. One reason is that would-be sellers of single-family homes are becoming landlords in the probably vain hope that prices will soon rebound. In many cases, they are simply subsidizing renters while their equity shrinks. These frustrated sellers are adding more rental stock to a glutted market. According to Statistics Canada, the vacancy rates among multi-family rental units averaged 6% last year. This resulted in rents for modern apartments inching up just 1%. The vacancy rate is even higher among some luxury rentals.

- The elimination of the $100,000 capital gains exemption for secondary real estate in February 1992 means that all capital gains after March 1, 1992, are subject to taxation. The question that arises is whether you should sell or hold onto your cottage or investment property.

- If the value of the investment property remains flat, or even declines, your tax-free gain diminishes every month. If this is your situation, selling the property as soon as possible would make sense.

- If you are in a position to utilize a tax-free gain but don't want to lose the use of the property, one strategy is to "crystallize your exemption" by selling the property to another member of your family. However, an important consideration in this case is that the transaction must take place at fair market value. Also consider the potential costs associated with the transaction, such as land transfer taxes and legal fees.

- Consider other components of your overall portfolio. For example, if you also own stocks that qualify for the $100,000 capital gains exemption, your priority may be to claim the exemption by selling these assets first and holding off selling your investment property.

The only good news is that, except in British Columbia, there has been little if any capital gains on real estate since March 1992, so you have little to worry about.

Older Canadians looking for a better cash flow have used what is called a "reverse mortgage" where essentially an annuity is created out of the equity in the real estate with a mortgage company. The home-owners pay themselves a monthly income, drawing out principally their capital. Most of these mortgages are 10- or 15-year terms. By the time you are 90, the equity is gone and you are out of cash and assets. You should only consider reverse mortgages if you are above age 75. If you are in good health and hope to live past 90, the reverse mortgage is not really a good idea because you will not have an estate left when you pass on if your house is your principal asset.

To me, reverse mortgages are a last resort for cash flow if you have no further options. This kind of financing has been grossly oversold as an idea and many people in the United States have been sold on it. The best approach is to sell the house and get the cash; then, with the help of your financial planner, work on a strategy that provides tax-reduced payment from a withdrawal plan that incorporates capital gains and capital. See the treatment of this issue in the chapter on mutual funds. The yield should be about 12% to 15% per annum and mostly tax-free.

SOME KEY REAL ESTATE QUESTIONS

I surveyed RE/MAX, Century 21, Royal LePage, and Royal Trust to get the following information so here is the best advice they have to offer.

Q. How should home buyers and sellers respond to today's sluggish appreciation?

A. Buyers should plan on owning a home for at least five years. Otherwise, becoming a home-owner probably will not make financial sense, given today's modest price gains and a real estate agent's normal sales commission of about 6%. The key for sellers is to set a price that attracts buyers and agents. You want to sell the house within 45 days of when you put it on the market. After that, a house can take on the feeling of used merchandise, and agents grow less interested in showing it. Pricing a house at more than 5% to 7% above what comparable homes have been selling for really turns off buyers and agents.

Q. How can you tell whether your market is getting hotter or colder?

A. For starters, look at how long the **FOR SALE** signs are staying on front lawns. If the same signs have been up for three to six months, you know properties are not moving. For a more precise diagnosis, get a market analysis from an agent. He or she should be willing to tell you exactly how many homes are on the market in your price range, how long such homes tend to remain on the market before they are sold, and how sales prices compare with asking prices. Moreover, the agent can tell you how those figures have changed over the past three to six months.

Q. How do you find the right agent?

A. Whether you are a buyer or a seller, you want to work with an agent and a real estate office that do at least 50% of their business in your immediate area and in your price range. They know your market the best. Interview three agents from different offices and ask each for a written market analysis to see whose work seems most useful. If you want help selling your home, before signing an agent's contract (which typically commits you to work with the agent for three to six months) call a few of the agent's recent clients. Ask them how responsive the agent was to their phone calls and how attentive to details he or she was during the closing process.

Q. How negotiable are real estate agents' commissions today?

A. Somewhat. There are some agents who will drop their commissions by a percentage point or so on higher-priced homes in the area. Consumers should ask for such discounts. On the other hand, sellers in some tough markets now offer agents bonus commissions of about 1% to make sure they get a top marketing effort.

KEY FACTORS TO REMEMBER

When making real estate decisions, remember that the Canadian real estate market will be strongly and negatively affected by the following factors for the rest of the 1990s.

1) Canadian demographics are changing. There are fewer new households being formed, so demand for houses will drop and prices will continue to decline.

2) The federal government took back the $100,000 capital gains exemption on all properties you own except your principal residence. This will further hurt the market.

3) A lot of people got burned on real estate that they purchased during the boom years of the late 1980s. It will take a long time to restore confidence in real estate.

4) Due to taxation, government regulation, and wage scales, Canada (especially Ontario) has now become the "highest cost" environment in North America for business, which has a major negative impact on the willingness of new companies to locate in Canada or existing companies to expand.

5) The current degree of oversupply of real estate in central Canada ranges from 12% for residential to 27% for commercial. That means that in many markets the oversupply is somewhere between a five- to 10-year inventory.

6) Geographical location and type of use are critical factors in evaluating real estate investments. The only growth markets in North America over the next two to three years are in the southern United States in places such as Atlanta, Orlando, Dallas/Fort Worth, and Phoenix. Several of these locations are in "tax-free" states and all are experiencing a significant influx of people, so demand is increasing and prices are rising. In these regions, the type of real estate that will appreciate in value most rapidly is the multi-unit residential investment.

THE CYCLE OF REAL ESTATE

Phase I, the stage we find ourselves in now, is an unfavourable real estate environment. Vacancies are high, the media is negative, and most capital is fleeing from new developments. In Phase II, vacancies begin to decrease and rents rise, but there is little new construction. In Phase III, the turnaround occurs with low vacancy rates, favourable tax legislation, favourable publicity, and a large amount of new capital for development. When the market peaks toward the end of Phase III, a period of increased construction takes place and a rising vacancy rate will follow. If you understand this real estate cycle, you will see the potential in certain markets around the world and you will see the potential for investing effectively in real estate.

The first thing to do is look at a market that meets the eight basic criteria.

1) A flexible high-quality workforce is readily available in the surrounding area.

2) The market is located close to many other major Canadian or U.S. markets.

3) There is a strong local pro-business attitude.

4) There is a good solid public education system generating a high-quality labour force.

5) There is convenient air service to key cities from the particular city.

6) There is an efficient highway system for ease of distribution and transportation.

THE CYCLE OF REAL ESTATE

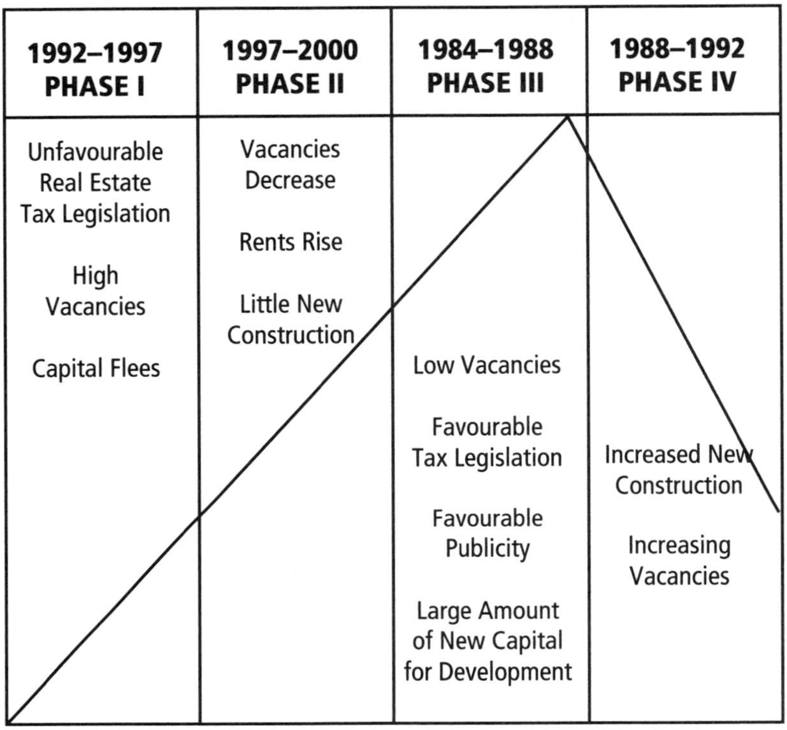

1992–1997 PHASE I	1997–2000 PHASE II	1984–1988 PHASE III	1988–1992 PHASE IV
Unfavourable Real Estate Tax Legislation High Vacancies Capital Flees	Vacancies Decrease Rents Rise Little New Construction	Low Vacancies Favourable Tax Legislation Favourable Publicity Large Amount of New Capital for Development	Increased New Construction Increasing Vacancies

FIGURE 11–1

7) All cost structures, housing, labour, facilities, and taxes are relatively low, therefore making it a highly favourable environment for dynamic growth.

8) There is a whole host of intangibles amounting to what is called "quality of life."

To identify markets that meet these criteria, I have looked at a number of different sources. *The New York Times* did an analysis of job growth by market and indicated which markets would grow dynamically for the balance of the decade. *Fortune* magazine did its own analysis of the best environments for growth potential for business. In addition, *The Washington Post* looked at the markets that had changed the most and increased the most in terms of real estate prices. And finally, in 1992 Andersen Consulting did a national survey that analysed the best markets and also the best commodities to invest in— that is, types of buildings.

Needless to say, the bulk of my attention is focused on the United States because I have little confidence in the performance of Canadian real estate values, but I don't want to ignore the potential still in Vancouver because it is a Pacific-rim area and it has similarities in many ways to the environment in Seattle and Spokane except without many of their tax benefits. However, Vancouver is getting over-built and the peak should occur in 1995.

The real potential for growth occurs where there is a combination of all the variables I have mentioned. *The New York Times* analysis of forecasted job growth indicates that the largest sector for job growth will be in the South-Central United States— essentially, the areas in and around Texas. It will average about 2.4% per annum. The next highest category will be the Pacific Northwest. The entire region around Washington, Oregon, and Idaho, which will certainly be an area of dynamic potential, currently has low unemployment. These are attractive investment locations.

The South Atlantic region from the Mason-Dixon line south to Florida will also be an area of reasonable growth over the balance of the decade. With at least 2% per annum real growth in jobs, although unemployment is around 6%, there still is substantial potential in central and northern Florida and all the way up to Virginia.

The *Fortune* magazine analysis, which was done in April 1993, indicated that the 10 top markets in the United States were as follows:

Top 10 U.S. Cities

1) Atlanta

2) Dallas/Fort Worth

3) Pittsburgh

4) Houston

5) Las Vegas

6) Salt Lake City

7) Charlotte

8) Florida Gulf Coast—Dunedin to Naples

9) Austin/San Antonio

10) Phoenix

These results ranking best environments for business growth were quite similar to *The Washington Post* February 1993 identification of markets responding with the strongest potential growth in real estate values. It's nice to see that there is still double-digit potential return in the markets.

In the survey conducted by the national firm Andersen Consulting, 1,724 developers, investors, lenders, managers, and corporate real estate personnel were interviewed. The analysis not only placed Canada dead last, among the regions surveyed, in terms of the most attractive places to invest in, but the results placed the Southwest U.S., Pacific Northwest U.S., and the Southeast U.S. as the best places where money could grow, particularly in terms of real estate investment.

The Andersen Consulting survey was highly skeptical of investment in suburban office development, industrial development, and major retail and hotel properties, but recommended multiple-unit residential housing—primarily rental apartment developments—because these areas would be in substantial need of new rental accommodation, due to their dynamic growth potential. Many of these units are located in tax-free states, such as Texas, Utah, and Nevada—places that hold excellent potential, according to the interviewees.

When asked what regions over the next three years would be the most attractive areas for development, the Andersen Consulting study rated the Southwest U.S. as being unquestionably the best place for investment. When asked to name the metropolitan areas that would have, over the next three years, the most potential for return on real estate investment, Dallas/Fort Worth was rated number 1, Atlanta number 2, Houston number 3, followed by Las Vegas, Seattle, Charlotte, Orlando, Denver, Chicago, Honolulu, and Phoenix.

When analysing multiple-unit residential developments, it is important to realize that there are a number of criteria to consider. The development should be:

- in a major suburban centre that has direct access to major factories, office complexes, and shopping;

- managed by a major national name, such as Hyatt, Westin, Four Seasons, or Sheraton;

- in an area free of rent-control legislation;

- in an area where the population is growing and demand for residential accommodation exceeds existing supply; and

- purchased at a price significantly below appraised value.

FOREIGN REAL ESTATE INVESTMENT

My long-time friend and real estate adviser Allan Shim has developed real estate in Toronto, Dallas, Florida, and China. He seems to be embarrassingly accurate in his market predictions as to where the real estate lightning bolt will strike next. Allan is a conservative and negative thinker. He reads all of the alarmist and Armageddonist literature, which seems to have accurately guided him ever since 1973 in predicting market trends.

As I earlier had mentioned, in real estate, the need to be ahead of the pack is critical to investment returns. Most people buy behind the market and miss the peak.

In Southeast Asia, Allan and I found the world's next major upturn. The Great Wall of China is no longer one of the great wonders of the earth. The pace of current development in Guangdong province in the southern part of China is an even greater wonder. In the '60s, we had the Cultural Revolution in China. Now we have the Industrial Revolution, which will lead China into the position of being the world's number 1 economic power in 10 years. The facts are irrefutable.

There was 7.5% growth in 1991, 12.9% in 1992, and (even with the government slowing things down to control 17% inflation), 1993 will yield 10% growth—the best in the world. Trust me on this one—I toured many towns and cities myself. A number of China-based mutual funds have been created in the past year and all are yielding 25% to 30% annual returns. Look for new ones to be out in Canada in the next few months. They are excellent buys as part of a portfolio, perhaps taking up as much as 10% of your assets. Such an investment could also fall into the foreign content portion of your RRSP.

When I recommended Asian funds in 1990, 1991, 1992, and 1993, the ones I picked produced returns of 21%, 27%, 31%, and 34% for the first nine months of 1993.

Action Plans

"Action plans" is another term for "financial strategies." In other words, to achieve your financial objectives, you need specific measurable courses of action to follow. Throughout this book, I have tried to explain financial, tax, and investment concepts, as well as highlighting overall strategies for you to follow with your financial adviser.

This chapter is meant to be a series of action check-lists that can be observed on a daily basis. They are gathered from lists of financial-strategy truism, gleaned from financial advisers and added to by me. The central theme of these concepts is to act. You will never get rich if you choose to do nothing. It is very much like the tale of the individual who prayed to God for 20 years to help him win the lottery. One evening, God himself appeared in a dream and said to the person, "Do you mind doing me a small favour? To win the lottery, have you ever considered buying a ticket first?"

Certain basic principles do work. This is not to say that investing and personal finance are precise sciences, but there are basics that seem to be reliable long-term concepts that when followed, improve your cash flow, reduce your risks, and enhance returns on your investments.

TAX-PLANNING STRATEGIES

1) Keep complete and accurate files to the most minute detail.

2) Pay close attention to federal and provincial budget announcements each year.

3) Look to tax-ameliorated income sources wherever possible, such as dividends from Canadian sources.

4) Claim all possible allowable deductions and act in an aggressive manner.

5) Tax-plan as a family on an annual basis.

6) Have a detailed will and estate plan updated every three years.

7) Maximize deductible interest expense and minimize non-deductible interest such as credit-card interest.

8) Establish a source of entrepreneurial income both to augment your cash flow and increase your tax-planning options.

9) Learn how to complete your own tax return and carefully check all your work. Even if you have a tax preparer or an accountant do it, you should review the work to make sure it's right.

10) The six dimensions of personal financial planning are interrelated and synergistic. If you do all six together, you will have a higher net cash flow and pay a lot less tax throughout your entire life.

TEN EQUITY STRATEGIES

1) Plan first how you want to allocate your money across broad categories; then select companies within each category.

2) Match investments with personal financial objectives.

3) Within your portfolio, construct a core holding (50% or more) of stock that you rarely tinker with.

4) Emphasize stocks for retirement. Top investors have an average of 53% of their investments in stocks; most individuals have less than 10% in stocks.

5) Develop a stock picking style.

6) Focus on prospects, not past results.

7) Formulate a strategy for when to sell—an exact formula. What happens when a stock drops 20%? Buy more or sell?

8) Review your holdings regularly—at least once a quarter.

9) Diversify into foreign markets.

10) Monitor your results against industry benchmarks. For example, small-cap growth stocks did an average of 12.5% in 1992. How did yours do?

ARE YOU HEADING TOWARD BANKRUPTCY?

Never take the threat of bankruptcy lightly. It is always a bad experience and you should try to avoid it at all costs. However, if you think you are heading toward bankruptcy, read and answer (honestly) the following questions.

1) Are you able to make only the minimum payments on your revolving charge accounts or existing bank loans?

2) Are you already at or near your credit limits?

3) Have you ever needed a loan simply to meet existing loan repayment commitments?

4) Excluding your mortgage payments, do your current loan obligations account for more than 25% of your take-home pay?

5) If you lost your job today, would you be in immediate financial difficulty?

If you answered no to at least four of these questions, you are doing relatively well during these tough economic times. Seeking bankruptcy protection is probably not necessary and you are likely overreacting to perceived financial strain. However, if you answered yes to two or more of these questions, then you do need some professional assistance. Take immediate action to cut spending, reduce expenses, develop and adhere to a budget, and obtain the help of a financial adviser in monitoring your expenses closely.

The counsellor will set up a plan and help you get out of debt. If you are a spendaholic, you will never get rich. Control all impulse spending and avoid that non-deductible credit-card debt like the plague.

TEN STEPS TO FINANCIAL SAFETY AND SECURITY

1) Pay off credit-card debt now. Lower your living expenses; make and keep a budget.

2) Reserve six months' income for emergencies. It will disaster-proof your family.

3) Refinance your house at a lower mortgage rate and invest the savings.

4) Establish a home-equity line of credit rather than use credit-card debt to finance major expenditures.

5) Use rate searches for all fixed income investments.

6) Restructure your insurance: disability and term.

7) Make regular automatic contributions to your savings and retirement plans (e.g., use pre-authorized deductions for mutual funds).

8) Use tax-deferred savings plans to their maximum.

9) Invest in education—your own. Each year of post-secondary education adds 16% to lifetime earnings.

10) Work with an independent financial planner. Review your last three years' tax returns and recover cash (i.e., reduce your monthly tax deductions at source to conserve cash).

ACTION PLANS FOR SAVING AND INVESTING

1) Automate.
   - Invest in regular increments by using dollar-cost averaging techniques (i.e., buy less when prices are rising and more when prices are falling).
   - Pre-authorize investments through electronic funds transfers.
   - Re-invest dividends and tax refunds.
   - Have all cash earning interest in daily interest accounts.

2) Invest in a "build wealth slowly" plan.
   - Invest each and every year to the maximum allowable RRSP limits.

3) Invest in yourself (your best long-term investment may be staring at you in the mirror).
   - Re-educate.
   - Re-train.
   - Re-build your skills.
   - Be prepared to work part-time after your retirement.

WHY MONEY IS NOT EVERYTHING!

Style is!

Living well is the best revenge. Money is not everything. It is a means to an end. To live in the style you wish and to enjoy life because of your personal financial security is important.

Listeners and readers send me all sorts of quotes and tips about life. These thoughts are not original. They come from many books, sources, newspapers, and advisers. But I think they are worth their weight in gold.

1) Drive inexpensive cars, but have the best house you can afford while you have children at home.

2) The large print giveth and the small print taketh away.

3) If in a fight, hit first and hit hard.

4) Vote.

5) Whistle.

6) Slow-dance.

7) Forget the Joneses.

8) Choose your life's mate carefully. From this one decision will come 90% of all your happiness or misery.

9) Tell your kids often that they are terrific and that you trust them.

10) Remember people's names.

11) Let people know what you stand for and what you won't stand for.

12) Strive for excellence, not perfection.

13) Don't scrimp in order to leave money to your children.

14) Give people a second chance, but not a third.

15) Learn to recognize the inconsequential; then ignore it.

16) Be romantic.

17) Never go grocery shopping when you're hungry.

18) Don't major in minor things.

19) Never pay for work before it's completed.

20) Be modest. A lot was accomplished before you were born.

21) Remember that overnight success takes about 15 years.

22) Keep overhead low.

23) Don't expect life to be fair.

24) Don't think a higher price always means higher quality.

25) Don't let anyone talk you out of a great idea.

26) Work hard to create in your children a good self-image. It's the most important thing you can do for them.

27) Forget committees. World-changing ideas always come from one person working alone.

28) Be entrepreneurial.

29) Get your priorities straight. No one ever said on their death bed, "Gee, if only I'd spent more time at the office."

30) Steer clear of restaurants that rotate.

31) Cherish your children for what they are, not for what you'd like them to be.

32) Call your mother.

33) Never deprive someone of hope; it may be all this person has!

A FINAL WORD

This is a dynamic and frightening time for most Canadians. The rapid market change, low interest rates, and poor economic performance have inhibited thousands of individuals from acting or taking back control over their financial future. This has been a book about acting, not reacting. You must learn to say "yes" and not "no" to new ideas. Money is not everything, but it is critical toward achieving a better sense of freedom and flexibility. You need independent financial advice and you must learn constantly about money, investment, and finance. The only income increases will be from investing. As a strategic investor you will both mitigate risk and increase your returns.

You make many conscious and subconscious choices in life. Choose to act and choose to be rich. The process outlined in this book is only useful if it is utilized, not left dormant on the page. If you do choose to be rich, remember Voltaire, who wrote, "Better is the enemy of good." You *will* be better.

DATE			

BLOOM'S

M A J O R

SHORT
STORY

W R I T E R S

Henry

James

EDITED AND WITH AN
INTRODUCTION BY HAROLD BLOOM

CURRENTLY AVAILABLE

BLOOM'S MAJOR SHORT STORY WRITERS

Anton Chekhov

Joseph Conrad

Stephen Crane

William Faulkner

F. Scott Fitzgerald

Nathaniel Hawthorne

Ernest Hemingway

O. Henry

Shirley Jackson

Henry James

James Joyce

D. H. Lawrence

Jack London

Herman Melville

Flannery O'Connor

Edgar Allan Poe

Katherine Anne Porter

J. D. Salinger

John Steinbeck

Mark Twain

John Updike

Eudora Welty

BLOOM'S MAJOR WORLD POETS

Maya Angelou

Robert Browning

Geoffrey Chaucer

Samuel T. Coleridge

Dante

Emily Dickinson

John Donne

T. S. Eliot

Robert Frost

Homer

Langston Hughes

John Keats

John Milton

Sylvia Plath

Edgar Allan Poe

Poets of World War I

Shakespeare's Poems & Sonnets

Percy Shelley

Alfred, Lord Tennyson

Walt Whitman

William Wordsworth

William Butler Yeats

BLOOM'S
MAJOR
SHORT STORY
WRITERS

Henry

James

DITED AND

First Printing
1 3 5 7 9 8 6 4 2

Library of Congress Cataloging-in-Publication Data

Henry James : Henry James's short stories / Harold Bloom, editor.
       p. cm. — (Bloom's major short story writers)
    Includes bibliographical references and index.
    ISBN 0-7910-5943-X (alk. paper)
      1. James, Henry, 1843–1916—Criticism and interpretation—
Handbooks, manuals, etc. 2. James, Henry, 1843–1916—Examinations—
Study guides. 3. Short story—Examinations—Study guides.
4. Short story—Handbooks, manuals, etc. I. Bloom, Harold. II. Series.
  PS2117 .H46 2001
  813'.4—dc21   00-065914

Chelsea House Publishers
1974 Sproul Road, Suite 400
Broomall, PA 19008-0914

The Chelsea House World Wide Web address is
http://www.chelseahouse.com

Contributing Editors: Erica DaCosta, Ellyn Sanna

Produced by: Robert Gerson Publisher's Services, Santa Barbara, CA

Contents

User's Guide

This volume is designed to present biographical, critical, and bibliographical information on the author's best-known or most important short stories. Following Harold Bloom's editor's note and introduction is a detailed biography of the author, discussing major life events and important literary accomplishments. A plot summary of each short story follows, tracing significant themes, patterns, and motifs in the work, and an annotated list of characters supplies brief information on the main characters in each story.

A selection of critical extracts, derived from previously published material from leading critics, analyzes aspects of each short story. The extracts consist of statements from the author, if available, early reviews of the work, and later evaluations up to the present. A bibliography of the author's writings (including a complete list of all books written, cowritten, edited, and translated), a list of additional books and articles on the author and the work, and an index of themes and ideas in the author's writings conclude the volume.

~

Harold Bloom is Sterling Professor of the Humanities at Yale University and Henry W. and Albert A. Berg Professor of English at the New York University Graduate School. He is the author of over 20 books, including *Shelley's Mythmaking* (1959), *The Visionary Company* (1961), *Blake's Apocalypse* (1963), *Yeats* (1970), *A Map of Misreading* (1975), *Kabbalah and Criticism* (1975), *Agon: Toward a Theory of Revisionism* (1982), *The American Religion* (1992), *The Western Canon* (1994), and *Omens of Millennium: The Gnosis of Angels, Dreams, and Resurrection* (1996). *The Anxiety of Influence* (1973) sets forth Professor Bloom's provocative theory of the literary relationships between the great writers and their predecessors. His most recent books include *Shakespeare: The Invention of the Human*, a 1998 National Book Award finalist, and *How to Read and Why*, which was published in 2000.

Professor Bloom earned his Ph.D. from Yale University in 1955 and has served on the Yale faculty since then. He is a 1985 MacArthur Foundation Award recipient, served as the Charles Eliot Norton Professor of Poetry at Harvard University in 1987–88, and has received honorary degrees from the universities of Rome and Bologna. In 1999, Professor Bloom received the prestigious American Academy of Arts and Letters Gold Medal for Criticism.

Currently, Harold Bloom is the editor of numerous Chelsea House volumes of literary criticism, including the series BLOOM'S NOTES, BLOOM'S MAJOR DRAMATISTS, BLOOM'S MAJOR NOVELISTS, MAJOR LITERARY CHARACTERS, MODERN CRITICAL VIEWS, MODERN CRITICAL INTERPRETATIONS, and WOMEN WRITERS OF ENGLISH AND THEIR WORKS.

Editor's Note

My Introduction reflects on Henry James's status as the major American writer of prose fiction and examines Spencer Brydon, protagonist of the fine short story "The Jolly Corner."

As there are some 24 Critical Views excerpted here, I will confine my comments to a few I find most illuminating. The eminent critic Harold C. Goddard provides a pre-Freudian reading of "The Turn of the Screw," while Robert Weisbuch probes James's conception of evil in that well-known story.

On "The Beast in the Jungle," Allen Tate discusses James's success with the short-story form, and Ruth Bernard Yeazell explains the metaphor of the beast.

Charles R. Smith provides an interpretation of "The Lesson of the Master," while Philip Horne uses the story to outline Henry James's goal of literary perfection.

Potentiality in "The Jolly Corner" is discussed by Millicent Bell.

The character of Daisy Miller is examined in essays on the story of that name by both William Dean Howells and Kenneth Graham.

Introduction

HAROLD BLOOM

The ghostly tales of Henry James enjoy such a masterful critique in the author's prefaces to the New York Edition that we do well to follow in the master's wake. "The Jolly Corner" is my own favorite among James's ghostly forays, where he sought "the strange and the sinister embroidered on the very type of the normal and easy." And yet James manifested a certain reticence on "The Jolly Corner," as he expresses:

> I was moved to adopt as my motive an analysis of one of the conceivably rarest and intensest grounds for an "unnatural" anxiety, a *malaise* so incongruous and discordant, in the given prosaic prosperous conditions, as almost to be compromising. Spencer Brydon's adventure however is one of those finished fantasies that. . . speak best to the critical sense for themselves—

"Almost to be compromising" is, for Henry James, a rather strong phrase, and implies here that Spencer Brydon's adventure could as easily be Henry James's.

Henry James is certainly the major American writer of prose fiction, outshining his precursor Hawthorne, and his antithesis, Faulkner. Perhaps only Emerson and Walt Whitman (to both of whom James condescended) should be regarded as more central to the American literary achievement than was Henry James. His "Jolly Corner" is a classic American ghost story, aesthetically superior to the more notorious "The Turn of the Screw," and also to Poe's "William Wilson," which is also a tale of the *doppelgänger*, the sinister double or *alter ego.*

What Spencer Brydon *sees* truly is compromising for Henry James, the grandson of the founder of the family fortune, since Brydon beholds the commercial alternative to himself. Henry James Sr. had lived as an Emersonian/Swedenborgian visionary, while William James became the major American philosopher-psychologist, and Henry James Jr. the major American novelist. James suffered from a peculiarly American guilt at having failed to make his own fortune, and he finds his surrogate in the equivocal aesthete Spencer Brydon.

What *can* happen in a good ghost story? Stephen King, the Edgar Allen Poe of our cultural decline, crowds his ghost-novels with grisly events, but then King belongs to our visually obsessed age, where everything is seen on a screen, including King's latest offering. Nothing *happens* in "The Jolly Corner" except that Spencer Brydon confronts his own image, and sees instantly the plutocrat he has failed to become. All of us have failed to become much that we desired, or thought we desired.

It is a curious irony that Henry James, who never married and apparently never wanted to, consigns Brydon to a likely marriage with the lady who has seen him through his ordeal. Whether this is to be reward or punishment is left unanswered by the story:

> Rigid and conscious, spectral yet human, a man of his own substance and stature waited there to measure himself with his power to dismay. This only could it be—this only till he recognized, with his advance, that what made the face dim was the pair of raised hands that covered it and in which, so far from being offered in defiance, it was buried as for dark deprecation. So Brydon, before him, took him in; with every fact of him now, in the higher light, hard and acute—his planted stillness, his vivid truth, his grizzled bent head and white masking hands, his queer actuality of evening-dress, of dangling double eye-glass, of gleaming silk lappet and white linen, of pearl button and gold watch-guard and polished shoe. No portrait by a great modern master could have presented him with more intensity, thrust him out of his frame with more art, as if there had been "treatment," of the consummate sort, in his every shade and salience. The revulsion, for our friend, had become, before he knew it, immense—this drop, in the act of apprehension, to the sense of his adversary's inscrutable manœuvre. That meaning at least, while he gaped, it offered him; for he could but gape at his other self in this other anguish, gape as a proof that he, standing there for the achieved, the enjoyed, the triumphant life, couldn't be faced in his triumph. Wasn't the proof in the splendid covering hands, strong and completely spread?— so spread and so intentional that, in spite of a special verity that surpasses every other, the fact that one of these hands had lost two fingers, which were reduced to stumps, as if accidentally shot away, the face was effectually guarded and saved.

The *other* Spencer Brydon, one hand mutilated, perhaps symbolizes less the unlived life than unattained power, more over others than over the self. James, a great dramatist of the self in fiction, failed always in his attempts at stage drama. There may be a link between the ghostly splendor of "The Jolly Corner" and the power Henry James never achieved over a theatrical audience. ✤

Biography of
Henry James

Henry James was born in New York City on April 15, 1843, the brother of William James, who would be a notable philosopher-scientist. The James family was wealthy and socially prominent, and the father, Henry James Sr., was interested in both theology and philosophy, as well as the cultural life of his own city. He exposed his sons to all the cultural advantages New York, New England, and even Europe had to offer. Henry was privately tutored in New York, and he received special schooling abroad from the time he was 12 until he was 17; during these years his family lived in London, Switzerland, France, and Germany. His father was drawn to any location where he could find intense intellectual activity.

Henry studied painting briefly, but his studies were interrupted by an accident that injured his spine when he was 18. The injury also, however, kept him from being drafted into service during the Civil War. At 19 he was admitted to Harvard Law School, and two years later he began writing and earned his way into the most prestigious literary magazines.

One of his short stories, "A Passionate Pilgrim," which appeared in *Atlantic,* described the cultural attraction and repulsion between England and America, an attraction and repulsion that was just as strong in Henry James's own mind. He continued to travel abroad often, and the "idea" of Europe is a central part of his fiction. He saw America as being illuminated by her European past. In his writing he returned again and again to what he called the "possibility of contrast in the human lot . . . encountered as we turn back and forth between the distinctively American and the distinctively European outlook."

In 1875, James published his first collection of short stories, *A Passionate Pilgrim and Other Tales.* The same year the *Atlantic* serialized his first important novel, *Roderick Hudson.* In this novel, a talented young American sculptor goes to Florence to study, where he is ultimately destroyed by the artificial materialism of the international society he finds there.

These works established James's first success and launched the early period of his career. During this first period, he continued to examine the American abroad, comparing the innocence and freedom of the New World with the experience and conventions of the Old World. He also wrote *The American, The Europeans, The Portrait of a Lady,* and *Daisy Miller* during these years. All of these works explore the contrasting social values of America and Europe.

In James's second period, the middle years of his career, he wrote "social" novels, turning from the international theme to complex social issues in both Europe and New England. He wrote *The Princess Casmassima* and *The Bostonians* during this phase, but these books were never as popular as his other works. As a result, his income dropped considerably, and he turned to writing plays for the stage.

For the last 15 years of his career, however, James turned his efforts back to fiction. His style became increasingly complex, filled with ambiguities and psychological symbolism. His characters were more intense (and also more abnormal), and the social situations in which they moved were more and more full of nuance and obscure significance. The short novels he produced during this period—*The Wings of the Dove, The Ambassadors, The Golden Bowl, What Maisie Knew,* and *The Turn of the Screw,* among others—are considered to be the peak of James's literary achievement.

James believed that prose, like poetry, could be invested with symbolic meaning. He was one of the first authors to use psychological devices to intensify a story's influence over the reader. By putting the reader "inside the narrator's head," he made the reader a part of the story's psychological process. He also influenced the shape that the novel would take in the years to come. Authors like D. H. Lawrence, James Joyce, Willa Cather, and Virginia Woolf would use his techniques and carry them still farther.

From the time James was 24 until his death, he lived mostly in England. When World War I began, he became impatient with America's unwillingness to become involved in the war, and in 1915 he became a British citizen.

Although Henry James was an accomplished author, successful in his own right, he lived most of his life in his brother's shadow. He always saw William as being better than himself; "I was always his absolute younger and smaller," he wrote, "hanging under the blest sense of his protection and authority." His brother's death was emotionally devastating, and yet William's death enabled Henry for the first time to possess the knowledge of his own authority and achievement. He was frequently referred to as "the Master" in literary circles, an acknowledgement of his genius.

In 1915, in London, Henry James suffered two strokes. He died shortly after of pneumonia. Throughout his life he had struggled with the contrast between innocence and evil. If he reached no definite answers, before his death he came to believe that life is a process of *seeing*; through true awareness we attain understanding. ✸

Plot Summary of
"The Turn of the Screw"

In 1897, after five years of writing almost exclusively plays, none of which were popular successes, Henry James was invited by *Collier's Weekly* magazine to write a twelve-part ghost story for serialization. He was happy to receive the commission, since his failed experiments with theater had been motivated specifically by financial woes. The product of this assignment was "The Turn of the Screw." It would eventually become one of James's most contentiously debated pieces of fiction, though James publicly declared in the 1908 preface to the story that it was nothing more than a "fairy-tale, pure and simple." The literary establishment has largely ignored this assertion, however, because the story is so layered with ambiguity, rife with conspicuous omissions, and set in a curious structure.

The narrator of the story opens in eager anticipation of hearing a ghost story, which will be read presently, by a man named Douglas. It is Christmas Eve, a fire is burning, and the narrator is one of a hopeful audience, waiting to be scared senseless. Douglas presents a ghost story, which he claims to be a piece of history rather than fantasy. He proceeds to read from the hand-written journal of a woman to whom all the incidents happened. It is not long before the woman's narrative winds itself around us, the readers, and we are allowed to forget completely that the story is a manuscript being read aloud. By the time the story ends, both Douglas and the original narrator have disappeared altogether from the consciousness of the reader, replaced totally by the woman who relates her chilling tale. We remember the first two layers of narration vaguely, if we remember them at all.

The woman who transcribed the terrible events begins her story when she takes a position as a governess on a sprawling country estate outside of London, called Bly. Her principal responsibility, a little girl named Flora, was orphaned some years prior, along with her brother Miles who is away at school. At the time of their parents' deaths, they became the legal charges of their uncle, an English gentleman. The uncle has left Bly completely to the care of the servants, however, living full-time in his London residence, and when he hires the new governess, one of the conditions of employment is that she never contact him for any reason.

The new governess is a replacement for a previous one, Miss Jessel, though the new one does not find this out for some time. Miss Jessel had left her position and then subsequently died of some obscure ill, not long after the valet at Bly, Peter Quint, had himself died by slipping and falling on some ice while drunk. Before their deaths, Quint and Miss Jessel had become intimate and had encircled little Miles and Flora in their lives. But Quint and Miss Jessel were, according to the domestic staff at Bly, a depraved pair. The children were exposed to any amount of evil the reader may choose to imagine, since the exact nature of their depravity is always foggy.

When the new governess arrives, she is greeted by lovely little Flora and Mrs. Grose, the housekeeper, who tends Flora temporarily. Only days after the governess's arrival, Miles returns to Bly from boarding school with a note of expulsion. The reason for the dismissal is not included and the governess is left to imagine the worst.

Miles and Flora turn out to be an angelic pair, however, and the governess is continually astonished by their contented and precocious sweetness. The tremendous pleasure she takes in the children is soon clouded, however, as she begins to see apparitions— a man with red hair and a woman in black. The housekeeper informs her that Quint and Miss Jessel fit these descriptions, and the governess concludes that they have returned to possess the souls of the innocent children.

The governess becomes obsessed with protecting the children from Quint and Miss Jessel. Everything begins to fall under suspicion, including the very fact that the children have so few problems. She finds them to be too happy, and strangely satisfied to continue just as they are. She also notices that they never mention the names of Quint or Miss Jessel. The governess tries to keep them within her view at all times and to shield them from the elusive poisons floating about Bly.

Her effort becomes more and more desperate, and the ghostly visitations more frequent, until finally she finds a way to rid both children of the demons. Unfortunately, in the process, Flora falls into a feverish delirium and Miles loses his life completely.

The precise sequence of revelations and the private logic the governess attaches to this sequence are both vital to any understanding of the story. The governess feels herself to have championed the good and saved her charges from demonic possession. But little Miles is dead, and we, the readers, cannot know exactly what killed him. "We were alone with the quiet day, and his little heart, dispossessed, had stopped," the story concludes. What made it stop?

By the end of the book, the governess's presentation of the events does not satisfy us any longer. In subtle ways, she has proved herself to be less than a completely reliable narrator. She, for example, is the only person at Bly to have seen the ghosts. Miss Grose believes her but does not see them herself.

There are dozens of interpretations of "The Turn of the Screw," but among the most popular and enduring is the theory that the governess is hysterical, or worse, that she has fantasized the whole situation against which she claims to battle. According to this interpretation, the governess, an unworldly country parson's daughter, is given so little support, so much responsibility and so many unexplained circumstances, that she finds herself perched continually on the edge of the discovery of some secret horror— which is to say, she is on the edge of insanity.

Another dimension to her alleged madness is her infatuated love for her employer. She barely has time to note it in her journal, but it is obvious that she is smitten. He exists, however, in a social sphere that he can never leave and she can never enter. Her desire to see him, in spite of his remoteness, is not insignificant. Add to this her insomnia and her unquestioning confidant, Mrs. Grose, and the combination is perfect to make an unbalanced young woman imagine ghosts and daydream about evil.

The story certainly offers some support for this interpretation, but this perspective does not eliminate all inconsistencies. We are still faced with numerous questions, amongst them the question of Douglas, the reader of the governess's story, who was himself once the charge of the governess in an entirely different setting. If she *was* insane at Bly, why would she have gone on to be the well-loved governess of Douglas and his sister? And how would the governess have been able to give such an accurate description of Quint, whom she had never seen? All variety of explanations have been provided by scholars and critics, but none are definitive.

The Freudian reading stresses the governess's repressed sexual desires as the source of her hysteria, even though James could have known very little about Freud at the time he wrote this piece. Most recently, critics have shied away from the "either/or" approach and placed supreme value on the story's ambiguity itself.

James would probably have been astonished at the volume of literary fervor generated by a work he considered insignificant. His own remark referring to it as a mere fairy-tale is, understandably, disregarded—the psychological complexity of the governess seems too great, whichever way she is interpreted. It cannot be denied, however, that James was writing a ghost story for popular consumption in a weekly magazine. Of all his numerous ghost stories, he wanted this one to keep his audience up at night. The late nineteenth-century reader, lacking the excess of high-voltage stimulation to which the modern reader is accustomed, did, in fact, find the story petrifying. As a tale of horror, "The Turn of the Screw" was a huge hit. The notorious obscurities and liberal blank spots were the tools of a master craftsman. James knew that the most terrifying ghosts he could summon were those we, the readers, create ourselves in the dark recesses of our own minds. ❀

List of Characters in
"The Turn of the Screw"

The Narrator must be identified even though he recedes completely before chapter one. He opens the story with childish excitement about hearing a ghost story.

Douglas reads the hand-written manuscript that he contends is a true account and not a story at all. The manuscript was written by a lovely woman he had known many years previous but who was now dead. The woman had been a governess to his sister after the events of the story. Douglas also disappears before chapter one.

The governess becomes the first-person narrator as chapter one opens. She is a high-strung young woman from the English countryside, who has answered an advertisement placed by a London gentleman concerning his niece and nephew. He offers her the position which is to be carried out at his country estate, Bly. There, she takes charge of little Miles and Flora and begins to sense evil and see apparitions.

The London bachelor is the rich uncle of Miles and Flora who sends the governess to her position with the explicit instructions that she is never to bother him about anything, ever. The governess never hears from him again.

Mrs. Grose is the head housekeeper at Bly, and the temporary caregiver for the children. She quickly becomes a sympathetic confidant to the governess.

Flora is the angelic little girl for whom the governess is originally commissioned to care.

Miles is Flora's brother who was away at boarding school until a few days after the governess's arrival. Miles is sent home with an expulsion notice but with no indication as to the reason.

Peter Quint is the former valet at Bly who died when he slipped, intoxicated, into some ice. The governess believes she sees his ghost first.

Miss Jessel is the former governess at Bly. She had been very intimate with Peter Quint while she was there, but had left and then died of some illness. This is the second ghost the governess sees. ✾

Critical Views on
"The Turn of the Screw"

[In this extract taken from his book *The Psychological Novel: 1900–1950* Edel discusses the influence of point of view on "The Turn of the Screw."]

The governess's imagination, we see, discovers "depths" within herself. Fantasy seems to be reality for her. Anything and everything can and does happen, in her mind.

The attentive reader, when he is reading the story critically, can only observe that we are always in the realm of the supposititious. Not once in the entire story, do the children see anything strange or frightening. It is the governess's theory that they see as much as she does, and that they communicate with the dead. But it is the governess who does all the seeing and all the supposing. "My values are positively all blanks save only so far as an excited horror, a promoted pity, a created expertness," James explained in his Preface. But we have one significant clue to the author's "blanks." In his revision of the story for the New York Edition he altered his text again and again to put the story into the realm of the governess's feelings. Where he had her say originally "I saw" or "I believed" he often substituted "I felt."

We have here thus in reality two stories, and a method that foreshadows the problems of the stream-of-consciousness writer. One is the area of fact, the other the area of fancy. There is the witness, in this case the governess and her seemingly circumstantial story, and there is the mind itself, the contents of which are given to the reader. The reader must establish for himself the credibility of the witness; he must decide between what the governess *supposed* and what she claims she saw. Read in this fashion, "The Turn of the Screw" becomes an absorbing study of a troubled young woman, with little knowledge or understanding of children, called upon to assume serious responsibilities for the first time in her life. She finds support for her own lack of assurance by telling herself she is courageous and "wonderful." Yet in reality and by her own admission, she is filled with endless fears: "I don't know what I *don't* see—what I *don't* fear!"

The life she describes at Bly is serene enough outwardly: the servants are obedient and devoted to their master and the children. The children are on the whole well behaved at Bly—and sufficiently normal to indulge in a measure of mischief. It is the governess who sees ghosts and reads sinister meanings into everything around her. It is she who subjects the children to a psychological harassment that in the end leads to Flora's hysteria and Miles's death.

In the controversies that have raged about this work, certain critics have argued that James was telling us a ghost story pure and simple, that there *are* ghosts in the tale, and that to attempt to explain the governess is to be "over-rationalistic." The ghosts, of course, are there: they belong to the experience of the governess. But to attempt to dismiss any weightier critical consideration of the tale on grounds of too much "rationalism" is to overlook the art of the narrator. Regardless of what any clinical diagnosis of the governess might be, or any judgment of her credibility as a witness, there remains her sense of horror and the extent to which it is communicated to the reader. And it is because there is this question of her feeling, and its communication to the reader, that there has been so much critical argument: for each reader feels the story differently and fills in the Jamesian blanks in accordance with these feelings.

—Leon Edel, *The Psychological Novel: 1900–1950* (New York: J. B. Lippincott Company, 1955): pp. 66–68.

HAROLD C. GODDARD ON A PRE-FREUDIAN READING

[In this extract taken from his essay "A Pre-Freudian Reading of 'The Turn of the Screw'" Goddard offers a psychological interpretation.]

Fear is like faith: it ultimately creates what at first it only imagined. The governess, at the beginning, imagines that the actions and words of the children are strange and unnatural. In the end they become strange and unnatural for the good and sufficient reason that the children gradually become conscious of the strangeness and unnaturalness of her own attitude toward them. They cannot put it into words: they have never heard of nervousness, still less of insanity. But they sense it and grow afraid, and she accepts the abnormal condition into which their fear of *her* has thrown them as proof of their intercourse with the two specters. Thus do her mania and their fear feed and augment each other, until the situation culminates—in a preliminary way—in two scenes of shuddering terror.

The first of these is the occasion when the governess comes at night to Miles's bedside and tries, without mentioning the dreaded name of Quint, to wring from the child a confession of the infernal intercourse which, she is convinced, he is guilty of holding. Forget, for the moment, the governess' version of the occurrence and think of it as it must have appeared to the child. A little boy of ten, who had for some time felt something creepy and uncanny in the woman who has been placed in charge of him and his sister, lies awake in the dark thinking of her and of the strangeness of it all. He hears steps outside his door. At his call the door opens, and there, candle in hand, is this very woman. She enters and sits beside him on the edge of the bed. For a moment or two she talks naturally, asking him why he is not asleep. He tells her. And then, quite suddenly, he notices in her voice the queer tone he has felt before, and the something in her manner, excited but suppressed, that he does not like. As they go on talking, this excitement grows and grows, until in a final outburst she falls on her knees before him and begs him to let her *save* him! Visualize the scene: the hapless child utterly at a loss to know what the dreadful "something" is from which she would "save" him; the insane women on her knees almost clasping him in her hysterical embrace. Is it any wonder that the interview terminates in a shriek that bursts from the lips of the terror-stricken boy? Nothing could be more natural. Yet, characteristically, the governess interprets the boy's fright and outcry as convincing proof of the presence of the creature she is seeking to exorcise. Utterly unconscious of the child's fear of *her*, she attributes his agitation to the only other adequate cause she can conceive.

The corresponding scene in the case of Flora occurs the next day by the lake. Once more, think of it from the angle of the child. A little girl, too closely watched and confined by her governess, seizes an opportunity for freedom that presents itself and wanders off for half an hour in the grounds of the estate where she lives. A little later, the governess and the housekeeper, out of breath with searching, come upon her. A half-dozen words have hardly been exchanged when the governess, a tremor in her voice, turns suddenly on the child and demands to know where her former governess is— a woman whom the little girl knows perfectly well is dead and buried. The child's face blanches, the housekeeper utters a cry, in answer to which the governess, pointing across the lake and into vacancy cries out: "She's there, she's there!" The child stares at the demented woman in consternation. The latter repeats: "She's there, you little unhappy thing—there, there, *there*, and you know it as well as you know me!" The little girl holding fast to the housekeeper, is frozen in a convulsion of fear. She recovers herself sufficiently to cry out, "I don't know what you mean. I see nobody. I see nothing. I never *have*," and then, hiding her head in the housekeeper's skirts, she breaks out in a wail, "Take me away, take me away—oh take me away from *her!*"

"From *me?*" the governess cries, as if thunderstruck that it is not from the specter that she asks to be delivered.

"From you—from you!" the child confirms.

Again, is not the scene, when innocently taken, perfectly natural? Yet again the governess is incapable of perceiving that the child is stricken with terror not at all at the apparition but at *her* and the effect the apparition has had upon her.

—Harold C. Goddard, "A Pre-Freudian Reading of 'The Turn of the Screw,'" *Nineteenth-Century Fiction* 12, no. 1 (June 1957): pp. 22–24.

DORTHEA KROOK ON THE FATAL FLAW

[In this extract taken from her book *The Ordeal of Consciousness in Henry James*, Krook writes about the fatal weakness of the governess.]

The Turn of the Screw is then chiefly (though not exclusively) a fable about the redemptive power of human love: the power of love—here the governess's love for the children—to redeem the corrupt element in a human soul, and so to ensure the final triumph of good over evil; though (as so often in tragedy) at the cost of the mortal life of the redeemed soul.

To recognise this as the basic theme is not yet, however, to exhaust the meaning of the story. There is still a further and final aspect to consider—one last turn of the screw, as it were, that the traditional Faustus *motif* receives; and to understand this is to understand the full scope of James's achievement in this story and the range, depth and subtlety of the insight into the nature of man and the conditions of man's salvation it exhibits.

This last aspect has to do with the prevailing ambiguity and with the matter of the governess's guilt; and it is best approached by considering the problem of little Miles's death at the very end. For it *is* a problem: Why (one finds oneself impelled to ask) does Miles die? Why does he *have* to die? Why, if he has renounced the devil, as religious people would say; if he has embraced, or is about to embrace, God again; if he has thrown himself upon God's mercy through the agency of the good angel in the shape of the governess—why then must he die? Where is the moral necessity; where therefore the artistic inevitability? ⟨. . .⟩

It is the governess who directs us to the answer. ⟨. . .⟩

> He turned to me again his little beautiful fevered face. 'Yes, it was too bad.'
> 'Too bad?'
> 'What I suppose I sometimes said. [Too bad] to write home.'

If only she could have stopped there, even there. But she cannot:

> I can't name the exquisite pathos of the contradiction given to such a speech by such a speaker; I only know that the next instant I heard myself throw off with homely force: 'Stuff and nonsense!' But the next after that I must have sounded stern enough. 'What *were* these things?'

'My sternness,' she adds, 'was all for his judge, his executioner.' But— 'What were these things?' she demands, though she can see that the child is collapsing under the pressure. 'What were these things?' And as she brings this out, Peter Quint reappears: 'There again, against the glass, as if to blight his confession and stay his answer, was the hideous author of our woe—the white face of damnation.' And from this point the scene proceeds to the tragic catastrophe.

What are we to understand by all this? It is plain, I think, that we are to understand that the governess herself is directly responsible for the return of Peter Quint; that she is therefore indirectly responsible for Miles's death; that she is, in short, guilty of some awful moral lapse which precipitates the final catastrophe. And this lapse (we come now to see) is only the last and most disastrous expression of something in the governess of which we have been uneasily conscious all the time: some flaw, some fatal weakness, in her moral constitution that has, in some elusive way, been present throughout in all her relations with the two children.

The nature of this 'fatal flaw' is now not difficult to see. Its generic name is what Christians call spiritual pride; and the specific form it takes here is, first, the desire to know all—to 'get all' (in the governess's own phrase) in the sense of putting herself in complete possession of the child's soul by a complete knowledge of all that he has done. This is the aspiration after complete and perfect knowledge which by Christian definition belongs only to God and not to man; and this, which in the traditional Faustus story is shown as the glorious and damnable sin of Faustus himself, the soul that had sold itself to the devil, is here transferred to God's own emissary, the 'good angel' of the Faustus story.

—Dorothea Krook, *The Ordeal of Consciousness in Henry James*
(Cambridge, U.K.: Cambridge University Press, 1962): pp. 121–22,
123, 124–125.

MARTHA BANTA ON THE GHOSTLY ENCOUNTER

[In this extract taken from her book *Henry James and the Occult*, Banta writes about meeting ghosts.]

James's contemporaries thought "The Turn of the Screw" was about real ghosts in the good old-fashioned tradition; to most the governess was a beleagured maiden set in dire peril. It has been a long time since readers have been content with this impression. As superstition disappears in the daily lives of those who read James, so does their ability to consider the possibility that the ghosts they know do not exist in the world could exist in the pages of a story. Naturally, this is meant as a high compliment to James—just as one is offered to Shakespeare whenever someone says, "Of course, Hamlet was mad; there was no ghost of his father, because Shakespeare's was a *modern* mind." It is logical, if unwise, for modern, intellectually responsible readers to insist that James as a modern, intellectually responsible man could not have intended the apparitions to be real. According to this syllogism, if it is obvious to us there could be no ghosts, but the governess asserted she saw them, the only conclusion is that she "saw" them through the eyes of an hallucinated imagination. And people who hallucinate are mad.

Yet James wrote the story so that it may be taken as possessing ghosts seen by anyone capable of seeing them because they are there. "The Turn of the Screw" ought at least to be considered in context with the rest of James's work in its genre. In story after story James used real apparitions for his haunted characters to see. There is no reason to believe he suddenly turned fastidious in 1898; not with "The Jolly Corner" and *The Sense of the Past* still to come. At the time James wrote the bulk of his supernatural tales, people wanted ghosts; taken straight or explained scientifically, but not necessarily "explained away" as Mrs. Radcliffe had done to the detriment of the artistic atmosphere of her fiction. As a professional carefully eyeing his market, James understood the commercial need for the delightful sense of hackle-raising horror that ghosts provided his readers; like those who first heard Douglas read the governess's manuscript, he saw this story as "gruesome, as on Christmas eve in an old house a strange tale should essentially be. . . ." Further, James had respect for the effects he could obtain by dramatizing the dead in confrontation with the living; he did not feel the need to apologize whenever he decided to use real ghosts. ⟨. . .⟩

In his mind the form of the ghost story stirred many responses, was therefore interesting, was therefore a success, "a perfect example of an exercise of the imagination unassisted, unassociated—playing the game, making the score . . . off its own bat." Alas, this self-confidence was diminished by the time he set down his preface to the New York Edition. Artistic satisfaction had been disturbed by the story's reception; it "shook" his "artistic" and "ironic heart" "almost to breaking" to realize the public wanted the very thing he had renounced.

James had written his story under one set of rules; his readers too often wished to play another game under another set of rules.

If James felt certain delayed pangs of apprehension over the way his ghosts were being received, he also experienced anxiety over the governess. He had been concerned only with what she said she observed. He wanted to keep "crystalline her record of so many intense anomalies and obscurities—by which I don't of course mean her explanation of them, a different matter. . . ." What we have here is James typically standing against a black or white position; he clearly implies that there are several ways to assess why the governess saw what she saw if one wants such explanations, as he did not. If one is eager to make absolute conclusions based upon the partial evidence the governess provides, what can one end with but that she is mad or she is sane? To James it was not the mere choice of insanity or sanity; his was rather the artistic decision to provide ghosts to be seen by people whether those people are mad or not, and whatever their mad or sane explanations for seeing what they do.

—Martha Banta, *Henry James and the Occult* (Bloomington: Indiana University Press, 1972): pp. 116–17, 118–19.

T. J. LUSTIG ON SIGNIFICANT BLANKS

[In this extract taken from his book *Henry James and the Ghostly*, Lustig offers a perspective on voids in meaning.]

If 'The Turn of the Screw' is concerned with slippages and turns of meaning, it is also deeply preoccupied with gaps and voids: James wrote in his Preface that the 'values' of the story were 'positively all blanks.' Shlomith Rimmon has argued that 'The Turn of the Screw' constructs its ambiguity around 'a central informational gap.' But this notion of an absent core, a single and central enigma, seems to secure its lucidity by avoiding any explication of the teeming voids which haunt 'The Turn of the Screw.' Few fictions deploy such extensive and disparate lacunae, and 'The Turn of the Screw' uses its blanks to undermine all attempts to establish relations and to join references into a coherent pattern. One could even argue that the tale blanks its overt blanks. 'Blankley' is the name of a country house in 'The Wheel of Time.' In 'the Turn of the Screw,' by contrast, the revealing blank is elided and contracted into 'Bl. . .y,' a placename as suggestive as 'Paramore,' though a more reticently monosyllabic one.

'The Turn of the Screw' is repeatedly concerned with the act of telling. More often than not, however, its predicament is that of not being able to tell. Fragmented and vestigial, the existing text looks like the ruined remains of a fuller story. The introductory chapter of 'The Turn of the Screw' begins just after a story has been told and ends just before a story is about to begin. It occupies a space between two acts of telling, framing and mediating a narrative which, as Douglas points out, takes up the tale 'at a point after it had, in a manner, begun,' and which ends in the air, with a death whose consequences are not registered in the narrative of the governess, except in the sense that her narrative is the effect of that death. The formal beginning and ending of the introductory chapter and of the main narrative do not conclude with actual, absolute, chronological beginnings and endings: they are, as Christine Brooke-Rose puts it, 'truncated, at both ends.'

The frame chapter serves to mediate a further mediation, since it seems that the events at Bly do not constitute a complete and discrete story so much as a border between a past defined in terms of social relations and a future made up of literary or textual relations. Miles and Flora are passed from their dead parents to their disappearing uncle and on to Quint and Jessel, who die to make way for an evanescent nursemaid, a temporary school, Mrs Grose and the governess herself. Some time after the events of the main narrative the governess tells her story directly to Douglas. The story is subsequently written down by the governess and sent to Douglas before her death. Douglas reads the governess's narrative to the circle gathered in the old house and in turn transmits it, before his own death, to the narrator of the introductory chapter, who finally makes an 'exact transcript' of the manuscript. The events at Bly thus form the mid-point in a sequence of transmissions, each of which begins and ends in death or absence, all of which lead away from genetic sources and reproductive pairs to single parental substitutes and from primary spoken narratives to written, read and copied ones.

—T. J. Lustig, *Henry James and the Ghostly* (Cambridge, U.K.: Cambridge University Press, 1994): pp. 115–117.

ROBERT WEISBUCH ON HENRY JAMES AND THE IDEA OF EVIL

> [In this extract taken from his chapter "James and the Idea of Evil" in *The Cambridge Companion to Henry James*, Weisbuch discusses the ambiguity of the evil in "The Turn of The Screw."]

Commentators have so often cited the various sexual shadings of the Governess's visions that it seems almost shameful to rehearse them, but every sighting of the ghosts includes a potentially sexual implication: Quint's phallic appearance takes place just as the Governess wonders if she is to see her desirable employer; the Governess sees Miss Jessel in communion with Flora as Flora makes a toy boat by sticking a mast-like stick into a flat piece of wood. This is truest in the final scene, where the Governess's forcing Miles to view the apparition of Quint—"the devil," "the hideous author of our woe"—is rendered in a language suffused with double entendres ("with a moan of joy, I enfolded, I drew him close") and energized by orgiastic, superhot syntax. What is interestingly anomalous to these exclusively sexual readings is the presence of an equally inappropriate language: that of a cold yet egomaniacal scientist. In the final, fatal confrontation with Miles, she is "so determined to have all my proof": contradicting utterly her earlier attempt to keep the specter from Miles's sight, she requires him to view Quint "for the demonstration of my work." Both qualities—the eroticism, the unnatural intellectual removal—are functions of egotism, as the Governess is by now far more concerned with her own dramas than with protecting her charges. Flora goes mad and Miles dies in her arms; she imagines the latter as a creature hurtling over an abyss: "I caught him, yes, I held him—it may be imagined with what a passion" and yet "his little heart, dispossessed, had stopped."

The tale will not tell us whose evil is responsible for this death—perhaps his corruption has been so utter that salvation required it, perhaps her possessive clutching of him is suffocating, both figuratively and literally. Whatever one feels, the language of blindness supplants that of vision to measure the Governess's self-incriminating complicity with evil: "My equilibrium depended on my rigid will, the will to shut my eyes as tightly as possible to the truth that what I had to deal was revoltingly against nature"; Quint's return outside the window "reduced me to the mere blind movement of getting ahold of [Miles], drawing him close"; and finally, "I was infatuated, I was blind with victory," where again lover and logician combine in egotism at a mothering seduction turned suffocatingly murderous. One finally asks whether the striking absence of a final framing device is James's way of leaving meaning utterly open—as many critics have hypothesized—or whether the Governess's tale swallows the frame text narcissistically, as her subjectivity has suffocated all else.

James dares to warp the very form of his tale, then, to dramatize even in its structure the evil he is defining there. This damnation begins with a worrisome but not terrifying desire to be loved, which leads to what we might consider a prurient perception, to a final, self-confirming, self-advertising narrative told to sustain a self's sense of worth. Much of this is what one might want to call fault, or even error: what raises itself to the level of Evil is not merely egotism but egotism's disregard of the Otherness of other people, even and especially helpless children. Authentic hauntings or no, the evil is the forcing of children to confront what their psyches, tender or corrupted or tainted, cannot bear; whether or not Quint or Jessel began the ruin of their childhood, the Governess ends it, and ends it for reasons all her own.

—Robert Weisbuch, "Henry James and the Idea of Evil," in *The Cambridge Companion to Henry James*, Jonathan Freedman, ed. (Cambridge, U.K.: Cambridge University Press, 1998): pp. 107–108.

Plot Summary of
"The Beast in the Jungle"

John Marcher, the central figure of "The Beast in the Jungle," lives life by waiting. He believes he is destined for something enormous, not necessarily good or bad. He is absorbed so thoroughly in this non-activity that he manages to lose a whole lifetime. He remains until the very last completely static. "The Beast in the Jungle" is perhaps the prime example of James's theme of the "missed opportunity."

John Marcher meets May Bartram while visiting an old country house where May gives tours, and she reminds him that in fact, they are not strangers but have met ten years before in Naples. She also reminds him of a secret he had imparted to her at that time: "You said you had had from your earliest time, as the deepest thing within you, the sense of being kept for something rare and strange, possibly prodigious and terrible, that was sooner or later to happen to you, that you had in your bones the foreboding and the conviction of, and that would perhaps overwhelm you."

The two enter into a long friendship, in which they watch closely for signs of Marcher's fate. It is always part of their mutual consciousnesses. "She had in fact a wonderful way of making it seem, as such, the secret of her own life too." It occurs to Marcher only once to ask her "doesn't it sometimes come to you as time goes on that your curiosity isn't being particularly repaid?"

Recognition of his own profound selfishness flickers occasionally but the true meaning of it cannot be reached because he is blinded by "selfness." The two of them continue this way for many years until Miss Bartram becomes ill, at which time she considers offering what she has recently discovered about the nature of Marcher's secret. He does not understand her hints, however, and May dies, having had to face the monster alone.

Marcher is despondent over her death, and visits her grave obsessively. He searches for something. His grief feels somehow inadequate. "It was as if, in the view of society he had not been markedly bereaved, as if there still failed some sign or proof of it, and as if none the less his character could never be affirmed nor the deficiency ever made up."

He soon gives up waiting for the beast, as he cannot see how it matters any longer. One day he visits May's grave, and witnesses a stranger grieving over a nearby grave. The heightened and exquisite quality of the man's grief suddenly causes Marcher to be envious. At last, the stealthy demon pounces: he realizes that "no passion had ever touched him, for this was what passion meant; he had survived and maundered and pined, but where had been his deep ravage?" He had held his life in pause for that which lay in the grave before him: May Bartram.

The missed chance for a life with May is a sort of inverse beast, from which Marcher finally receives a terrible mauling. The tragic irony of it is the sharpest pain to Marcher. Conversely, it is not difficult to imagine that Marcher himself is also the beast, circling in on May, but never pouncing until the end of her life. "He circled about it at a distance that alternately narrowed and widened and that still wasn't much affected by the consciousness in him that there was nothing she could 'know' after all, any better than he did." He seals the truth of his fate by refusing to embrace her when she offers herself to him finally during her illness. He has forced the beast upon her, too.

Fear and hope are the same for Marcher. He does not look forward to the future without a paralyzing mix of the two. Marcher is a very modern literary creation—a desperately self-involved man, whose constant waiting is a metaphorical search for the existential self. Marcher cannot truly remember when he and May first met, which signifies his inability to concentrate on anything but himself. It is May who must supply this information. When she reminds him of the secret he told her, he must immediately, though unconsciously, give up any idea of romantic involvement with her. He cannot marry a woman who knows he is waiting for some terrible fate, a woman he cannot know for sure even believes in his foreknowledge. "It was always open to him to accuse her of seeing him but as the most harmless of maniacs, and this, in the long run— since it covered so much ground—was his easiest description of their friendship."

Homosexuality is, naturally, one way to understand Marcher's strange passionless relationship with May. This is an idea put forth by several modern critics, but it is important to recognize the abstract quality of this story. James dramatizes a highly philosophical idea in "The Beast in the Jungle," not intending that this story be one of pure psychological realism. There are many gaps in the story, which indicate James's reluctance to make his ideas concrete. James never discusses, for example, the original source of Marcher's obsession. Marcher is simply obsessed.

Throughout the story, Marcher and May interact with no one but each other. Their lives seem to exist only in relation to the other. Again, James uses this technique to focus the reader on the moral elements of the story, rather than the narrative line, of which there is, after all, very little.

The lack of narrative progress in the story puts us in the same position as our protagonist, Marcher—we are waiting. As Marcher waits for the beast, so do we. That the story has very little plot is exactly the point, because Marcher is the man to whom nothing happens. James draws us into the stagnation of Marcher's universe both by exposition and by story structure. The man who cannot act must have an ending in which he does not actively participate. When Marcher discovers the nature of the beast, which is actually a lack of a beast, James is providing us with a lesson on endings rather than a completely literal ending. As the end of the story arrives, so does the revelation that no one ever escapes the inevitability of fate, or the story that must necessarily lead up to it. ❀

List of Characters in
"The Beast in the Jungle"

John Marcher is the man who spends his life waiting for "the beast in the jungle" to appear. He is obsessed by the idea of meeting some dreadful fate, and in the process misses the opportunity to spend his life with May. Not until she dies does he understand that his lost life is itself the beast.

May Bartram is the woman who spends her life with Marcher, waiting with him for the mystery to appear. When she grows older and becomes ill, she finally offers herself to him, giving him an opportunity to escape the beast, but he does not understand her offer, and she goes to her grave knowing that the monster will spring on him while he mourns her. ❀

Critical Views on
"The Beast in the Jungle"

[In this extract, taken from his commentary in *The House of Fiction: An Anthology of the Short Story with Commentary*, Tate gives a perspective on the story itself.]

Are we to conclude that the very nature of James's problem in "The Beast in the Jungle," the problem of dramatizing the insulated ego, of making active what in its essence is incapable of action, excluded the use of an active and searching intelligence in the main character?

The first of the two scenes appears in part IV when years of waiting have driven May Bartram to something like desperation. She cannot overtly break the frame of their intercourse, which permits her only to affirm and reaffirm her loyalty to the role of asking nothing for herself; in the act of a new reaffirmation,

> "No, no!" she repeated. "I'm with you—don't you see—still." And as to make it more vivid to him she rose from her chair—a movement she seldom risked in these days—and showed herself, all draped and all soft, in her fairness and slimness. "I haven't forsaken you."

We return to Marcher's mind, in which this reflection is all that the moment can give him:

> . . . He couldn't pity her for that; he could only take her as she showed—as capable even yet of helping him. It was as if, at the same time, her light might at any instant go out; wherefore he must make the most of it. . . . "Tell me if I shall consciously suffer."

Here we get a special case of James's Operative Irony, which "implies and projects the possible other case." But the "possible other case" is not in the awareness of Marcher ⟨. . .⟩; it is manipulated by James himself standing beside Marcher and moving May Bartram up close to imply her virtual offer of herself, her very body—an offer of which Marcher is not aware, so deeply concerned is he with his "problem." As May Bartram stands before him, "all soft," it is Marcher's Beast which had leaped at him from the jungle; and he doesn't know it.

It is a fine scene, unobtrusively arrived at, and it has a certain power. It is perhaps sounder in its structure than the second and climactic scene. Marcher's frequent visits to Miss Bartram's grave are occasions of a developing insight into his loss, his failure to see that his supreme experience had been there for him day after day through many years. But James must have known that, to make the insight dramatically credible, it must reach the reader through a scene; and to have a "scene" there must be at least two persons and an interchange between them. He thus suddenly introduces, at the last moment, what he called in the Prefaces a *ficelle*, a character not in the action but brought in to elicit some essential quality from the involved characters. The stranger haunting the other grave is such a *ficelle*; but not having been "planted" earlier and disguised, he appears with the force of a shock, and could better be described as a *deus ex machina*—a device for ending an action by means of a force outside it; here it serves to render scenically, for the eye and ear, what had otherwise been a reported insight of Marcher's. James could not let himself merely tell us that Marcher had at last seen his tragic flaw; he must contrive to show him seeing it.

If this story is the greatest of the James *nouvelles*, as it probably is, one must reconsider the generally held belief that it is his special form, in which he scored greater triumphs than he ever did in the novels.

> —Allen Tate, "Henry James: 'The Beast in the Jungle,'" in Caroline Gordon and Allen Tate, *The House of Fiction: An Anthology of Short Story with Commentary* (New York: Charles Scribner's, 1954): pp. 229–230.

ELISABETH HANSOT ON IMAGINATION AND TIME

[In this extract, taken from her essay "Imagination and Time in 'The Beast in the Jungle'" Hansot discusses Marcher's experience of imagination.]

Marcher's detachment from ordinary experience, James tells us, comes from his conviction that an extraordinary experience awaits him which, like a supernatural event, is expected to dislocate, supersede, or render meaningless the normal incidents and attitudes which make up a good part of everyday life. In the course of his narrative James describes some of the attitudes and beliefs which enable Marcher to establish and maintain a distance between himself and the everyday experience available to him, and suggests how, in turn, these dispositions come to constitute the substance of Marcher's own character. One of the most noteworthy concomitants of Marcher's detachment is the curiously passive attitude he adopts toward his own past and future. This passivity—whether it be a cause or a consequence of his detachment—has among its effects a gradual and unperceived impoverishment of his own sensibility, for Marcher maintains toward his own past and future the attitude of a spectator viewing events that he cannot influence. He seems to view both these dimensions of time as discrete, self-contained objects, endowed with their own independent value and bearing little or no relationship to himself in the present.

When Marcher does try to conceive of himself as an active agent he chooses the paradigm of the hero. The hero's singularity might be said to consist in his ability to dominate events by his perfectly timed and conceived actions. James describes this kind of abrupt shift in Marcher's concept of himself as a sudden passage from one extreme of consciousness to another. The images James uses to portray Marcher's rapid, almost unconscious transitions from passive spectator to heroic actor offer important clues to Marcher's attitude toward time.

In his opening sentence, James indicates that Marcher is not interested in questions of causality. "What determined the speech that startled him in the course of their encounter scarcely matters, being probably but some words spoken by himself quite without intention. . . ." Marcher at this juncture is wondering what had brought May to remind him of a long forgotten intimacy, a confession made to her ten years ago. Both the past confession and the present rediscovery of it appear to be fortunate accidents, explained, if explanation is needed, by some words spoken by Marcher without intent or purpose. Marcher seems to be a man to whom accidents—including accidents of memory—occur easily. As James portrays him, both in his initial setting at Weatherend and subsequently, Marcher does not conceive of himself as an active agent capable of initiating changes or causing events to occur in his everyday world. He is a man who lacks intentions, perhaps because he lacks desires and purposes by which to define himself and furnish his corner of the universe.

When Marcher does look to the past, it is because he desires to find a groundwork strong enough to support further intimacy with May in the future. He had, James remarks, most curiously forgotten the events of their encounter. The explanation may be that for Marcher these events seemed, in the strongest sense of the word, to be mere accidents, episodes which did not mark him, or even annoy or amuse him enough to recollect them in the intervening years. Marcher's past, seen in this light, might be described ·as a collection of incidents without continuity or form.

> —Elisabeth Hansot, "Imagination and Time in 'The Beast in the Jungle,'" in *Twentieth Century Interpretations of The Turn of the Screw and Other Tales*, Jane P. Tompkins, ed. (Englewood Cliffs, N.J.: Prentice-Hall, Inc., 1970): pp. 88–89.

Ruth Bernard Yeazell on the Imagination of Metaphor

[In this extract, taken from her book *Language and Knowledge in the Late Novels of Henry James*, Yeazell discusses the metaphor of the beast.]

Marcher the tiger-hunter is in reality Marcher the terrified. The image which haunts him implies a readiness to confront exotic horrors, but all the while that he pursues his beast, Marcher flees in terror from ordinary human contact and from love. On a late April afternoon in a quiet London town house, May Bartram offers herself to him; but Marcher, obsessed with metaphors of distant jungles and mysterious beasts, utterly fails to understand what is happening. Through the metaphor of the beast in the jungle, apparently a talisman of hidden knowledge, Marcher actually retreats from knowledge—both sexual knowledge of May and conscious knowledge of himself. Metaphoric thinking allows him to evade immediate reality and its demands, to avoid the risk of passionate confrontation.

Yet even the frustratingly obtuse Marcher at last comes to perceive the pattern of his life, to understand the meaning of his escape and his loss. After May Bartram has died, Marcher haunts her grave, and it is during one such autumn vigil that the truth finally dawns. Shocked into awareness by the grief-stricken face of a fellow visitor to the graveyard, by "the deep ravage of the features he showed," Marcher asks himself, "What had the man *had*, to make him by the loss of it so bleed and yet live?" In typically Jamesian fashion, the very form of the question calls forth the answer: "Something—and this reached him with a pang—that *he*, John Marcher, hadn't; the proof of which was precisely John Marcher's arid end. No passion had ever touched him, for this was what passion meant; he had survived and maundered and pined, but where had been *his* deep ravage?" Too late comes "the truth, vivid and monstrous"; in this long-delayed moment of illumination Marcher finally grasps the missing tenor of his metaphor:

> The Beast had lurked indeed, and the Beast, at its hour, had sprung; it had sprung in that twilight of the cold April when, pale, ill, wasted, but all beautiful, and perhaps even then recoverable, she had risen from her chair to stand before him and let him imaginably guess. It had sprung as he didn't guess; it had sprung as she hopelessly turned from him, and the mark, by the time he left her, had fallen where it *was* to fall. He had justified his fear and achieved his fate; he had failed, with the last exactitude, of all he was to fail of; and a moan now rose to his lips as he remembered she had prayed he mightn't know. This horror of waking—*this* was knowledge, knowledge under the breath of which the very tears in his eyes seemed to freeze.

The exotic is brought home, and in this painful moment of awakening Marcher recognizes that May's offer of love and his own failure to respond marked the true spring of the beast. Paradoxically, the metaphor through which Marcher has escaped comes in the end to signify both the experience which he fled and the very flight itself. The beast sprang when May made her humble gesture of love; it sprang again when the self-absorbed Marcher failed to comprehend her gesture. And it springs once more, most horrifyingly, at this final moment of full awareness: "He saw the Jungle of his life and saw the lurking Beast; then, while he looked, perceived it, as by a stir of the air, rise, huge and hideous, for the leap that was to settle him. His eyes darkened—it was close; and instinctively turning, in his hallucination, to avoid it, he flung himself, face down, on the tomb." Marcher's beast—a distant cousin of that tiger with the gleaming eyes which in *Death in Venice* crouches in Aschenbach's hallucinatory jungle—is at once sensual love, the failure of self-knowledge, and the pain of that knowledge come too late.

Marcher clings to his metaphor in order to distance reality, to postpone the anguish of knowledge, but when knowledge at last overwhelms him, the metaphor turns sickeningly real; the beast which leaps in the final lines of James's tale may be hallucinatory, but for Marcher the effect of its last spring is a condition virtually indistinguishable from death.

—Ruth Bernard Yeazell, *Language and Knowledge in the Late Novels of Henry James* (Chicago: The University of Chicago Press, 1976): pp. 37–39.

Millicent Bell on the Inaccessible Future

[In this extract, taken from her book, *Meaning in Henry James*, Bell looks at the idea of the inaccessible future.]

"Nothing happens," as readers impatiently protest—which is just the point. Marcher's aging appearance through the years, his modest career, are only simulations of the progress of ordinary life history, and as for May, "beneath her forms as well detachment had learned to sit, and behavior had become for her, in a social sense, a false account of herself." Of course, *she* does have a story, unknown to Marcher; she is in love with him. Stepping for a moment beyond the boundary of Marcher's masculine awareness, his inability to feel the female side of experience, the narrator remarks, "There was one account of her that would have been true all the while and that she could give, directly, to nobody, least of all to John Marcher."

For the eyes of the world Marcher and May pretend the history of a love affair. "What saves us, you know, is that we answer so completely to so usual an appearance: that of the man and woman whose friendship has become such a daily habit—or almost—as to be at last indispensable." For Marcher in particular their "habit" of keeping each other company "saves"; as May tells him, "It makes you, after all, for the vulgar, indistinguishable from other men. What's the most inveterate mark of men in general? Why the capacity to spend endless time with dull women—to spend it I won't say without being bored, but without minding that they are, without being driven off at a tangent by it; which comes to the same thing. I'm your dull woman, a part of the daily bread for which you pray at church. That covers your tracks more than anything."

Literally interpreting James's story we can, if we wish, see Marcher as a man who fears the most intimate human communion and commitment, the sexual bond. At the same time, one may say, he is not unwilling to accept the protection of a woman's friendship, a friendship which makes him seem normal, helps him "to pass for a man like another"—though it denies her what the appearance implies. Eve Kosovsky Sedgwick has interestingly suggested that something more positive than a mere *lack* of sexual desire is the matter with Marcher. She thinks that Marcher's "pretense" of an ordinary sexual affair must conceal an unavowable motive of another sort, and that "to the extent that Marcher's secret has a content, that content is homosexual." "The apparent gap of meaning . . . is far from being a genuinely empty one," she says. "It refers to the perfectly specific absence of a prescribed heterosexual desire." The "nothing" that is Marcher's fate, on the other hand, is "male homosexual genitality," which can only be referred to by pretermission—that is, as the "love that dare not speak its name." In her interesting speculative reading of the story Sedgwick goes on to see May's long patience with Marcher as an unsuccessful attempt to free him from "homosexual panic" by helping him to understand his own desires. Yet sexual nullity, rather than homosexual desire, serves as an appropriate sign of the refusal of enacted being.

But perhaps the "gap" of psychological explanation for Marcher's behavior needs to remain unfilled, however eagerly our imaginations *will* fill it, in this parable, which, like Hawthorne's tales upon which it is modeled, is an abstract moral statement without psychological depth. Hawthorne's notebooks are full of one- or two-sentence summaries of proposed stories which will fail to gain realistic substance even when he writes them; for "Ethan Brand" the writer first set down the following idea: "The search of an investigator for the Unpardonable Sin;—he at last finds it in his own heart and practice"—which completely summarizes the story. Or one can say that the gap of exact knowledge about Marcher's life is like the unfillable gap of undenoted "evil" in "The Turn of the Screw," which also (and perhaps even more plausibly if we read it as more realistic than it is) can suggest the covert homosexual subject.

—Millicent Bell, *Meaning in Henry James* (Cambridge, Mass.: Harvard University Press, 1991): pp. 267–269.

Plot Summary of
"The Lesson of the Master"

The theme of the "missed opportunity" surfaces again in "The Lesson of the Master." Paul Overt, a young writer, misses his chance to marry the lovely and sympathetic Marian Fancourt, but in this story the blame does not belong strictly to Paul. A very subtle variety of coercion might have played a part, and if so, the culprit is Henry St. George, the famous writer of great fictions. The question of Mr. St. George's motivation is never truly resolved, however. One of James's favorite strategies—ambiguity—is fully employed in this tale. All possible answers to the question of blame are raised but none are completely convincing.

This is also a story about the tensions between life and art. Paul Overt meets the man commonly known as "the Master," Henry St. George, at a weekend gathering on a friend's country estate. It is a huge moment for the burgeoning young author, preceded by a great deal of eagerness and anxiety. When Paul first arrives and discovers that St. George is somewhere in the vicinity, he suppresses the desire to seek him out immediately. He waits for an opportunity to meet and talk to him at some length, and in the interim he encounters Mrs. St. George.

She is a sickly woman who is singularly unimpressed with her husband. She mentions, casually, a manuscript that she insisted he destroy because of its sheer badness. Paul is privately horrified. The great writer and his unimaginative wife seemed to be pulling in opposite directions.

Marian Fancourt, the beautiful and highly literate daughter of a general, is another member of the ensemble who is innocently interested in both writers: Henry St. George and Paul Overt. She takes pains to meet Paul and he is charmed by her vibrancy, her beauty, and her spontaneity. She describes Mr. St. George as "delightful" and promises to bring the two of them together. Marian proves herself to be someone of high intellectual curiosity and striking naturalness. In general, she is highly sympathetic to the act of literary creation.

The three of them become good friends, and much to Paul's delight, St. George takes it upon himself to counsel Paul regarding his literary career. In chapter five, St. George asks Paul to remain after all the dinner guests have left his home in Ennismore Gardens. He brings Paul into his study to conduct a serious "lesson."

"'Isn't it a good big cage for going round and round? My wife invented it and she locks me up here every morning,'" says the Master as he goes on to detail the sacrifices and indignities of marriage. He tells Paul that he has given up the pursuit of perfect art long ago and instead now concentrates strictly on writing popular successes in order to support his family. He tells Paul "'I'm a successful charlatan. . . . I've been able to pass off my system.'" Paul is horrified. He does not see compromise at all; he sees only greatness enjoying the fruits of its labors. St. George insists. "'I've got a loaf on the shelf; I've got everything in fact but the great thing.' 'The great thing?' Paul kept echoing. 'The sense of having done the best.'"

The subject of Marian Fancourt surfaces and Paul confesses that he does love her. St. George insists that to marry her would mean to dishonor his calling. Paul takes this conversation very much to heart. He takes the Master's advice and leaves soon thereafter for Switzerland to concentrate on his work. Several months pass and Paul writes to Marian, who responds with the news that Mrs. St. George has died. Paul then immediately writes to St. George, who in turn sends him a letter describing the loss of his wife as "irreparable." Paul wonders if his "inspired advice had been a bad joke and renunciation was a mistake." St. George declares that "she carried on our life with the greatest art, the rarest devotion, and I was free, as few men can have been, to drive my pen, to shut myself up with my trade." Their intimate conversation about the nature of marriage suddenly falls into question. But Paul presently catches "a glimpse of certain pages he hadn't looked at for months, and that accident," caused him to be "struck with the high promise they revealed." Paul perseveres.

When Paul returns to London after an absence of two years, he learns that Marian Fancourt is engaged to be married to Henry St. George. The shock of the news is compounded by the lack of recognition St. George seems to have concerning their fateful conversation. The Master is happy to receive him, and when the subject is raised, he is eager to assure Paul that his romance with Marian was something no one could have foreseen. He tells Paul that he has given up writing altogether, another shock, which Paul, by now, is incapable of interpreting. His mentor has tricked him into banishing his true love, has married her himself, and has given up the very art that drew Paul to him in the first place.

As for Marian, Paul observes, "She was so happy that it was almost stupid—it seemed to deny the extraordinary intelligence he had formerly found in her. Didn't she know how bad St. George could be, hadn't she recognized the awful thinness—? If she didn't she was nothing, and if she did why such an insolence of serenity?"

St. George does appear to give up writing when he marries Marian. Though Paul's own book becomes a critical success, he still waits in dread for St. George to write and publish something new. Paul's meager sense of vindication would then evaporate immediately. The story concludes with an assurance from the narrator that Paul's true nature is purely artistic and not vengeful: "if this event [a new work by St. George] were to occur he would really be the very first to appreciate it: which is perhaps proof that the Master was essentially right and that Nature had dedicated him to intellectual, not personal passion." The Master has not, by the end of the story, published anything however, and Paul has not been put to the test. But two lines previous to the last excerpt the narrator has just invited us to believe the opposite about Paul, when he tells us that, "Greatly as he admired [St. George's] talent, Paul literally hoped such an incident wouldn't occur, it seemed to him just then that he would scarcely be able to endure it."

In succeeding brilliantly, Paul hopes to avenge his defeat in love, but the Master has already won both sides of the game, if, in fact, he is playing a game at all. If Paul becomes a celebrity, St. George will know that he played a large role. If Paul fails, the Master will have at least rescued Marian from poverty and obscurity. Another possibility is that St. George's malevolence is a figment of Paul's, and therefore our own, imagination.

Is it truly necessary to be "a mere disfranchised monk . . .[who] can produce his effect only by giving up personal happiness"? Even if St. George's intentions were good, is he right about the incompatibility of marriage and art? This was a subject James raised repeatedly throughout his life.

For himself, Henry James chose the solitary life. His unexpressed homosexuality probably played a role in his decision. Witnessing his brother William frequently drown in familial duties and crises, James's fear of intimacy was re-enforced. Paul Overt, who gives up love rather easily, seems himself rather timid in matters of love, but he is certainly not James's biographical self in "The Lesson of the Master."

James can also be identified with St. George in numerous ways. James too was referred to as "the Master" and was not completely foreign to the experience of writing purely for money. Here again is the classic Jamesian brew of ambiguity with specificity.

Whatever his intentions, the master of fiction, St. George, must necessarily be also the master of manipulation. This is an essential tool for any novelist. Perhaps St. George's talent and energies did not stop at fiction but enabled him to script lives as well, designing fates in reality as he did on the page. The lessons are manifold for Paul, regardless of the Master's motivation: the power of persuasion, the necessity of single-mindedness, the difficult mix of life, love, and art, the weaknesses in his own personality, and perhaps the greatness of his own art. ❀

List of Characters in
"The Lesson of the Master"

Paul Overt is an emerging young writer who idolizes Henry St. George, a famous and highly praised novelist. His chance to meet St. George presents itself during a weekend on a country estate, at which time he also meets Marian Fancourt. He is very impressionable at this state in his career and awed by St. George's talent.

Henry St. George is commonly known in literary circles as "the Master." He is at the pinnacle of success when he meets Paul Overt and gives him advice about matters of art and love. His advice becomes a bone of contention between Paul and himself, however, and his motives remain always mysterious.

Marian Fancourt is the lovely daughter of General Fancourt, whose great interest in literature makes her particularly interesting to both Overt and St. George. She is young and beautiful, but her sympathy for the literary life and her understanding of the action of creation make her irresistible.

Mrs. St. George is the sickly, unimaginative wife of Henry. Paul finds her to be astonishingly opposite to her great husband. She seems small and petty. St. George practically confirms this by telling him that she locks him up in his study every morning to induce him to produce money rather than literature. ❀

Critical Views on
"The Lesson of the Master"

MAXWELL GEISMAR ON *LA CRISE DU DRAME*

[In this extract taken from his book, *Henry James and the Jacobites*, Geismar analyzes the story's crisis.]

Dealing with the effect of marriage on an artist, the deterioration of his work through overproduction and the need for money, it reflected the underlying fear of love and of women in the Jamesian temperament. Henry St. George is the popular novelist, or the "Master" of the story—and James was now beginning to see human relationships in an almost feudal pattern of masters and disciples—while the background was again a sort of eighteenth century royal British elegance. At the estate of Summersoft, young Paul Overt, the disciple, meets the St. Georges and the bright young Miss Fancourt. Somewhat as in "The Author of Beltraffio," Mrs. St. George has never interfered with her husband's work except once—"when I made him burn up a bad book."

The wealthy, respected and admired St. Georges represent just that literary position and "success" which James himself had yearned for, but which now, from the depths of his own failure, he described with a more cutting satiric edge. For Overt soon discovers the real truth. The great popular novelist is chained to his writing desk, in his prison cell, in order to support his social position. Mrs. St. George has given him a study without windows, a good big cage for going round and round. "My wife invented it and she locks me up here every morning." There is the familiar "revelation scene" between master and disciple; but St. George is remarkably honest about his position, and his wife's "influence." He warns the young writer to avoid such dangers to his craft as embodied in the alluring shape of Miss Fancourt. "I refer to the mercenary muse whom I led to the altar of literature. Don't, my boy, put your nose into *that* yoke." And here occurs one of the most notable, if unintentional, passages in James's work: "It must be delightful to feel that the son of one's loins is at Sandhurst," says Paul Overt enthusiastically . . . "It is—it's charming," says St. George. "Oh I'm a patriot!"

Still, he warns Overt away from his own path, since the writer must heed not the chatter of society, but "the incorruptible silence of Fame"—a fine phrase that *was* intended. And the faithful, worshiping, devout and naïve Overt abandons Miss Fancourt in order to take "a long trip abroad"—always the Jamesian formula for frustrated love affairs, if hardly the recourse of the less comfortably situated broken heart. He profits by the "advice of the master"—only to discover on his return to London that Mrs. St. George has died, that St. George is to marry Miss Fancourt, and that they are both blooming, happy, and "stupid." The older novelist even tells the younger one that he has stopped writing altogether, and will content himself by reading Overt's masterpieces. "He *was* the mocking fiend."

It is just this ambiguity in the master's "lesson" which makes the story so entertaining. If James was dealing with obsessional themes in his work—the temptations of the world, the dedication to writing, the lure and the trap of women—here the balance of emotions was still maintained. The tone of this little parable of life and art was excellent, and life, however "stupid," won out. Both "the great misguided novelist," St. George, and the devout and dedicated young apostle, Overt—who was hardly capable of seizing or enjoying a creature like the story's heroine—were described with ironic insight.

—Maxwell Geismar, *Henry James and the Jacobites* (Boston: Houghton Mifflin Company, 1962): pp. 112–114.

CHARLES R. SMITH ON INTERPRETING THE STORY

[In this excerpt taken from his article "'The Lesson of the Master': An Interpretive Note," Smith explores his interpretation of James's story.]

Another important Jamesian attitude emerges when St. George encourages Overt to make the necessary sacrifices for the sake of art and perfection. Overt hesitates, "'The artist—the artist! Isn't he a man all the same?'" "'[Don't you] allow him the common passions and affections of men?'" St. George answers, "'Hasn't he a passion, an affectation, which includes all the rest?'" Similarly, James records in the preface (1908) to *The Tragic Muse* (1889), "What I make out from the furthest back is that I . . . must in fact practically have always had, the happy thought of some dramatic picture of the 'artist life' and of the difficult terms on which it is best secured and enjoyed, the general question of its having to be not altogether easily paid for." A few pages later in the same preface James concludes, "There need never, at the worst, be any difficulty about the things advantageously chuckable for art; the question is all but of choosing them in the heap."

If even the delightful Marian Fancourt might advantageously be "chucked" for art, the student of this tale should not look for a "humanistic" resolution to the conflict between the artist's life and his art. James spells out his rigorous concept of the artist in "The Lesson of Balzac" (1905). In trying to explain Balzac's inscrutable genius, James begins by setting up an opposition between art and life as he asks himself how one man could have experienced and at the same time created so much life, "lived at large so much" and still "so much abstracted and condensed himself." As James answers this question, he continues, "The elements of the world he set up before us . . . were not, for him a direct revelation. . . . He could so extend his existence partly because he vibrated to so many kinds of contact and curiosity. To vibrate intellectually was his motive, but it magnified, all the while, it multiplied his experience. He could live at large, in short, because he was always . . . astride of his imagination. . . . always fencing himself in against the personal experience in order to preserve himself for converting it into history. . . ." James sides here with the Master; "life" for the dedicated artist is not, as Overt would have it, to be a "man all the same," personally and directly experiencing "the common passions and affections of men." The artist does not, indeed, must not live so much by doing as by intellectual vibration and by experiencing imaginatively. James's 1891 notebook entry describing his own aspiration is interesting in this connection: "To live in the world of creation—to get into it and stay in it—to frequent it and haunt it—to *think* intently and fruitfully—to woo combinations and inspirations into being by a depth and continuity of attention and meditation—this is the only thing. . . ." It is thus that the Master assures Overt that he will "live" in the greatest sense if only he will make the sacrifice.

Persuaded by the Master, Overt then chooses to make the sacrifice, to free himself for art. Given his vibrating sensitivity and devotion to perfection, he appears potentially capable of measuring up to James's artist ideal. Indeed, even before the Master warns him, Overt saw the contradiction between an "ink-stained table" and the "life" embodied by Marian Fancourt; her "aesthetic toggery," in fact, at first had "made him shrink not as a man of starch and patent leather, but as a man potentially himself a poet. . . ." Later, as Overt begins to fall in love with Marian, he again thinks "with some alarm of the muddled palette of the future." Finally, with her marriage to the worldly Master, Marian apparently fulfills her destiny as one made, according to Overt himself, "not for a dingy little man of letters" but for the "world." But if Overt is potentially a type of the Jamesian ideal, he has not yet reached that ideal; for even as he determines to free himself from the world for the sake of art, he fails to free himself from dependence on his patron saint, the flawed St. George. Overt's compromised position thus stands revealed when he gives up his thoughts of marriage to Marian only to return two years later to feel "sold" over her impending marriage to the Master. Ideally, the Master's reversal should have worked no change in Overt's resolve to make the sacrifices necessary for art, and in as much as the Master recognizes not only Overt's artistic potentiality but also his liability here exposed, he goes far to clear himself of duplicity when he protests to Overt, "'I wanted to save you, rare and precious as you are.'" The vindication of the Master's lesson seems to come, however, as the narration changes from the third person to the first in the last sentence: "I may say for him [Overt], however, that if . . . [the Master were to begin publishing again, Overt] would really be the very first to appreciate it: which is perhaps a proof that the Master was essentially right and that nature had dedicated him to intellectual, not to personal passion."

The historical context appears thus to support internal evidence that "The Lesson of the Master" employs neither humor nor irony to question the Master's lesson. Biographically, the story evinces James's persuasion that the artist must be "always fencing himself in against the personal experience in order to preserve himself for converting it into history. . . ." Artistically, the story and its dénouement dramatize both the characteristic spinelessness of the Master and the difficult terms on which Overt must achieve the artist ideal. Nor does the irony of the dénouement call the lesson into question. All it really does is illuminate the weakness of both characters; for as James notes in the preface, "this is exactly what we mean by operative irony. It implies and projects the possible other case, the case rich and edifying where the actuality is pretentious and vain." The Master's reversal thus becomes the perfect conclusion to a carefully-wrought tale.

—Charles R. Smith, "'The Lesson of the Master': An Interpretive Note," *Studies in Short Fiction* 6, no. 5 (Fall 1969): pp. 657–658.

Shlomith Rimmon on the Concept of Ambiguity

[In this extract from *Henry James: Critical Assessments*, Rimmon examines James's use of narrative ambiguity.]

A creditable view of the Master is encouraged by the two confession scenes. We tend to take St. George's realization of the declining quality of his work and the courage he shows in admitting it as evidence of integrity, of something in his personality which rebels against the prostitution of his creative gifts for the sake of financial gain. The seemingly gratuitous nature of the whole confession strengthens our inclination to see it as sincere, an inclination which we have no reason to check until we learn about St. George's decision to marry Marian. The Master's choice of Paul as someone who deserves to be made privy to his innermost feelings, based as it is on a realization of the quality of the young man's work, as well as St. George's high-pitched offer, "Ask me anything in all the world. I'd turn myself inside out to save you" inevitably strike the note of sincerity.

Jarring notes, however, are not absent, arousing some suspicion even in the first reading and completely balancing the creditable ones in retrospect. It is by means of contradiction that the discreditable possibility is suggested: contradiction between what the Master says and what he does or between what he says on one occasion and what he says on another. Meeting St. George with Marian at an exhibition, Paul reflects the novelist's "manner of conducting himself toward her appeared not exactly in harmony with such a conviction," the conviction expressed earlier by St. George that "She's not for me!" Going back to this earlier conversation, we discover that it is in fact doubly directed. The Master and Paul are discussing the beauty of Marian's personality, and Paul says, "One would like to paint a girl like that." To this St. George answers: "Ah, there it is—there's nothing like life! When you're finished, squeezed dry and used up and you think the sack's empty, you're still spoken to, you still get touches and thrills, the idea springs up—out of the lap of the actual—and shows you there's always something to be done. But I shan't do it—she's not for me!" Paul now asks, "How do you mean, not for you?" And St. George replies, "Oh, it's all over—she's for you, if you like." But Paul modestly explains, "She's not for a dingy little man of letters; she's for the world, the bright rich world of bribes and rewards. And the world will take hold of her—it will carry her away." In the context of this conversation, "She's not for me" can be taken either as "She's not for me as a literary subject" or as "She's not for me as a woman." The first reading does not contradict the Master's subsequent demeanor toward Marian, the second reading does.

The two other contradictions do not even have the potentially "redeeming" quality of double-edgedness. On Paul's first visit to Manchester Square, Marion informs him that St. George has decided not to come: "He said it wasn't fair to you [to Paul]," but the minute Paul leaves the house, he sees Henry St. George stepping out of another hansom. Thus, what first seemed an act of generosity on the Master's part now becomes a possible trick devised to enable St. George to be alone with Miss Fancourt.

Equally perplexing is St. George's attitude toward his wife. This time, the contradiction is between what he says about her on different occasions. Whereas in the confession scene St. George describes his wife as an interference with his art, as a person whose good worldly intentions pave the way to an artistic hell, after her death he writes to Paul: "She took everything off my hands—off my mind. She carried on our life with the greatest art, the rarest devotion, and I was free, as few men can have been, to drive my pen, to shut myself up with my trade. This was a rare service—the highest she could have rendered me. Would I could have acknowledged it more fitly!"

These remarks strike Paul "as a contradiction, a retraction" and arouse doubt in his mind about the validity of St. George's doctrine of renunciation. While understanding the soreness and sorrow expressed in St. George's letter and seeing its fitness, Paul still wonders: "if she was such a benefactress as that, what in the name of consistency had St. George meant by turning *him* upside down that night—by dosing him to that degree, at the most sensitive hour of his life, with the doctrine of renunciation? If Mrs. St. George was an irreparable loss, then her husband's inspired advice had been a bad joke and renunciation was a mistake." These contradictions point to a possible insincerity on the part of Henry St. George, an insincerity which anticipates his final act, but they are never allowed to become definitive, fully balanced as they are by suggestions of integrity and genuine concern about Paul's career.

A similar coexistence of creditable and discreditable clues emerges from a retrospective scrutiny of the genuineness of Marian's interest in literature and perfection. But whereas the ambiguity of the Master is achieved mainly by the balance of singly directed clues (with one example of a doubly directed conversation), in the case of Marian doubly directed clues become more prominent, although not so prominent as to outweigh the balance of singly directed clues, which remains the central technique employed in "The Lesson of the Master" to create narrative ambiguity.

—Shlomith Rimmon, "The Lesson of the Master," in *Henry James: Critical Assessments,* Volume IV, Graham Clarke, ed. (East Sussex, U.K.: Helm Information Ltd., 1991): pp. 435–437.

Philip Horne on Perfection

[In this excerpt, taken from his book, *Henry James and Revision: The New York Edition,* Horne outlines James's goal of literary perfection.]

Part of what takes Paul Overt's fancy in Marion Fancourt is her sympathy with the aspirations of the artist; in their most intimate *tête-à-tête* they are to be found 'discussing, with extreme seriousness, the high theme of perfection,' and more precisely 'the perfection . . . of which the valid work of art is susceptible.' Miss Fancourt is shocked at, and seems unlikely to lapse into, the philistinism of Mrs St George, who boasts of having got her husband to 'burn up a bad book' and speaks of his writing 'a few' with desolating casualness. Paul Overt's response to these remarks is to ask himself: 'Didn't she, as the wife of a rare artist, know what it was to produce *one* perfect work of art?' The one thing St George has reportedly said of his wife to Miss Fancourt is 'that she didn't care for perfection'; whereas the younger woman exclaims 'Ah, perfection, perfection—how one ought to go in for it!'

This contrast forcibly suggests that *The Lesson of the Master* is far from presenting its women as uniform, and raises doubts about the general applicability of the law St George enunciates, 'that one's children interfere with perfection. One's wife interferes. Marriage interferes.' In an essay on 'Edmond Rostand' in 1901 James sketches a comparable ironic general law about artistic quality—that the great popular success will never be the distinguished work of art—only to qualify it with some germane warnings.

> The insidious part of the perplexity is that acclamation may swell to its maximum, and the production acclaimed, the novel, the poem, the play, none the less truly *be* the real thing and not the make-believe. It is so often the make-believe that we are all but driven comfortably to generalise—so great is the convenience of a simple law. The law, however, ceases to be simple from the moment even one book in five hundred does appeal, distinguishably, to a critical sense. The case, though of the rarest, occurs, and it thereby deprives the conscientious student we have postulated of the luxury of a hard-and-fast rule.

If St George's 'hard-and-fast rule' is to be broken, we might think, surely so exceptional a woman as Marian Fancourt will be a likely candidate to do it. Paul indeed asks St George, 'Isn't there even *one* who sees further?' but is assured by the authority: 'Of course I know the one you mean. But not even Miss Fancourt.' For Paul at this point his elder speaks with the disinterested voice of experience, and the Master makes enough allowance for Marian Fancourt's uniqueness to save the law from ludicrous rigidity; yet the reader is unlikely to be convinced by this alone that she is necessarily ruled out by St George's grim regulation. What may be more relevant is the treatment of the young woman elsewhere, the possible presence of hints that she is superficial; and as Shlomith Rimmon points out every clue we have may point in *either* direction. If we are to hold it against her that she is so keen on St George, since he hasn't achieved the highest perfection, why can't we hold the same thing against Paul Overt, who is equally thrilled to receive the Master's attention? If it seems shallow of her to marry St George and not to 'wait for' Paul Overt, how could she be expected to do otherwise when Overt has not told her of his love and has left the country, without telling her, for a two-year absence?

Such insidious questions surround *The Lesson of the Master* with a perplexing hinterland of missing elements, realistic puzzles vividly recreating the conditions under which major personal decisions usually have to be made; or, as James puts it in 'The Art of Fiction,' 'Catching the very note and trick, the strange irregular rhythm of life.' For this particular story we might say that the achievement of an engaging but irresoluble knotting of impulses around the central action—of the sort that the insidious questions conjure up—constitutes in itself 'a decent perfection,' as the *NYE* revision calls the McGuffin of this artistic tale. James himself, in this light, would have attained 'the great thing,' as St George eloquently defines it:

> The sense of having done the best—the sense, which is the real life of the artist and the absence of which is his death, of having drawn from his intellectual instrument the finest music that nature had hidden in it, of having played it as it should be played.

James's *NYE* revisions, moreover, sent to Scribners in July 1908, exactly twenty years after the story began to appear in the *Universal Review*, indicate in their measure that unlike St George James has not undergone 'any decline,' or as they more precisely phrase it, 'any decline of talent or of care.' The 'care,' as the conditions of fiction make it, is both a care for the details of the text *and* a care for the feelings and situation of the characters which the text enshrines. Since the work is an ambiguous secular parable of the talents, moreover, such care in this case will involve *imagining* those talents convincingly—a task difficult, as James points out in the Preface, discussing his invention of great writers, 'from the moment . . . that one worked out at all their greatness; from the moment one didn't simply give it to be taken on trust.' St George benefits from such a working-out in the story's final scene, where as Marian Fancourt's fiancé he is confronted by an accusing Paul Overt, and with supreme urbanity does his best to see the young man's point of view: he

> went on, as if, now that the subject had been broached, he was, as a man of imagination and tact, perfectly ready to give every satisfaction—being able to enter fully into everything another might feel.
>
> —Philip Horne, *Henry James and Revision: The New York Edition* (Oxford: Clarendon Press, 1990): pp. 295–298.

Plot Summary of
"The Jolly Corner"

James returned to the United States in 1904 after a 20-year absence. The United States, and New York in particular, had changed dramatically. New York was no longer a quaint little town but a grand metropolis, supported by vast entrepreneurial wealth. Everybody was playing the money game. He, however, was now practically British, and in a few more years would be officially British. In 1908, "The Jolly Corner" was published—the story of a man who meets the ghost of what he might have been.

Though it is impossible not to see "The Jolly Corner" in the context of James's visit to the United States in 1904, this observation is little more than an interpretive footnote to yet another Jamesian tale about the missed opportunity or the life unlived. In "The Jolly Corner," Spencer Brydon comes face to face with an apparitional creature who lives in his abandoned family home. The creature is his own American self.

James employs one of his favorite forms, the ghost story, in "The Jolly Corner," but only in a broad sense. This ghost is not malevolent. It is just a latent being, a creature within Brydon who never expressed itself, and ultimately it is a metaphor for a crisis of identity.

When Spencer Brydon returns to the United States after an absence of 33 years, he is overwhelmed by "the newness, the queerness, above all the bigness" of what was the little town of his youth. "Proportions and values were upside-down," he says. His values have indeed been inverted since his are the values of the old world.

He has come to evaluate his two properties: a row house, which he sublets, and his family home. The lease on the row house has supplied him with income during his years abroad, which many acquaintances think he has spent in a frivolous way. Certainly he has not managed to accumulate much money, and his recent encounters with the highly productive, dazzlingly prosperous American men has made him question himself.

For a couple of months he has remained in the constant company of his old friend Alice Staverton. He has also visited his family home daily, taking in all that lingers there silently. One day he takes Alice with him and they begin to contemplate aloud an idea that has already taken Brydon hostage: "He found all things come back to the question of what he personally might have been, how he might have led his life and 'turned out' if he had not so, at the outset given it up." This is the beginning of the Jamesian adventure, which is always a journey into the self.

Alice tries to convince Brydon that nothing has been ruined by his being away, that everything is as it was meant to be. "Do you believe then—too dreadfully—that I am as good as I might ever have been?" he demands. Brydon is completely attached to the idea of his other self and offended by the possibility that the repressed Brydon does not exist. Alice and Brydon begin a playful dialogue about the other creature, an alternate Brydon, whom Alice claims she has actually seen in her dreams.

"He isn't myself. He's the just so totally other person. But I do want to see him," Brydon tells her. The need to confront the literal other self becomes an obsession for Brydon, and he decides to stand vigil one night until he sees the creature. His waiting is not passive, however, as he actively tunes his instrument of ghostly perception. He "cultivates" an awareness. His attention is acute, and by the end of the night, very skilled. "People enough, first and last, had been in terror of apparitions but who had ever before so turned the tables and become himself, in the apparitional world, an incalculable terror?"

Brydon's extrasensory perception begins to tell him that he is being followed just as he is following. "It made him feel this acquired faculty like some monstrous cat." Brydon goes upstairs to find a door closed that he had left ajar. Aside from this, he has still seen nothing; frustrated, he renounces his hunt. He descends to the first floor to find a door open which he had left closed, and finally he is rewarded with the presence of the other Brydon.

The ghost is described as a man of his own "substance and stature" but with some obvious differences. One of the hands of the apparition has only three fingers, while the others are cut to stumps.

His mutilation is symbolic of his active, combative, American self—the self who jumps into the fray rather than out of it. Brydon can tell from his dress, that he is also a man of great wealth.

The vision is a hideous one to Brydon, however. It is a stranger; it is expended, vulgar and piteous. It is not a self Brydon would ever want to have been. The ghostly self covers its face in shame and flees Brydon. In "The Jolly Corner," Brydon is the pursuer and the ghost is the victim. Brydon decides that the other self is not ultimately himself.

When Brydon relays what he saw to Alice, she does not entirely agree with him. Alice feels deeply for both Brydons. She has pity on the other self while Brydon does not. "He has been unhappy, he has been ravaged," she says. "And haven't I been unhappy? Am not I—you've only to look at me!—ravaged?" pleads Brydon vying for the highest place in her affections.

Brydon recognizes that Alice is the person she was always meant to be. Her evaluation of the other self is evidence of her intelligent, thoughtful love for Brydon. Now that he has returned, she feels he has fulfilled himself and that nothing is lost. The story implies that they will marry.

"The Jolly Corner" is layered with another meaning, however: the creation of art itself. In formulating a story, exclusion is the principle task. In the critical preface to "The Jolly Corner," written years after the original publication (for the New York Edition of his works), James laments the possibilities the artist must pass over. The story must deny all other stories, all other course of events, and all other endings, except the one chosen, and it is in suppressing these other potential plots that an artist both creates and destroys. ❀

List of Characters in
"The Jolly Corner"

Spencer Brydon has returned to America for the first time in several decades and is confronted by a very different place than he left. Upon his return, he becomes obsessed with the idea of what he might have been if he had stayed in the country. He goes to his empty family home to hunt down the ghost of his other self, who he is sure resides there.

Alice Staverton is Brydon's old American friend. She believes in Brydon's other self as well and has seen him herself in a dream. But to Alice the other Brydon is not hideous, only rough and brutalized.

The Ghost is Brydon's "other self." He is the object of Brydon's pursuit and he turns out to be an ugly creature, with a disfigured hand due to some accident, but a man of great wealth. This other Brydon flees in shame when he is confronted with the real Brydon. ❀

Critical Views on
"The Jolly Corner"

F. O. MATHIESSEN ON THE RELIGION OF
CONSCIOUSNESS

[In this extract from his book, *Henry James: The Major Phase*, Matthiessen discusses the consciousness of Spencer Brydon.]

Here James presented, in Spencer Brydon, a man in his middle fifties who has been away from America for over thirty years, and who returns at last to look after his small property. In the eyes of his New York contemporaries he has spent 'a selfish frivolous scandalous life,' with nothing to show for it. He now senses in himself what he had formerly never suspected, a real flair for business, and begins to wonder what he would have been like if he had stayed here all his life. Would he have been 'one of those types who have been hammered so hard and made so keen by their conditions?' He finds himself brooding on this *alter ego* as he visits his old house downtown on 'the jolly corner,' as he fondly describes it. The question becomes obsessive as he begins to haunt the now unoccupied house at night, as though he was tracking down a ghost. Once again James' evocation of a house depends on his incredibly developed pictorial skills. This time he presents the interior almost entirely by means of the light shining in from the street-lamps through the half-drawn blinds of the high windows, gleaming across the polished floors, picking out the massive silver door knobs, and dissolving into dark pools in the vast recesses. After many vigils in this setting Brydon finally encounters his quarry, only to wish that he had not. As he descends the stairwell, there lurks beneath the fan-lights of the outer door a figure in full evening dress. But his hands are spread across his face, and, with the flash of revulsion of which James is such a master, Brydon suddenly sees that two of the man's fingers are gone. Those bare stumps are of a piece with the horror that strikes Brydon when the stranger drops his hands and confronts him with a face that is blatant and odious in its evil.

But the man is no stranger, though Brydon faints away at the sight of him. This is the man Brydon himself would have become through the tensions of American life. James has created the revulsion here more compellingly than he was to do even with Graham Fielder's, since, imaging a house that was unquestionably destined to be torn down soon to make way for apartments, he was drawing on a peculiarly intimate sense of his own past, on his memories of the leisurely old New York that he felt had been obliterated by the rising city.

This sense of loss is pervasive through James' latest work. It can be traced back, to be sure, to the outset of his career, to his essay on Turgenieff (1874), for instance, an essay that helps define James' own aims even better than his many critiques of Balzac and Flaubert. For James discovered several resemblances between American and Russian life, particularly in the artist's relation to social change. Turgenieff struck him as being quite 'out of harmony with his native land—of having what one may call a poet's quarrel with it. He loves the old, and he is unable to see where the new is drifting. American readers will peculiarly appreciate this state of mind; if they had a native novelist of a large pattern, it would probably be, in a degree, his own.'

—F. O. Matthiessen, *Henry James: The Major Phase* (New York: Oxford University Press, 1944): pp. 136–138.

WILLIAM A. FREEDMAN ON UNIVERSALITY IN THE STORY

[In this extract taken from his article in *Texas Studies in Literature and Language* (1962), Freedman looks at the use of universal quantifiers in "The Jolly Corner."]

Any message in James's fiction is of course not likely to be presented as such; it is not didacticized, for James deplored the use of art for purposes of overt moral instruction. Instead the message will be carefully woven into the texture of the work, and the weave must often be deliberately undone before it can be found. It is my intention in the next few pages to play Penelope with "The Jolly Corner."

"Everyone asks me what I *think* of everything," said Spencer Brydon, "and I make answer as I can—begging or dodging the question, putting them off with any nonsense." This is the opening sentence of "The Jolly Corner," and as is almost always the case with James's first sentences, it carries a special weight. For the recurrence of universal quantifiers, here "Everyone," "everything," and "any," presages the pervasive appearance of a vocabulary abounding in such exhaustives. The word *all*, for example, appears no fewer than 66 times, 10 times in the combination *above all*. And when we add to this the number of appearances of *ever* and *every* (16), *everything* (10), *any* (13), *anything* (5), *whole* (8), *never* and *none* (15), and *nothing* (10), we are provided with a vocabulary of generalizations which makes up a large part of the fictional and ideational pattern of the story. James's fiction, existential at least to this extent, rests on the premise that existence precedes essence. For James, terms often had no pre-existent essence or meaning, and the work of art itself was necessary to establish it. As a result, meanings are supplied by and emerge from the stories themselves. On one level, this explains the abundant use of this all-encompassing, hence indefinite, terminology. From the first, Spencer Brydon knows that for him "everything" is some sort of self-knowledge. Thus, with regard to everyone's asking him what he thinks about everything, he remarks: "It wouldn't matter to any of them really, . . . for, even were it possible to meet in that stand-and-deliver way so silly a demand on so big a subject, my 'thoughts' would still be almost altogether about something that concerns only myself." "He found all things come back to the question of what he personally might have been." Yet it is not until much later that he is to discover, to define as it were, the "might have been," and it is thus labeled only as "all things" or "everything." At the moment of perception, therefore, when the object of his quest has been literally and figuratively cornered, "everything" and "everyone" become "something" and "somebody": "It gloomed, it loomed, it was something, it was somebody, the prodigy of a personal presence." The all-inclusive has become particular, hence meaningful. To affix a label of "something" or "somebody," however, is still not to define fully, and while this figure of the Spencer Brydon that might have been is subsequently described in some detail, he turns out not after all to have been the search's ultimate end: Recovering in the lap of Alice Staverton from his swoon of self-perception, Brydon "had come back, yes—come back from further away than any man but himself had ever travelled; but it was strange how with this sense what he had come back *to* seemed really the great thing, and as if his prodigious journey had been all for the sake of it." And what he has come back to is Alice Staverton, the woman he had left thirty years before, along with a chance for a prodigious fortune, to pursue a prodigal existence on the continent. Thus the final specific definition for Spencer Brydon of "all," of the "everything" and "everyone" of the first sentence is having Alice and being himself—as he is. And it is contained in the final lines of the story, thereby completing the unravelment of the cognitive tapestry: "'He [the Brydon that might have been] has a million a year,' he lucidly added. 'But he hasn't you!' 'And he isn't— no, he isn't—you!' she murmured as he drew her to his breast." In this sense, therefore, "The Jolly Corner" represents an untypically jolly counterpart to James's "The Beast in the Jungle." John Marcher, the passive protagonist of that story, has missed his "everything." By waiting inactively for his something big to happen, his beast to spring, Marcher has missed the one positive thing in his life—the love he might have shared with May Bartram. As a result, the positive something for which he had waited all his life and which had become for him an obsessive "everything" emerges as "Nothing" itself: ". . . he had been the man of his time, the man to whom nothing on earth was to have happened. That was the rare stroke— that was his visitation." Spencer Brydon, on the other hand, has confronted his beast in the jungle. He has stalked and trapped the monster (the imagery is even more consistent with the jungle motif) he might have been, and having done so, he has won the prize which evaded John Marcher. He has won Alice Staverton, the May Bartram of "The Jolly Corner"—his everything.

—William A. Freedman, "Universality in 'The Jolly Corner,'" *Texas Studies in Literature and Language* 4, no. 1 (Spring 1962): pp. 12–13.

KRISHNA BALDEV VAID ON THE TRIPTYCH

[In this excerpt from *Technique in the Tales of Henry James*, Vaid examines Brydon's obsession with his ghost.]

Brydon's obsessive probe into the "mystical other world . . . of all the old baffled forsworn possibilities" is shown as it progresses from stage to stage. At first by his "hushed presence" he wakes "them [the "possibilities"] into such measure of ghostly life as they might still enjoy." Then these possibilities take "the Form" he imagines himself to be hunting; the Form then is pictured by him as a Beast, "the conviction of [whose] probable, in fact [whose] already quite sensible, quite audible evasion of pursuit grew for him from night to night, laying on him finally a rigour to which nothing in his life had been comparable." The image of the chase is presented as elaborating itself in his mind until, after many nights of daring pursuit, he begins to strike himself as "some monstrous stealthy cat." This transference of the beast image to himself is another fine stroke; it perhaps would take a "monstrous stealthy cat" to waylay that other beast. The crucial stage in this preparatory phase of his adventure is reached when he becomes conscious of a partial reversal of the roles played by himself and the still invisible Form of his alter ego. He becomes aware "of his being definitely followed, tracked at a distance carefully taken and to the express end that he should the less confidently, less arrogantly, appear to himself merely to pursue. It worried, it finally broke him up, for it proved, of all the conceivable impressions, the one least suited to his book." When Brydon has reached this stage of his probe, which allegorically speaking represents his developed awareness of the survivals of his other self within him—he is both the haunter and the haunted—the author switches the narrative from a summary to a fully sustained scene.

Since, however, there is no other visible character in the greater part of this scene—even when toward the end of it the "presence" appears in a visible form, it is not vocal—it resembles what we may call, taking our cue from Brydon's own image of Pantaloon and Harlequin, a pantomime. We watch his movements and overhear his thoughts as he accomplishes his fateful ritual in the dark. What passes in his mind is dramatized through the use of inverted commas: "I've hunted him till he has 'turned': that, up there, is what has happened—he's the fanged or the antlered animal brought at last to bay." A later writer would perhaps have rendered such thoughts in the hero's mind by an attempted emulation or adaptation of Joyce's stream-of-consciousness technique. James employs an earlier convention and does not flinch from commenting on the limitations of his method: "There came to him, as I say—but determined by an influence beyond my notation!—the acuteness of this certainty; under which however the next moment he had broken into a sweat that he would as little have consented to attribute to fear as he would have dared immediately to act upon it for enterprise." It may be mentioned here that the presence of the author throughout this scene is clearly noticeable even when it is not so obvious as in the authorial "I" of the above quotation.

The first striking moment in the scene is when Spencer Brydon experiences a "duplication of consciousness" and rejoices in the fear that his hitherto frightened other self has begun to cause in him: "It was as if it would have shamed him that a character so associated with his own should triumphantly succeed in just skulking, should to the end not risk the open; so that the drop of this danger was, on the spot, a great lift of the whole situation." This lift, however, is compatible with the brief spell of panic that he masters and after which "the room, the other contiguous rooms, extraordinarily, seemed lighter—so light, almost, that at first he took the change for day." Thus the picture of struggle with his fears is achieved with an exceptional psychological realism and vividness and its successful outcome reflected in the increase he sees in the surrounding light.

—Krishna Baldev Vaid, *Technique in the Tales of Henry James* (Cambridge, Mass.: Harvard University Press, 1964): pp. 239–241.

EARL ROVIT ON THE GHOSTS

[In this extract from his article, "The Ghosts in James's 'The Jolly Corner,'" Rovit explores the use of Brydon's alter ego.]

One fruitful line of approach can be found on a quasi-psychoanalytical level of interpretation. Spencer Brydon's original departure from America at the age of twenty-three ("almost in the teeth of my father's curse") suggests a fictional rehearsing of the archetypal rebellion against the father—a revolt against the paternal establishment of discipline, authority, and the continuity of tradition. He has "followed strange paths and worshipped strange gods" in the intervening thirty-three years, surveying the world through the cold egotistical round of his monocle, leading a "selfish frivolous scandalous life" while he supports himself parasitically on the accrued capital of his "property" as absentee landlord and reluctant inheritor. In his search for the "forsworn possibilities" of his youth, Brydon is involved in an exhumation of the corpse of himself and of his father as well, since the *alter ego* is both the what he might have been and was not, the what he had actually become without realizing it, and the slaughtered progenitor of what he ultimately became. If the child is in some degree father to the man—and James's consistent moral faith in "experience" would require his acceptance of that Romantic axiom—then the *alter ego* is, among other possibilities, Brydon's father and the climactic meeting on the black and white marble squares of his childhood is the long postponed settlement of the original crime of parricide. For Spencer Brydon's flight to Europe was in part an evasion of the moral and psychic obligations which his denial of the father had laid upon him. He had symbolically slain his father, but he has failed to acknowledge his crime; his action has led him, not into the responsibilities of maturity, but, instead, into a pervasive and paralyzing state of guilt. His egotism is witheringly social; it cuts him off from any mutually fructifying relationships with other human beings. But this egotism is fragmentizingly *internal* as well as social. He is impotent in the profoundest sense—affectionally castrated, unable to use his native powers, divided (and, indeed, subdivided) within himself, and hence, morally and physically destitute. The mechanics of the rebirth of Spencer Brydon (the renovation of house and psyche) demand that the primal crime be resolutely faced, and that the "self," the "other," and the "spirit" be fused into a new union and communion in order for life to flow again wholly and creatively.

Thus the *alter ego* functions on two distinct although closely related levels of identity. His crippled vision and maimed hand—the two distinguishing characteristics of his appearance—effectively relate him to both levels. The *alter ego* is slaughtered father (ineffectually castrated by the son) and an image of Brydon's own truncated development. And the imagery with which New York City is dramatically realized (images drawn from economics, finance, accounting, construction, and silver coinage) is an elaborate extension of the billionaire figure whom Brydon finally faces in "the watery under-world" of his gropings for identity. The "money-madness" which is Brydon's characterization of the world outside the house on "the jolly corner"—a "money-madness" which embraces all of New York except Alice Staverton—is condensed into what is an essentially excremental portrait of the *alter ego*, "evil, odious, blatant, vulgar." He is a figure of colossal accumulation and physical possession. On the other hand, the antithetical imagery of the novelle (music and flower images) links Brydon to Alice Staverton who—as "spirit"—is able to cope with the area of the excremental when the need arises, without becoming compromised or corrupted by her liaison. But we must note that a corollary of the excremental is *power*, and Brydon lacks power, both financially and existentially. His revulsion from the *alter ego* (thematically prepared for by his dissociation from the vulgarities of New York) is a sign not so much of refined sensibilities as of an abortive disengagement from the libidinous sources of energy which alone can give him the power to create, to love, and to escape the imprisonment of his frozen egotism.

—Earl Rovit, "The Ghosts in James's 'The Jolly Corner,'" *Tennessee Studies in Literature* (Knoxville, Tenn.: University of Tennessee Press, 1965): pp. 67–69.

MILLICENT BELL ON THE PRESENCE OF POTENTIALITY

[In this extract from her book, *Meaning in Henry James,* Bell reviews the concept of potentiality in "The Jolly Corner."]

James was certainly aware that the storyteller arbitrarily suppresses all but a few potentialities of story in his materials. He speaks of such potentialities in the already familiar preface to the first volume of the New York Edition, in which he describes life as a "vast expanse" of canvas with "its boundless number of distinct perforations . . . for the needle" of the tapestry maker. Confronted with innumerable solicitations to design, the artist-weaver feels "terror" or at least an "ache of fear . . . of being unduly tempted and led on by 'developments'" that might not, after all, contribute to the pattern he has decided upon. In actuality, "relations stop nowhere," but art pretends otherwise as the artist picks out one design or another on the canvas. In the preface to the volume that contains "The Jolly

Corner," James reflects that he found himself rediscovering in his notebooks possibilities passed by as well as some taken up, and those taken up suggesting other outcomes than he had later given them. But he feels more than the artist's tenderness for literary opportunities passed by—his language suggests James's sympathy with bypassed alternatives, with suppressed potentialities in any individual life, a theme felt again and again in his stories and novels.

The discrepancy between available social role and the self's best expectations is made more absolute in the fable of "The Jolly Corner," probably the latest work to be included in the New York Edition. In 1908, when the story was published, James was already looking squarely at the kind of personal options open to the seeking self in the twentieth century—especially on that frontier of the future, his own America, which he had recently revisited after an absence of twenty years. "The Jolly Corner" is a fictional twin of *The American Scene*, with its vision of a rapidly changing New York full of new opportunities for entrepreneurial energy—a scene bustling with the physical evidence of a multiplied alertness to business opportunity. The Manhattan to which Spencer Brydon has returned is a physical metaphor of finance—its numerous cross-ruled streets and new buildings are described as "the dreadful multiplied numberings which seemed to him to reduce the whole place to some vast ledger-page, overgrown, fantastic, of ruled and criss-crossed lines and figures." In bringing his sensitive expatriate back to America, James confronted the idea of what such a man would have *had* to be in this place, this new age. It was an intensely personal way of thinking, which gives a special, autobiographical sense to those sentences in the preface in which he seems to be talking only about artistic projects: "We chance on some idea we *have* afterwards treated; then, greeting it with a tenderness, we wonder at the first form of a motive that led us so far and to show, no doubt, to eyes not our own, for so other; then we heave the deep sigh of relief over all that is never, thank goodness, to be done again. Would we have embarked on *that* stream had we known?—and what mightn't we have made of this one *hadn't* we known! How, in a proportion of cases, could we have dreamed 'there might be something'?—and why, in another proportion, didn't we *try* what there might be, since there are sorts of trials (ah indeed more than one sort!) for which the day will soon have passed?"

"The Jolly Corner" is James's final fable dealing with the presence of the unlived life in the life that is lived. It is a final settling of the problem of potentiality in its relation to act, of character and its expression, mutilating or improving, in plot. Spencer Brydon, the *déraciné* who has returned after half a lifetime away from his native New York, is assailed at first by the "great fact" of "incalculability" in the world that might have been his. Unimaginable also is the man he would have been if he had stayed at home. But in his new situation he feels compelled to imagine an alternate self, an alternate life. "He found all things came back to the question of what he personally might have been, how he might have led his life and 'turned out,' if he had not so, at the outset, given it up." The mysterious other whom Brydon pursues in his old house on the "jolly corner" may be thought of as representing his growing sense of his own nature and its potentialities. But it is, more precisely, a summoning out of an imagined but possible past of a history that could have been his. The self who never was figures in the story as a ghost of a special sort, not a revenant of the dead, a spook such as the cleaning woman, Mrs. Muldoon, fears to encounter in "the ayvil hours." He is a hypothesis made visible, the unenacted alternative comprehended as a "presence"—the word used in an ambiguous sense throughout the story—because what we can or could be is always *present* in what we are, and yet it is ghostly, immaterial. In "The Jolly Corner," James exploits the "fantastic" doubt that hovers between the real absence of unenacted possibility and its ghostly, hypothetic realization.

—Millicent Bell, *Meaning in Henry James* (Cambridge, Mass.: Harvard University Press, 1991): pp. 275–277.

Plot Summary of
"Daisy Miller"

While visiting his aunt at an inn, in Vevey, Switzerland, Mr. Winterbourne meets Daisy Miller, the bright, beautiful young American girl from Schenectady, New York. Daisy is, as her name implies, an innocent. She is Henry James's quintessential American girl, the girl he would write about repeatedly, possessing that unique American sense of freedom, which in Europe, at the turn of the century, was nothing less than scandalous. Daisy has no familiarity with the rigidity of European social convention nor, it turns out, any capacity to develop sensitivity to complicated social mores.

Winterbourne is himself American-born, but has lived abroad most of his life and has become more European than American. His perspective is, however, best described as international, and this makes his approach to Daisy particularly complex. He is immediately charmed, struck by her openness, which is at the same time ignorance.

Shortly after they meet, she insists that he take her on a tour of the Castle of Chillon, just the two of them. Winterbourne is confused. The idea of taking the girl without a chaperone is both inviting and shocking, though neither Daisy nor her tepid little mother even take it into consideration. Daisy does not particularly act like a flirt, nor does she blush when European girls would normally blush, so he decides to withhold judgment. The outing is a success, but they soon all part ways, with a tentative agreement to meet again in Rome in several months.

Winterbourne's excessively proper aunt, Mrs. Costello, knows that the Millers, consisting of Mrs. Miller, Daisy, little Randolph, and their courier Eugenio, are to be avoided at all cost. Mrs. Costello represents the most unattractive aspect of European convention. He who is ill mannered is, in Mrs. Costello's opinion, necessarily bad. Winterbourne assures her "They are very ignorant—very innocent only. Depend upon it they are not bad."

Winterbourne does meet up with Daisy again in Rome, where he watches her unwittingly destroy her reputation. Many attempts are made to warn her about spending so much time alone with a lower-class Italian of dubious reputation, Mr. Giovanelli, but the warnings do not impress her as being anything more than excessive concern. Daisy's mother is as oblivious as Daisy, and Mrs. Walker, an American acquaintance residing in Rome, feels she must step in. "Did you ever see anything so imbecile as her mother?" she asks Winterbourne. The only threat Mrs. Miller understands is the threat of Roman fever.

Mrs. Walker goes to such lengths as to pursue Daisy by way of carriage, as Daisy and Mr. Giovanelli carelessly walk the streets of Rome at night. Daisy rebuffs Mrs. Walker's attempts however, continuing with her "inscrutable combination of audacity and innocence."

When Daisy finally goes too far, and brings her unsavory Italian friend to a society function at Mrs. Walker's home, Mrs. Walker leads the way in Daisy's ostracism. Winterbourne witnesses Mrs. Walker openly turn her back to Daisy when she is about to offer thanks for the invitation. "He said to himself that she was too light and childish, too uncultivated and unreasoning, too provincial, to have reflected upon her ostracism or even to have perceived it. Then at other moments he believed that she carried about in her elegant and irresponsible little organism a defiant, passionate, perfectly observant consciousness of the impression she produced."

Daisy's association with Mr. Giovanelli is not curbed in the least. Speculation begins to emerge that they are engaged, which only serves to worsen her reputation. Winterbourne goes to her on a fateful night at the Roman Coliseum where she and Giovanelli are walking. He tries to convince her that her behavior is reckless. Besides the risk of being so near the water and catching Roman fever, everyone is shocked by her "going around" with Mr. Giovanelli. She declares simply that she doesn't believe that they "care a straw" what she does and that she does not care about catching anything. Winterbourne's unflappable opinion of Daisy finally takes a turn for the worse. That night, however, she catches the Roman fever. During her brief illness she sends a letter to Winterbourne to assure him that she and Mr. Giovanelli are not engaged. Within a few days she is dead.

Winterbourne ultimately defers judgment until it is too late for Daisy to be saved. He watches her closely for signs of insincerity and calculated indifference, but finding none, he still does not take action to save her. Her exasperating and sometimes mysterious behavior causes him to waffle between good and bad opinions of her motives. His attempts to intervene are sometimes forceful, but never so forceful that he conquers the situation. He remains passive, and in the end he is implicitly sorry for it.

Winterbourne is as much the subject of "Daisy Miller" as Daisy. He has been in Geneva for many years, occupying himself with things that remain obscure. His pretence for existence is "to study," but James leaves his occupation intentionally shadowy. Men of nineteenth-century, upper-class Europe often had ambiguous occupations that consisted of simply leisure or "study." That Winterbourne is not a man of industry, points to the fact that he is not essentially American. He is, furthermore, associated with an older woman in Geneva. There is only a brief reference to this relationship, and it is cast in the light of a rumor. Whether rumor or fact, past or present, this alliance, again confirms his European character. The ambiguity of the relationship would have made it very difficult to manage in the American moral landscape.

Winterbourne is not so Europeanized that Daisy's naiveté repulses him, however. Daisy's free spirit, in fact, captivates him. Rather than engaging in a relationship with her, though, he observes her. Even his name signals the cold, passionless stance he takes toward Daisy, as so many Jamesian men take toward their women, but her tragic end does touch him. He seems sure then of his own misperception, and regrets that he did not do more. He tells his aunt, "'She sent me a message before her death which I didn't understand at the time. But I have understood since. She would have appreciated one's esteem.' 'Is that a modest way' asked Mrs. Costello, 'of saying that she would have reciprocated one's affection?' Winterbourne offered no answer to this question; but presently said, 'you were right in that remark that you made last summer. I was booked to make a mistake. I have lived too long in foreign parts.'"

Winterbourne is now not only convinced of Daisy's innocence but also that the Byzantine moral code of Europe is evidence of depravity and not, as Europeans contend, of sophistication. Finally, striking a classic Jamesian chord, the narrator concludes the story by telling us: "Nevertheless, he went back to live at Geneva, whence there continue to come the most contradictory accounts of his motives of sojourn; a report that he is 'studying' hard—an intimation that he is much interested in a very clever foreign lady." Just as the reader comes to a full understanding of Daisy, Winterbourne becomes the enigma. ❁

List of Characters in
"Daisy Miller"

Daisy Miller is the young American girl from Schenectady, New York who travels with her mother and small brother to Europe for an extended stay. Her unaffected innocence makes her an object of Winterbourne's affection, but her ignorance gets her into trouble with European society whose strict societal rules are mysterious to her.

Winterbourne is an American-born European who lives in Geneva, Switzerland. He meets Daisy and observes her carefully, defending her reckless actions to everyone until the last when he gives up on her seeming determination to ruin herself.

Mrs. Miller is Daisy's mother and is even more ignorant of European social customs than Daisy. She does not function as a mother, and thus several others find themselves trying to fulfill the role of Daisy's protector. She is Daisy's double but with less vibrancy and youth.

Randolph Miller is Daisy's vivacious ten-year-old brother who is not at all interested in the castles and museums around him but very interested in candy.

Eugenio is the Miller's Italian courier. He shepherds them from one inn to the next, one town to the next, and guides them through historical sites. The Millers act very familiar with Eugenio, which shocks the Europeans who customarily treat couriers as servants.

Mrs. Costello is Winterbourne's aunt who disdains the Millers and anyone with even a touch of commonness. She refuses to even be in their company, even though Winterbourne defends them to her.

Mrs. Walker is another Europeanized American living in Rome. She represents the rigidity of European social convention and ultimately ostracizes Daisy.

Giovanelli is the lower class Italian with whom Daisy spends most of her time while in Rome. Daisy is repeatedly warned against spending evenings alone with him, but she does not take heed. Giovanelli finds Daisy to be wonderful, and since he is not himself restricted by aristocratic strictures, he does not discourage her company. When Daisy dies, he declares that she was the most innocent girl he had ever known. ❀

Critical Views on
"Daisy Miller"

[In this extract taken from *Discovery of a Genius: William Dean Howells and Henry James,* Howells discusses the character of Daisy.]

The story of Daisy Miller is as slight as Mr. James delights to make the frame of his picture, which depends so very little for its quality upon the frame. She is first seen at Vevey in Switzerland, with her young but terribly mature little brother and their mother, a little, lonely American group in the rather impertinent custody of a courier whom they make their domestic if not social equal; and she is seen last at Rome (where indeed she dies of the fever) the wonder of the international and the opprobrium of the compatriotic society. Such drama as arises from the simple circumstances precipitates itself in a few spare incidents which, in the retrospect, dwindle to nothing before the superior interest of the psychology. A girl of the later eighteen-seventies, sent with such a mother as hers to Europe by a father who remains making money in Schenectady, after no more experience of the world than she got in her native town. Cultivated but not rude, reckless but not bold, inexpugnably ignorant of the conventionally right, and spiritedly resentful of control by criterions that offend her own sense of things, she goes about Europe doing exactly what she would do at home, from an innocence as guileless as that which shaped her conduct in her native town. She knows no harm and she means none; she loves life, and talking, and singing, and dancing, and "attentions," but she is no flirt, and she is essentially and infinitely far from worse. Her whole career, as the reader is acquainted with it, is seen through the privity of the young Europeanized American who meets her at Vevey and follows her to Rome in a fascination which they have for each other, but which is never explicitly a passion. This side of the affair is of course managed with the fine adroitness of Mr. James's mastery; from the first moment the sense of their potential love is a delicate pleasure for the reader, till at the last it is a delicate pang, when the girl has run her wild gantlet and is dead not only of the Roman fever but of the blows dealt her in her course. There is a curious sort of fatality in it all. She is destined by innate and acquired indiscipline to do the things she does; and she is not the less doomed to suffer the things she suffers. In proportion to the offence she gives by her lawless innocence the things she does are slight things, but their consequence breaks her heart, and leave the reader's aching, as Winterbourne's must have ached life-long.

—William Dean Howells, "Mr. James's Daisy Miller," in *Discovery of a Genius: William Dean Howells and Henry James*, Albert Mordell, ed. (New York: Twayne Publishers, Inc., 1961): pp. 185–187. Reprinted from *Harper's Bazaar* (January, 1902).

CAROL OHMANN ON CHANGING INTENTIONS

[In this excerpt from her article, "'Daisy Miller': A Study of Changing Intentions," Ohmann looks at the fluctuating nature of the characters' intentions.]

Presented with the collision between the artificial and the natural, the restrained and the free, we side emotionally with Daisy. We sympathize with Winterbourne, too, to the extent that he seems capable of coming "alive" and to the extent that he speaks up in favor of Daisy to Mrs. Costello in Vevey and, later, in Rome, to Mrs. Costello and also to Mrs. Walker, another American who has lived in Geneva. For the rest, however, our emotional alliance with Wintebourne is disturbed or interrupted by his Genevan penchant for criticism. At his first meeting with Daisy in Vevey, Winterbourne mentally accuses her—"very forgivingly—of a want of finish." But when Daisy blithely announces that she has always had "a great deal of gentlemen's society," Winterbourne is more alarmed. He wonders if he must accuse her of "actual or potential *inconduite*, as they said at Geneva."

In Rome, although Winterbourne defends Daisy to the American colony publicly, he is, privately, increasingly shocked by her friendship with the "third-rate" Italian Giovanelli. Her walks with Giovanelli, her rides with Giovanelli, her tête-à-têtes in her own drawing room with Giovanelli—all worry Winterbourne. He imitates Mrs. Walker in scolding Daisy. And so he removes himself farther and farther from her. When he finally comes upon her with Giovanelli in the Colosseum at night, he thinks that she has certainly compromised herself. And he is relieved. For his personal feelings for Daisy have gradually been overwhelmed by his intellectual involvement in the problem of Daisy. He is relieved and "exhilarated" that the "riddle" has suddenly become "easy to read." He promptly judges Daisy by her manners—as Mrs. Costello and Mrs. Walker have already done—and condemns her. "What a clever little reprobate she was," he thinks, "and how smartly she played at injured innocence!"

He learns otherwise too late. He knows, for a moment at the end of the nouvelle, that he has made a mistake; he knows he has wronged Daisy because he has stayed too long abroad, has become too rigid in his values. Yet his knowledge does not change him. The authorial voice concludes the tale by mocking Winterbourne's return to the narrow social code of restraint and prejudice:

> Nevertheless, he went back to live at Geneva, whence there continue to come the most contradictory accounts of his motives of sojourn: a report that he is "studying" hard—an intimation that he is much interested in a very clever foreign lady.

Like so many Jamesian heroes, Winterbourne has lost the capacity for love, and he has lost the opportunity to come to life.

As Winterbourne judges Daisy, judges her unfairly, and completes her expulsion from the American set in Rome, our sympathy for her naturally increases. But I think James does not—save through a certain pattern of symbolic imagery to which I wish to return in a moment—guide us to any such simple intellectual alignment with his American heroine.

Daisy's sensibility has very obvious limitations, limitations we hear very clearly in the statement that Europe is "perfectly sweet." Daisy is more intensely alive than anyone else we meet in Vevey or Rome. But James hints from time to time at a possible richness of aesthetic experience that is beyond Daisy's capabilities—a richness that would include an appreciation of the artificial, or the cultivated, not as it is represented by the mores of Geneva but by the "splendid chants and organ-tones" of St. Peter's and by the "superb portrait of Innocent X. by Velasquez."

And Daisy has other limitations. The members of the American community abroad are very much aware of one another's existence. True, they use their mutual awareness to no good purpose—they are watchbirds watching one another for vulgarity, for any possible lapse from propriety. But Daisy's social awareness is so primitive as scarcely to exist. At Rome, in the Colosseum, Winterbourne's imagination cannot stretch to include the notion of unsophisticated innocence. But neither can Daisy's imagination stretch to include the idea that manners really matter to those who practice them. She never realizes the consternation she causes in Rome. "I don't believe it," she says to Winterbourne. "They are only pretending to be shocked." Her blindness to the nature of the American colony is equalled by her blindness to Winterbourne and Giovanelli as individuals. While Winterbourne fails to "read" her "riddle" rightly, she fails to "read" his. She feels his disapproval in Rome, but she is not aware of his affection for her. Neither does she reveal any adequate perception of her impact on Giovanelli. To Daisy, going about with Mr. Giovanelli is very good fun. Giovanelli's feelings, we learn at the end, have been much more seriously involved.

James therefore hands a really favorable intellectual judgment to neither Geneva nor Schenectady. He gives his full approval neither to the manners of restraint nor to those of freedom. His irony touches Daisy as well as the Europeanized Americans. And the accumulation of his specific ironies hints at an ideal of freedom and of vitality and also of aesthetic and social awareness that is nowhere fully exemplified in the nouvelle. To be from Schenectady, to be from the new world, is to be free from the restrictions of Geneva. But merely to be free is not enough.

—Carol Ohmann, "'Daisy Miller': A Study in Changing Intentions," *American Literature* 36, no. 1 (March 1964): pp. 4–6.

Motley Deakin on Winterbourne

[In this extract taken from his article in *The Henry James Review*, Deakin analyzes the character of Winterbourne.]

To begin with Winterbourne, James introduces him as a dillentantish aesthete "addicted to observing and analysing" feminine beauty, but also possessing a passion, somehow comparable, for a lovely landscape or a melancholy ruin. His habit is to categorize; he sees the type, not the individual. When Daisy first appears before him, his response is not "How pretty she is," but "How pretty they are." And as she exhibits her talkative amiability, he concludes that he had never "encountered a young American girl of such a pronounced type as this." Unwilling to accept her in her charming uniqueness, he searches for a term to typify her, until "almost grateful for having found the formula that applied to Miss Daisy Miller," he concludes that she is a flirt. He approaches his interests with this habit of making comparisons, even to the extent of trying to balance the attractions of the Italian cities Bologna and Florence against those other, quite different charms of Daisy.

Winterbourne's purpose is to please his fancy, not to stir his soul. His attitude is mild, suggesting that he is committed because he thinks it is the proper thing to do rather than because he feels any great passion. His interests involve very little personal risk. Even his attraction to the pretty but socially *déclassé* Daisy leaves no blemish on him, for that ultimate bastion of social standards, his aunt, recognizes that "of course a man may know every one." Winterbourne does risk malaria to see the Colosseum by moonlight, but one wonders how much of a chance he thought he took when he presents the experience in terms of its giving him "satisfaction" and of being "well worth a glance." A "lover of the picturesque" he may be, but only when his search for it is without loss of comfort and the social amenities. And how ironic the term "lover" here seems for him when one considers the unsatisfactoriness of his performance as understood in the usual sense of that term.

Winterbourne is presented as the captive of women, not their protective gallant. He is "at liberty to wander about" when his aunt wishes to be alone with her headache. "He had imbibed in Geneva the idea that one must always be attentive to one's aunt," certainly in part because the code requires it, but also in part, one would suspect, because she was in control of the "social sway," in part too because, being anything but a self-made man, Winterbourne's nebulous means of monetary sustenance seems peculiarly vulnerable to a matriarchic image as overwhelming as Mrs. Costello. He is the captive as well of—or, one should say, "extremely devoted to"—a mysterious, older, foreign lady in Geneva who, with her erotically ambivalent significance, seems a most satisfactory and safe choice—if he indeed made the choice—for one so lacking in initiative as Winterbourne. But then we do not know whether she really exists, for only his enemies—or, as the interpolative author hastily interposes, "but after all he had no enemies. . . . What I should say is, simply, that . . . certain persons"—affirm her existence. Real or not, she seems the appropriate symbol of that dominance from which Winterbourne emerges at the beginning of the story only to recognize that "he had engagements which, even within a day or two, would force him" to return. He emerges a second time, once more on the command of his aunt, only to retreat again at the end of the story.

—Motley Deakin, "Two Studies of 'Daisy Miller,'" *The Henry James Review* 5, no. 1 (Fall 1983): pp. 19–20.

ROBERT WEISBUCH ON WINTERBOURNE AND THE DOOM OF MANHOOD

[In this extract from his chapter in the book, *New Essays on Daisy Miller and The Turn of the Screw,* Weisbuch examines the relationship between Winterbourne and Daisy.]

Henry James is like the modern jazz masters in this: He begins with the simplest romantic themes, then builds intricacies upon them until the once-clichés speak to all the subtle richness of social existence. With Daisy Miller and her reluctant suitor Frederick Winterbourne, the theme is no more than "opposites attract," and the trick is that one pole of that opposition is so constructed as to make the attraction deadly. "Stiff" Winterbourne brings doom to Daisy and a different doom to himself; through him, James tallies the evils of a misconstructed masculinity.

It's a multifaceted opposition between the failed lovers, but at base simple as motion through the world. Daisy Miller moves. She "goes on," "goes round," "goes too far," well over a hundred times in the text. "She goes on," a particular persecutor remarks, "from day to day, from hour to hour, as they did in the Golden Age." No enthusiast of the dynamic, Mrs. Costello "can imagine nothing more vulgar." Too blithely regardless, alive, American, and unknowing amidst the miasma of history, "strolling along the top of one of those great mounds of ruin that are embanked with mossy marble and paved with monumental inscriptions," Daisy comprehends her life principle lightly and perfectly: "If I didn't walk I should expire," she tells an inaptly named Mrs. Walker. Mrs. Walker, representative of a society of parlors, never does walk, but chases Daisy in her carriage to persuade her against walking. "If I didn't walk I should expire," says the girl of gardens and the vibrant moment, surprised into opposition; and when she cannot walk any longer, she dies, a latest Roman sacrifice to a world of rooms and rules.

These too are simple, her perfect understanding and her nasty doom. Daisy begins simply, fills out only to defend that simplicity, and expires into mythy apotheosis: the "most innocent" of all young ladies by the account of the cured opportunist Giovanelli, whose judgment is unimpeachable in an assessment that holds no stakes for him. James, amazed that readers followed Winterbourne in making Daisy's innocence a point of dispute, ever after seconded the Italian's judgment.

Daisy's continuing and finally ennobled simplicity is not what we usually expect from fiction, where characters generally complicate themselves in the course of their experiences. But James means for us to see Daisy's complexity as not inherent. The terrible ambiguity, the vexing mystery of her status as innocent or vixen, have nothing to do with her inherent quality, simple as a Daisy can be; they are all evoked by Winterbourne's misshapen assessment. It is not really her story but Winterbourne's, and there the complications are killing.

Frederick Winterbourne does not go on or go too far, as he too accuses Daisy of doing. After his first words with Daisy, "He wondered whether he had gone too far; but he decided that he must advance farther, rather than retreat." But his advances *are* half-retreats, and he vacillates throughout: hesitating to visit Daisy on his arrival at Rome once he hears of her as "surrounded by half-a-dozen wonderful moustaches" or running comic opera between Mrs. Walker's carriage of imperial respectability and the scandalously free-walking Daisy. Progressively in the second, Roman half of the tale, Giovanelli succeeds Winterbourne as active suitor, and Winterbourne, retreating or receding, supplants the protective courtier Eugenio as eugenic guardian. Finally, spying Daisy with Giovanelli at night in the Colosseum, "as he was going to advance again, he checked himself; not from the fear that he was doing her injustice, but from a sense of the danger of appearing unbecomingly exhilarated by this sudden revulsion from cautious criticism. He turned away," seeking secrecy for his hideous emotion, relief that now he can find surcease from his vacillating movements in the sure (but wrong) knowledge that Daisy is corrupt.

—Robert Weisbuch, "Winterbourne and the Doom of Manhood in 'Daisy Miller,'" in *New Essays on* Daisy Miller *and* The Turn of the Screw, Vivian R. Pollak, ed. (Cambridge, U.K.: Cambridge University Press, 1993): pp. 65–67.

KENNETH GRAHAM ON THE STORY

[In this excerpt from *Henry James: The Drama of Fulfilment*, Graham analyzes the character of Daisy.]

Daisy is the figure who changes most through this story. Winterbourne, after his gyrations, stands still, even ossifies. She comes to have a tenderness for him; and she also moves towards a greater self-awareness that brings, if not maturity, at least a pained recognition of her own failure. She loses innocence without gaining wisdom, or even a reciprocated love. United to Winterbourne, one is meant to feel, she might well have developed out of her intellectual flimsiness. And he for his part would at least have escaped from the ethic of Geneva and the atmosphere of middle-aged ladies. As it is, what we feel about Daisy in the latter part of the story is her unprotected loneliness—she is virtually motherless—and even despair, in the face of ostracism. Her notorious behaviour becomes more assertive and more self-protective. Her 'spontaneity' turns into an impudent mask because the Rome of American exiles sneers at the 'Golden Age' in which she is seen to move, and because it cannot accept the most American of qualities in its pristine state. Hence the slightly frenetic note of her late appearance at Mrs. Walker's party with the unwelcome Giovanelli—a final act of defiance against the Mrs. Walker set, and a next-to-final attempt to exasperate Winterbourne out of his stiffness. All she moves him to is a comment on the possibility of her being in love with Giovanelli, which, to his bewilderment, offends a suddenly blushing Daisy by its indelicacy (Winterbourne tested against her natural sensibility once again, and found wanting). And when Daisy leaves the party in distress after being snubbed by the turned back of her hostess, Winterbourne's feelings of pity are the more damnable in that they are safely indulged from the distance, as a mere observer of the scene.

The last movement of the destruction of Daisy Miller, and James's last survey of all that is lost in that destruction, are given consummate expression by his use of the Roman landscape: a last progression, from the Palace of the Caesars, to the Colosseum, to the Protestant Cemetery (no novelist has ever used his impressions as a tourist to more functional, less merely picturesque effect than James).

> A few days after his brief interview with her mother, he encountered her in that beautiful abode of flowering desolation known as the Palace of the Caesars. The early Roman spring had filled the air with bloom and perfume, and the rugged surface of the Palatine was muffled with tender verdure. Daisy was strolling along the top of one of those great mounds of ruin that are embanked with mossy marble and paved with monumental inscriptions. It seemed to him that Rome had never been so lovely as just then. He stood looking off at the enchanting harmony of line and colour that remotely encircles the city, inhaling the softly humid odours and feeling the freshness of the year and the antiquity of the place reaffirm themselves in mysterious interfusion.

That 'mysterious interfusion' is lightly touched on—it just passes Winterbourne, and the reader, with a brush of its wings. But a great deal lies within it. What is interfused, so mysteriously, is history and the present moment, 'antiquity' and 'freshness'; the weightiness of a dead imperial society, 'paved with monumental inscriptions,' along with youth's spontaneity and spring; ruggedness with verdure; desolation with flowers; and all within 'the enchanting harmony of line and colour' that encircles Rome and the whole scene, with the figure of Daisy, strolling above the ruins, as the centre of the circle.

—Kenneth Graham, *Henry James: The Drama of Fulfilment* (Oxford: Clarendon Press, 1975): pp. 23–24.

Works by
Henry James

A Passionate Pilgrim and Other Tales. 1875.

Transatlantic Sketches. 1875.

Roderick Hudson. 1876.

The American. 1877.

Watch and Ward. 1878.

French Poets and Novelists. 1878.

The Europeans. 1878.

Daisy Miller. 1878.

An International Episode. 1879.

The Madonna of the Future and Other Tales. 1879.

Hawthorne. 1879.

The Diary of a Man of Fifty and a Bundle of Letters. 1880.

Confidence. 1880.

Washington Square. 1881.

The Portrait of a Lady. 1881.

The Siege of London, The Pension Beaurepas, and The Point of View. 1883.

Portraits of Places. 1883.

Tales of Three Cities. 1884.

A Little Tour in France. 1885.

Stories Revived. 1885.

The Bostonians. 1886.

The Princess Casamassima. 1886.

Partial Portraits. 1888.

The Aspern Papers, Louisa Pallant, and The Modern Warning. 1888.

The Reverberator. 1888.

A London Life, The Patagonia, The Liar, and Miss Temperly. 1889.

The Tragic Muse. 1890.

The Lesson of the Master, The Marriages, etc. 1892.

The Private Life. 1893.

The Wheel of Time. 1893.

The Real Thing and Other Tales. 1893.

Picture and Text. 1893.

Essays in London and Elsewhere. 1893.

Theatricals: Two Comedies—Tenants, and Disengaged. 1894.

Theatricals, Second Series. 1895.

Terminations, The Death of the Lion, etc. 1895.

Embarrassments. 1896.

The Other House. 1896.

The Spoils of Poynton. 1897.

What Maisie Knew. 1897.

The Two Magics, The Turn of the Screw, and Covering End. 1898.

In the Cage. 1898.

The Awkward Age. 1899.

The Soft Side. 1890.

The Sacred Fount. 1901.

The Bowl. 1904.

The Question of Our Speech and the Lesson of Balzac. 1905.

English Hours. 1905.

The American Scene. 1907.

Views and Reviews. 1908.

Julia Bride. 1909.

Italian Hours. 1909.

The Finer Grain. 1910.

The Outcry. 1911.

A Small Boy and Others. 1913.

Notes on Novelists. 1914.

Notes of a Son and a Brother. 1914.

Within the Rim and Other Essays. 1914–1915.

The Ivory Tower. 1917.

The Middle Years. 1917.

The Sense of the Past. 1917.

Collected Works: The Novels and Tales of Henry James. 1907–1917.
  (known as the New York Edition)

Gabrielle de Bergerac. 1918.

Travelling Companions. 1919.

Works about
Henry James

Allott, Miriam. "Form Versus Substance in Henry James." *The Review of English Literature* 3, no. 1 (1962): 53–66

Anderson, Charles. *Person, Place, and Thing in Henry James's Novels.* Durham, N.C.: Duke University Press, 1977.

Bloom, Harold, ed. *Henry James.* Philadelphia: Chelsea House, 1990.

———. *Henry James's* The Portrait of a Lady. Philadelphia: Chelsea House, 1996.

Brooks, Van Wyck. *The Pilgrimage of Henry James.* New York: Dutton, 1925.

Donadio, Stephen. *Nietzsche, Henry James, and the Artistic Will.* New York: Oxford University Press, 1978.

Edel, Leon. *Henry James: A Life.* New York: Harper and Row, 1985.

Fogel, Daniel Mark, ed. *A Companion to Henry James Studies.* Westport, Conn.: Greenwood Press, 1993.

Freedman, Jonathan. *The Cambridge Companion to Henry James.* Cambridge, U.K.: Cambridge University Press, 1998.

Fussell, Edwin Sill. *The French Side of Henry James.* New York: Columbia University Press, 1990.

Gordon, Lydall. *The Private Life of Henry James.* New York: Norton, 1998.

Graham, Kenneth. *Henry James: The Drama of Fulfilment.* Oxford: Clarendon Press, 1975.

———. *Henry James: A Literary Life.* New York: St. Martin's Press, 1995.

Hardy, Barbara Nathan. *Henry James.* Jackson, Miss.: University of Mississippi Press, 1998.

Hayes, Kevin J., ed. *Henry James: The Contemporary Reviews.* New York: Cambridge University Press, 1996.

Hutchinson, Stuart. *Henry James: American as Modernist.* New York: Barnes and Noble, 1982.

Kaplan, Fred. *Henry James: The Imagination of Genius*. New York: William Morrow, 1992.

Krook, Dorthea. *The Ordeal of Consciousness in Henry James*. Cambridge: Cambridge University Press, 1962.

Long, Robert Emmet. *The Great Succession: Henry James and the Legacy of Hawthorne*. Pittsburgh: University of Pittsburgh Press, 1979.

McCall, Dan. *Citizens of Somewhere Else: Nathaniel Hawthorne and Henry James*. Ithaca, N.Y.: Cornell University Press, 1999.

Moore, Harry Thorton. *Henry James*. New York: Thames and Hudson, 1999.

Norman, Ralf. *The Insecure World of Henry James's Fiction: Intensity and Ambiguity*. New York: St. Martin's Press, 1982.

Rimmon, Shlomith. *The Concept of Ambiguity: The Example of Henry James*. Chicago: University of Chicago Press, 1977.

Sears, Sally. *The Negative Imagination: Form and Perspective in the Novels of Henry James*. Ithaca, N.Y.: Cornell University Press, 1968.

Seltzer, Mark. *Henry James and the Art of Power*. Ithaca, N.Y.: Cornell University Press, 1984.

Stevenson, Elizabeth. *Henry James: The Crooked Corridor*. New York: Transaction Publishing, 2000.

Stowell, Peter H. *Literary Impressionism: James and Chekhov*. Athens: University of Georgia Press, 1980.

Tambling, Jeremy. *Henry James*. New York: St. Martin's, 2000.

Ward, Joseph A. *The Search for Form: Studies in the Structure of James's Fiction*. Chapel Hill: University of North Carolina Press, 1963.

West, Rebecca. *Henry James*. New York: Library Binding, 1994.

Winner, Viola Hopkins. *Henry James and the Visual Arts*. Charlottesville: University Press of Virginia, 1970.

Index of
Themes and Ideas